STUDIES ON THE CHINESE ECONOMY

General Editors: Peter Nolan, Sinyi Professor of Chinese Management, Judge Institute of Management Studies, University of Cambridge, and Fellow of Jesus College, Cambridge, England; and Dong Fureng, Professor, Chinese Academy of Social Sciences, Beijing, China

This series analyses issues in China's current economic development, and sheds light upon that process by examining China's economic history. It contains a wide range of books on the Chinese economy past and present, and includes not only studies written by leading Western authorities, but also translations of the most important works on the Chinese economy produced within China. It intends to make a major contribution towards understanding this immensely important part of the world economy.

Published titles include:

Bozhong Li
AGRICULTURAL DEVELOPMENT IN JIANGNAN, 1620–1850

Alfred H. Y. Lin
THE RURAL ECONOMY OF GUANGDONG, 1870–1937

Nicholas K. Menzies
FOREST AND LAND MANAGEMENT IN IMPERIAL CHINA SINCE THE SEVENTEENTH CENTURY

Ryōshin Minami
THE ECONOMIC DEVELOPMENT OF CHINA

Peter Nolan
STATE AND MARKET IN THE CHINESE ECONOMY

Yuming Sheng
INTERSECTORAL RESOURCE FLOWS AND CHINA'S ECONOMIC DEVELOPMENT

Hong Wang
CHINA'S EXPORTS SINCE 1979

Wang Xiao-qiang
CHINA'S PRICE AND ENTERPRISE REFORM

China's Trade Unions and Management

Ng Sek Hong
School of Business
University of Hong Kong

and

Malcolm Warner
Judge Institute of Management Studies
University of Cambridge

331.880951
N57c

First published in Great Britain 1998 by
MACMILLAN PRESS LTD
Houndmills, Basingstoke, Hampshire RG21 6XS and London
Companies and representatives throughout the world

A catalogue record for this book is available from the British Library.

ISBN 0–333–67841–9

First published in the United States of America 1998 by
ST. MARTIN'S PRESS, INC.,
Scholarly and Reference Division,
175 Fifth Avenue, New York, N.Y. 10010

ISBN 0–312–21029–9

Library of Congress Cataloging-in-Publication Data
Hong, Ng Sek.
China's trade unions and management / Ng Sek Hong and Malcolm
Warner.
p.   cm.
Includes bibliographical references and index.
ISBN 0–312–21029–9
1. Trade-unions—China.   2. Chung-hua ch'üan kuo tsung kung hui.
3. Trade unions.   I. Warner, Malcolm.
HD6837.N4 1997
331.88'0951—dc21
97–27116
CIP

This book is printed on paper suitable for recycling and made from fully managed and
sustained forest sources.

10   9   8   7   6   5   4   3   2   1
07   06   05   04   03   02   01   00   99   98

Printed and bound in Great Britain by
Antony Rowe Ltd, Chippenham, Wiltshire

Contents

v

List of Tables

List of Figures

List of Abbreviations

ACFIC   All-China Federation of Industry and Commerce
ACFTU   All-China Federation of Trade Unions
BWAF   Beijing Workers' Autonomous Federation
CASS   Chinese Academy of Social Sciences
CCP   Chinese Communist Party
CEDA   Chinese Enterprise Directors' Association
CFL   Chinese Federation of Labour (Taiwan)
CFIU   Chinese Labour Federation of Independent Union
CIC   Christian Industrial Committee
CTU   Confederation of Trade Unions
FEWC   Factory Employees' and Workers' Congress
FFE   Foreign-Funded Enterprise
FLUC   Free Labour Unions of China
FMC   Factory Management Committee
FOUC   Federation of Union Cadres (Taiwan)
FTU   Federation of Trade Unions (Hong Kong)
GDP   Gross Domestic Product
GNP   Gross National Product
HRM   Human Resource Management
ILC   International Labour Conventions
ILO   International Labour Organization
IR   Industrial Relations
JV   Joint Venture
KMT   Kuomintang (Guomindang) Nationalist Party
LRA   Labour Rights Association (Taiwan)
MNC   Multinational Corporation
MPF   Mandatory Provident Fund
NIE   Newly-Industrialized Economies
NFIU   National Federation of Independent Unions
NPC   National People's Congress
NTUC   National Trades Union Congress (Singapore)
NWC   National Wages Council (Singapore)
OECD   Organization of Economic Cooperation and Development
PAP   People's Action Party (Singapore)
PRC   People's Republic of China
RMB   Renmimbi

SAR	Special Administrative Region
SATU	Singapore Association of Trade Unions
SEZ	Special Economic Zone
SNEF	Singapore National Employer's Federation
SOE	State-Owned Enterprise
SSB	State Statistical Bureau
STUC	Singapore Trades Union Council
SWB	Short Wave Broadcasts (BBC Bulletin of)
TALM	Taiwan Association for Labour Movement
TALR	Taiwan Association for Labour Rights
TBW	T'ao-Chu-Miao Brotherhood Workers' Union (Taiwan)
TUC	Trade Union Council (Hong Kong)
TVE	Township and Village Enterprise

Preface

This book attempts to examine empirically the role of trade unions *vis-à-vis* management in the People's Republic of China from 1949 to the present day. It deals essentially with the evolution, reform and consolidation of the Chinese labour movement and, particularly, the role of the main arm of Chinese organized labour, the All-China Federation of Trade Unions (ACFTU) at both the apex and grass-roots levels. It not only covers the recent history of Chinese trade unions but also assesses their strategy, structure and membership as well as their legal context. After this, it goes on to consider their role *vis-à-vis* management in both the state-owned as well as the foreign-funded sectors. Last, it compares their activities with organized labour in three Overseas Chinese societies, namely Hong Kong, Singapore and Taiwan. A set of conclusions and a summary round off the book. We have also included the full official text of the Constitution of the ACFTU as an Appendix.

The study involved extensive field work in China over a number of years by the respective co-authors, as well as a study of 'Greater China'. The main research method we used involved interviewing Chinese respondents, whether civil servants, managers or trade union officials, as well as other representatives and members of the workforce. Documentary evidence and statistics were also collected and translated from the Chinese into English by research colleagues where required. The project, mostly focussing on the first half of the 1990s, was written up over the latter half of 1996, and the responsibility for both factual content and evaluation in the manuscript is entirely our own. The sources we have used in the text and set out at length in the bibliography include both Chinese and English language materials. The majority of these are in the latter category, as these are more accessible to a wider readership and those interested in the comparative industrial relations and human resource management. The division of labour in writing this book was as follows: Ng mostly drafted Chapters 2, 6 and 7, and Warner prepared the first drafts of Chapters 1, 3, 4, and 5 and the end-notes. Together, we added material to each of these and finally jointly wrote Chapter 8.

We hope that this book will not only appeal and prove useful to those studying Contemporary China at both undergraduate and postgraduate levels, but also to university teachers and researchers in the field. In addition, we have tried to make the material accessible to the non-specialist reader, particularly Western managers based in China or 'Greater China' or those doing business with companies there. There may also be others who are simply curious to find out more about the world's largest organized (and for that matter unorganized) labour force and how it is likely to evolve as China emerges as one of the next economic 'super-powers' in the coming millennium.

Hong Kong   NG SEK HONG
Cambridge   MALCOLM WARNER

Acknowledgements

We would like to thank the Exchange Programme of the British Council, as well as the Joint Exchange Programme of the British Academy, the Chinese Academy of Social Sciences (CASS), and the Economic and Social Research Council (ESRC), to whom we are deeply grateful for their past and present funding arrangements, and the many universities and research institutes in the People's Republic of China (PRC) which provided helpful assistance. We should also like to thank the innumerable Chinese academics, civil servants, managers, trade unions' officials and many others who gave generously of their time in order to help us. Special note should be made of the unreserved collaboration of Tsinghua University and the CASS Institute of Industrial Economics in Beijing, as well as, the All-China Federation of Trade Unions, the Hong Kong Federation of Trade Unions, the Ministry of Labour the Shenzen Labour Bureau and the Shenzen Municipal Trade Unions Council.

We would also like to acknowledge appreciation of the support of the University of Hong Kong School of Business and the Judge Institute of Management Studies at the University of Cambridge: all our colleagues at both academic institutions (and especially Jo Grantham for secretarial and administrative back-up) as well as the Presidents, Vice-Presidents and Fellows of Wolfson College, past and present. Next, we must mention the important role of the editorial staff at Macmillan, namely Tim Farmiloe and colleagues, as well as Professor Peter Nolan (the series editor) without whom this book would not have appeared. Last, but not least, we must thank our family members of their forbearance and patience during our absences on field trips in China: their unstinting support has proved invaluable.

The author and publisher would like to thank the editors and publishers of the following for giving permission to quote from earlier versions of our own work: particularly the *International Journal of Human Resource Management* and the *Journal of General Management*, as well as the Macmillan Press Ltd.

Part I
Evolving

'A greater movement naturally requires a greater union, and the greatest movement requires the greatest union. All such unions are more likely to appear in a time of reform and resistance.'

(Mao Zedong, August 1919 in Schram, 1963, p. 170)

1 Setting Out the Issues

1.1 INTRODUCTION

Why study Chinese trade unions and their role *vis-à-vis* management? There are several possible answers to this question. First, the Chinese economy is not only currently the fastest growing in the world but may also soon to gain economic 'superpower' status (Lardy, 1994).[1] Second, China has the world's largest industrial and aggregate labour force (Nolan, 1995). Third, it also has the largest trade union organization found in a single country (Warner, 1995). Fourth, since the demise of the former Soviet Union, it remains the last major example of a Leninist 'transmission-belt' model of trade unionism (Chan, 1995). There are no doubt many other reasons that could be adduced to study this phenomenon: we shall return to these later.

Since 1979, when Deng Xiaoping introduced the 'Open Door' policy, the Chinese economic structure and the management of its enterprises has undergone a major set of transformations (Naughton, 1995). Since the advent of the 'socialist market economy', the position of Chinese workers has been in state of flux (White, 1987; Han and Morishima, 1992; Yu *et al.*, 1993). True, the standard of living has greatly improved for most (see Table 1.1), but many have, either actively or passively, sacrificed employment-security and welfare-coverage for higher real incomes, particularly with the ongoing erosion of the 'iron rice bowl' (*tie fan wan*) employment system. On 1 May 1996, the Ministry of Labour announced somewhat optimistically that this practice would officially cease by the end of the year (*Xinhua News Agency*, 1 May 1996).[2]

As a linchpin of the emergent industrial sector, China's 'iron rice bowl' employment system (involving job-security and cradle-to-grave welfare coverage in its state-owned enterprises) had its roots in the early 1950s (see Brugger, 1976; Andors, 1977; Kaple, 1994). Derived from the Soviet management system with full, direct urban labour allocation, it had also been influenced by Japanese employment practices in prewar Manchuria and under the occupation (see Nakagone, 1989).[3] Designed to protect those in state-owned industrial enterprises (SOEs), it eventually spread to cover the majority of workers in urban employment (see Schurmann, 1966; Richman, 1969; Riskin, 1987). Although in some respects it resembled a 'lifetime employment system', comparisons with

3

Japanese companies may be as misleading as they are illuminating, as the two country-contexts markedly differed (see Chan, 1995; Warner, 1995). The 'iron rice bowl' system was centred on the work unit (or *danwei*) and resembled a 'total community'. As we shall see later, it constituted the main stronghold of Chinese organized labour, involving over 100 million workers. As the economic reforms have started to undermine the 'iron rice bowl', we now have to see what effects this might have on parallel labour institutions. It is not an overly-straightforward issue.

The main hypothesis of optimists might be that as the economic 'structure' of China has changed, so the 'infra-structure' may eventually move in a similar direction, albeit with a lag. As China has moved from a 'command economy' to a 'market-driven', albeit 'socialist market economy', it is therefore likely that the *institutional* framework of this new hybrid will move in an appropriate direction, whether we are dealing with enterprises, management or trade unions (cf. Boisot and Child, 1988; Child, 1994). The fact that there has already been significant decentralization of Chinese economic institutions supports the above assumption. On the other hand, economic decentralization has not always meant greater micro-institutional autonomy. Indeed, it has often involved provincial and city bureaux gaining greater

Table 1.1   Selected Chinese economic statistics, 1978–94 (year end)

	1978	1994	Average yearly % increase 1978–94
Population (millions)	962.59	1198.50	1.4
GNP index	100	446	9.8
GNP per capita* (US$)	250	522	12.2
Labour force (millions)	401.50	614.70	2.7
(of whom) staff and workers (millions)	149.90	148.49	2.8
Trade union membership** (millions)	51.60	104	11.9
Overall price index	100	121.70	7.3
Av. annual wage/staff & workers (RMB)	615	4 538	13.3
Per capita consumption/urban (RMB)	405	3 956	6.9
Unemployment (per cent)***	5.3	2.8	−3.1

Notes: * at prevailing exchange rates but not taking into account purchasing power parity
** based initially on 1979 figure
*** Unofficial estimates are much higher
Sources: Various, including State Statistical Bureau (SSB) 1995, World Bank, 1993.

power from the centre but not passing it on to the managers at enterprise-level. However, in the 1990s, there has been a real shift in the level of economic decision-making to the firm, both in the state-owned and the non-state sector, particularly in the case of joint ventures and foreign-funded enterprises (see child, 1994). Increasingly, the decision-making level with which workers or their representatives have to deal is increasingly 'down-stream', not only for day-to-day matters but also for more long-term concerns.[4]

1.2 CHINESE TRADE UNIONS IN THE 1990s

The peak trade union organizations in China, therefore, face a new world, both in economic and organizational terms (see Howell, 1995). The Chinese economy of the 1990s is very different from its formative years in the early 1950s, let alone the economic and social context of founding of the Chinese trade union movement (see Chesneaux, 1969) as we shall see next in Chapter 2. The ACFTU has had its organizational 'ups and downs' since the 'Liberation' in 1949 (for a brief chronology, see Table 1.2) including its dissolution during the Cultural Revolution, yet its revival did not lead to any fundamental degree of internal organizational change. Since the late 1970s, critics might allege it has more or less continued to function with a relatively unchanged strategy and structure. We will deal with its organizational structure in greater detail in Chapter 3 and elsewhere, suffice it to point out here that, in spite of the quite radical shifts in the nature and character of the Chinese economy and the relative shift of industrial weighting from the state to the non-state sectors, the 'peak' labour organization has remained for the most part a 'mirror image' of the economic management of the recent past. It is still, insofar as it is 'top-down' organization, a reflection of where economic power stood in the early 1980s.

At the same time, according to some authors (see Unger and Chan, 1995), there has been a step in the direction of 'corporatism'. China has long had a tradition of incorporation, passed on from the borrowed Soviet model to both the Guomingdang and the Chinese Communist Party. In principle, agencies with this structure were supposed to be two-way 'transmission belts', but in reality they were mainly 'top-down' ones, as we shall note in Chapter 3. Mao Zedong, at one stage, even dissolved the peak labour union federation altogether (ibid., p. 37). Since the 'Open Door' policy, however, tens of -thousands of 'bottom-up' associations have been registered. A new form of 'State corporatism' has evolved 'not as a mechanism for yet further strengthening the State's grip over the economy and society but rather the reverse through which the state's grip could be loosened' (ibid., p. 38). Indeed, the ACFTU has been more assertive to hold on to support from below and thus more eager to articulate demands from the arena where decision-making related to workers' interests takes place, whether at macro- or micro-levels. It could be argued, for example that the national union federation kept up the pressure in the late 1980s by lobbying for legislation to protect workers' incomes, conditions and welfare in both state and non-state-owned enterprises, and in the early 1990s to establish the five-day working week – as we shall see when we look at the 1994 Labour Law later in Chapter 4.

Table 1.2   Chronology of selected background events in China, 1949–95

1949	The 'Liberation': Communists take power
1950	Eight-grade wage system and Trade Union Law initiated
1951	Outbreak of the Korean War
1953	First Five-Year Plan announced
1955–6	Nationalization of industry and commerce
1957	Eighth Trade Union Congress convened
1958	The 'Great Leap Forward' begins
1960	Sino-Soviet split: Moscow recalls technicians
1966	The Cultural Revolution: years of strife follow
1976	Death of Premier Zhou En-Lai and later of Chairman Mao Zedong
1976–7	Launch of the 'Four Modernizations'
1978–80	'Open Door policy' initiated by Deng Xiaoping
1978	Reconvened Ninth Trade Union Congress
1979	Enterprise reforms extended to other areas
1980	Trial of the 'Gang of Four'
1981	Sixth Five-Year Plan (1981–5)
1982	Workers' Congresses set up in 95 per cent of large state firms
1983	Substitution of taxation for profit remittance
1984	New Law on enterprise management in urban factories
1985	Enterprise Responsibility Contract System approved
1986	Seventh Five-Year Plan (1986–90)
1986–7	Labour contract and wage reforms set out
1988	Zhao Ziyang approved as Party General Secretary: Li Peng as Premier
1989	Tiananmen Square student demonstrations and fall of Zhao Ziyang
1990	Eighth Five-Year Plan (1990–4)
1990–1	Policy of economic retrenchment
1992	New Trade Union Law introduced
1993	Comprehensive 'three systems' reforms of contracts, wages and social insurance
1994–5	Approval and implementation of new Labour Law

Sources: Adapted from Warner, 1992, p. 3; Takahara, 1992, p. viiff.

1.3 KEY QUESTIONS

In discussing a future for Chinese trade unions, several key questions come to the fore. First, will their future be linked to 'corporatism', whether the 'state' or 'societal' varieties? Or second, will they move the 'civil society scenario' with them 'asserting their independence from the State' (White, 1996, p. 3; White *et al.*, 1996). Third, is there in fact a half-way house or transitional stage between 'corporatism' and 'civil society' (see Perry, 1995)? Fourth, can the term 'corporatism' be stretched to the limit to encompass the realistic possibilities of change within the present *status quo*? Fifth, how far can they be seen as 'intermediaries' in a complex society (see Zhang, 1997)?

Even within such a corporatist framework, as White (1996) puts it, 'the analytical task is to discover the extent to which Chinese trade unions in the reform era have moved away from their previous position as a subordinated 'pillar of the Party' in the direction of some form of political and institutional arrangement in which they retain their close relationship with the Party-state while enjoying an expanded degree of representational autonomy' (White, 1996, p. 437). To institutionalize the maximum degree of such autonomy is therefore the challenge to the Chinese labour movement. The trade union's 'representational potential', as we may call it, was still evolving by the mid-1990s. Indeed, 'Wage earners had become more differentiated, partly in terms of growing conflicts of interests among state workers and partly in response to the segmentation between different ownership sectors' (ibid., p. 442). Younger workers had become more mobile, and older ones feared for their job-tenure.[5] As many as a third of those working in SOEs are under threat. We shall review the role of trade unions *vis-à-vis* management in the state-owned sector in Chapter 5. Those outside the 'iron rice bowl' domain who had for the most part not seen a trade union presence in their plants – whether in township and village enterprises (TVEs), private-owned, joint ventures (JVs) or foreign-funded ones (FFEs) – began to look for 'voice' regarding their grievances, as we shall see later in Chapter 6.

The mid-1990s were to see a realization that the current role of the ACFTU was in need of reorientation because of the diversification of enterprise ownership and the new 'constituencies' which these developments brought in their train. As the SOEs shrink in terms of its share of industrial production and as the non-state sector grows, the trade union representation pattern would have to adapt to this, if it was to survive. The lesson of other countries – where 'old' unionized sectors had attenuated – would point to a declining union-base that was not replaced with 'new' blood from other growing points of growth in the employment-structure.

A positive reorientation was encouraged not only by the union federation itself, but also by the Party and state authorities. The enactment of the amended Trade Union Law of 1992 and the Labour Law of 1994 reveals evidence of these new concerns, on the one hand. However, the long wrangles relating to the *detail* of such new legislation is testimony to the way differing perspectives of the players in the political drama, on the other hand. The way in which the above two developments related to a third – the enterprise reforms of 1984, 1988 and 1992 – was also to be crucial importance in what was increasingly to become a 'zero-sum' game.

We shall see later the way in which the 1994 Labour Law reflected the attempts by the 'technocrats' to encroach on the territory of the 'unionists' and how the latter resisted and in the eventual outcome achieved defensive concessions. Earlier, a similar logic of events had transpired *vis-à-vis* the 1992 Trade Union Laws (see Warner, 1995) Deconstructing the shifts in power between the players is not entirely straightforward as the Party and State authorities still wanted to strengthen union structures at one level or more, in order to maintain their social control in the workplace.

1.4 INSTITUTIONAL FRAMEWORK

One of the central themes of this book relates to the need for a 'fit' between economic and associated institutional structures. Stages of economic development shape appropriate institutional responses. In the early stages of industrialization, a set of industrial and labour institutions are generated. These then become 'stereotypical' of the regime, and sometimes more broadly of the society itself. China's institutional infrastructure, including its labour organizations, dates from the formative period of the PRC. The ACFTU in its modern form originates in the late 1940s and early 1950s, when the Chinese economy (and indeed many other social structures) was significantly different from today. It was then in the throes of industrialization, with the SOE sector as its rising star, and the workers employed therein, the new 'masters'. Indeed, 'in view of the significance of workers in rebuilding the nation, it is no wonder that the reconstruction of the trade union system was given meticulous attention after the formation of the PRC' (Lee, 1986, p. 33).

In the early 1950s, China adopted many aspects of the Soviet model, if somewhat eclectically (Kaple, 1994). The ACFTU had many similarities with its fraternal counterparts north of the border. The urban industrial workers were seen as an 'elite group' in China, as in the Soviet Union. As Lee (1986) notes:

The organizational principle of the ACFTU and its member unions, as stated in the 1948 constitution, was based on democratic centralism. By this, unions of the ACFTU had to observe the principle of the minority submitting to the majority, and lower organizations submitting to higher organizations. Structurally, it may be recalled that the guideline was that trade unions were to be formed on an industrial basis. (Ibid., p. 34)

Part of their new role was to support the Chinese Communist Party (CCP) in order to promote the industralization of China, and this could best be done by way of industrial unions on Soviet lines. At the time, there were few such unions – with only two national industrial unions and one handicraft union under the Federation as of 1949. The task was to build new industrial unions and in 1950 a Trade Union Law was promulgated to encourage such developments (ibid., pp. 34–48).

The institutional framework of the drive towards industrialization took form when China had a total population of well under half of what it is now. In 1950 it was 552 million, – just over 10 per cent was urban (11.2 per cent). The aggregate number of workers and staff was just over ten million (specifically 10 166 000) of which just under one fifth of the comparable Soviet total (see Kaple, 1994, p. 22, p. 42). It is clear, therefore, that the ACFTU would then be a relatively small-scale organization compared with its Soviet counterpart (or Western equivalents) even if it achieved the highest level of plant unionization possible. Indeed, the membership-density was quite elevated because in 1949 the membership figure had been 2 373 000 rising to 10 200 000 by 1953 (Lee, 1986, p. 48). The number of primary trade unions had soared from just under 100 000 to over 180 000 over a comparable period (ibid., p. 46).

As Kaple (1994) observes:

In October 1949 a self-proclaimed socialist government took control of China. It was a country so unprepared for socialism that its working class was almost non-existent. Therefore, one of the first tasks was to begin the process of socialist industrialization and, with it, to create a working class. (Ibid., p. 41)

Not only was the Chinese working class a small part of the population at the time of the Liberation, it was also 'not organized as a cohesive group' (Kaple, 1994, p. 42). The CCP had, after the events of 1927, failed to succeed with the Chinese proletariat and moved to reliance on the peasantry (see Wales,, 1945). The former was the 'weak link' in the revolutionary chain. Industrial workers were in a weak position for several reasons: factories had been foreign-owned; industry had been regionally fragmented; the labour market was dispersed; workers' consciousness was low and most were illiterate; and, in addition, work-organization based on the 'gang boss' system was decried as pre-capitalist and hence hampering the development of working class identity (see Kaple, 1994, p. 43). The task of creating an urban proletariat was thus daunting and the CCP chose to learn from the Soviet experience, adapted to Chinese circumstances. As in the USSR, they began to rely on three 'managerial players', namely the managers, Party officials and the trade unions' representatives.

As in the Soviet case, the union was held to be the link with the 'masses' and the Party–union nexus was crucial. The union's tasks paralleled those of the Party in the workplace, to help the former with worker-mobilization and mass political endeavours. Only the final task, the administration of day-to-day matters *vis-à-vis* the workers, was the union's 'full responsibility' (ibid., p. 47). As industrialization was one of the main goals, both Party and unions geared themselves to promote production. The Party used militant workers to boost workers' motivation and the union set up 'production conferences'. As we will see in greater detail later, the trade unions' role was a subordinate one throughout and there was very little scope for autonomous policy actions or initiatives that might diverge from what the Party ordained.

Mitigating the Stalinist model of the 'one-man management' (see Dobb, 1966; Merkle, 1980; Beissinger, 1988) adopted by the CCP, there were 'democratic' devices such as a Factory Management Committee (FMC) and a Factory Employees and Workers' Congress (FEWC) in each workplace to make the workers feel 'masters' (*zhuren*). The factory union chairman and key officials were to be seen on the FMC which discussed all production and related matters. The FEWC was headed by the union representatives from the early days, mainly acting as a 'watchdog' on management. The model, set up in early 1950s to achieve 'the dream of a red factory' (to use Kaple's (1994) book title), went through many modifications subsequently and into limbo during the Cultural Revolution, to be resurrected in a new guise by Deng's reforms. The dual responsibilities shared between Party and union persisted. The ACTFU's role as a Leninist 'transmission-belt' survives to this day – a theme we will return to repeatedly. Although the trade unions are less central in enterprise decision-making than they once may have been, they are still held up by the officialdom as the only representative bodies open to workers to join, not only in the state-owned sector, but also in the non-state-owned sector, even if in the latter their actual presence on site is variable.

The unions' role was explained by Lenin in 1920:

> In its work, the Party relies directly on the *trade unions* ... which are *formally non-party*. Actually, all the directing bodies of the vast majority of the unions ... consist of Communists and carry out all the directives of the Party. Thus, on the whole, we have a formally non-communist, flexible, and relatively wide and very powerful proletariat apparatus, by means of which the Party is closely linked up with the *class* and with the *masses*, and by means of which, under the leadership of the Party, the *dictatorship of the class* is exercised. (Cited in Harper 1969, p. 86)

The 'transmission-belt' function calls for the unions not only feeding directives downwards but also reflecting their members' wants and opinions upwards, the latter a position said to be echoed by not only ACFTU leeaders like Ni Zhifu and others, but also Deng Xioping and Zhao Ziyang in the late 1980s (see Zhang, 1997). To have legitimacy in the membership's eyes, the unions have to stand up for their interests if there is a potential conflict with either management or Party (or both). Otherwise, the unions will be seen as the 'tails of administration' (ibid., p. 108); yet to concede independence to the unions risks them building an independent power-base. Over the years, the Party normally prevailed. However, we must be careful here not to over-simplify the 'dependence of Chinese trade unions' thesis. Nor must we overstress the Party–union nexus. There were several past attempts by the unions to assert themselves including those of top officials Li Lisan and Lai Ruoru, but on each occasion the issue of autonomy by the ACFTU arose, it was defeated. It is clear that the degree of 'dependence' of the union must be seen in its context. Its role *vis-à-vis* other economic institutions in the PRC was from the start problematic at best, let alone *vis-à-vis* the political hegemony of the CCP.

It was perhaps only in the large urban conurbations such as Guangzhou or Shanghai that organized labour could achieve a momentum of its own. In such cities, we find a high proportion of all trade union members over many decades. For example, at the time of the Liberation nearly a quarter of a million workers were organized in Guangzhou and just under a million in Shanghai (Lee, 1986, p. 42). Perry (1993) has, for instance, convincingly shown the strength of workers organizations in the latter city, both over the pre-Liberation as well as post-Liberation periods.

Given the special circumstances of the Chinese Revolution and its subsequent development, compared even with other Communist regimes (see Meaney, 1988; Nolan, 1995) let alone Western (and Japanese) experience, it is not surprising that Chinese institutions generally, and enterprise managements as well as trade unions, should be so distinctive. Whether they are *sui generis* is another matter. The Chinese frequently claim the copyright on institutional developments 'with Chinese characteristics'. The emphasis on cultural specificity in cross-cultural and organizational analysis is, however, not restricted to the Chinese, although they do not go so far as to assert their overall absolute cultural distinctiveness, even 'uniqueness' as some Japanese writers have done.[6] Critical relativity may often be stretched too far if 'special' circumstances are claimed to justify shortcomings whether ethical or merely functional. Institutions must be judged comparatively and 'benchmarks' must be invoked. Sometimes this will lead to favourable comparisons; sometimes to the contrary.

1.5   COMPARISONS WITH UNIONS ELSEWHERE

In this light, Chinese trade unions clearly do have 'family resemblances' with their counterparts elsewhere, a theme we will return to later, especially in the context of overseas Chinese experience, particularly in 'Greater China' (Hong Kong, Singapore and Taiwan) as we shall discuss in Chapter 7. To assert this, however, raises questions as to what makes a trade union in the first place. The first working description of unions is to be found in the writings of the Webbs (see Warner, 1979). Sidney (1858–1943) and Beatrice Webb (1859–1947) were early British socialist intellectuals who helped to form the Fabian Society, and who were among the first to analyze the newly emerging labour organizations of the nineteenth century. They wrote two major tomes on this subject: *The History of Trade Unionism* (1894), and *Industrial Democracy* (1897).

   Their definition of a trade union went as follows:

> A Trade Union, as we understand the term, is a continuous association of wage-earners for the purpose of maintaining or improving the conditions of their working lives. (Webb and Webb, 1894, revised edition, 1920, p. 1)

Trade unions in China certainly fulfil several of the conditions laid down by the Webbs. First, they are clearly 'continuous associations of wage-earners', although they were in demise during the Cultural Revolution. Second, they consist of 'wage-earners' but clearly not all wage-earners, as noted earlier. Third, while they do exist for 'maintaining or improving the conditions of the working lives', these are not their only goals in the PRC. Then again, Western unions did not restrict themselves to a purely 'economistic' role in the past or do so in the present. Chinese trade unions have multiple goals, as do unions elsewhere (see Banks, 1974; Barling *et al.*,

1992). The key question relates to the hierarchy of such goals: that is, which are *primary* in the system and which are *secondary* (or *core* and *peripheral* if preferred).

Where they diverge, as we shall see in greater detail later, is in where they depart from the common (or at least Western) model. One authority (Lee, 1986, p. 159) stresses their lack of 'sub-system autonomy'. Their dependent role on the Party and indeed state organizations is an important point here. As it is argued there is no 'class antagonist' to negotiate with, the lack of collective bargaining is seen as another *lacuna*. Whether equality of bargaining power is precondition for such collective activities, is another matter. It is also not strictly true that 'bargaining' is entirely absent in Chinese enterprises or in the broader labour policy-arena. Such contracts of a sort were to be found in Chinese firms at various points in time, as they had been in their Soviet counterparts, even if only *vis-à-vis* fulfilment of plan norms. Collective contracts, which were introduced in the mid-1980s, have surfaced again recently in a new guise, as we shall see later. In this context, we will raise the question of the degree to which union-management relations have become more or less adversarial.

The requirement that such bargaining be 'free' raises broader questions which we hope to tackle later. Whether there is a 'right to strike' is entirely problematic, as for a while it was legally possible in China until it was removed from the Constitution in 1982. Even now, the fact that strikes are not formally forbidden in law is raised by some as evidence that Chinese labour relations can be compared with their Western counterparts. In the early 1980s for example, an ACTFTU spokesman envisaged the possibility of strikes albeit 'small-scale and short' if 'reasonable demands of workers' were ignored; here the unions had to look into such grievances and meet the 'justifiable demands of the strikers without jeopardizing the overall interests of China' (ibid., p. 164). We shall return to this point later in later chapters.

Taking many of the *prima facie* goals of China's trade unions, the reasonable observer might not only conclude that there were 'family resemblances' with unions elsewhere but that their goals or responsibilities were similar at least comparable. Critical observers are nonetheless often naturally cautious in taking 'official' constitutions, whether at state or sub-statal level, at their face-value even if their phraseology is normally 'benign' and 'worthy'. The experience of overseas visitors to the early 'Soviet experiment' makes for a cautionary tale: all too many such pilgrims – including prominent British Fabians in the 1930s (see Webb and Webb, 1935) – were to echo the phrase: we have 'seen the future and it works'. China was to prove no exception! During the height of Mao's influence, many a Western 'fraternal' delegation went to visit their

Chinese counterpart organizations, including trade unions, and reported with enthusiasm when they returned home that the Chinese workers were indeed 'masters'.

A high degree of unionization – we must emphasize at this point – does not *necessarily* mean anything positive in itself, either in terms of worker-power in an economy or indeed political pluralism: the former Soviet Union being a case in point. or does a low degree of union representation necessarily imply the existence of weak unions or a lack of pluralism: the United States being a prime example here. In some cases, pervasive union-ization and democracy may go hand in hand, as in the Scandinavian coun-tries. Trade unions may be promoted for a variety of reasons, for example where mobilization is to be encouraged in an emergent economy. The Chinese case may not be unique, as the circumstances in which the ACFTU emerged after 1949 were present elsewhere, at least in other developing countries' economies.

1.6   CONCLUDING REMARKS

Because strategies and structures develop in defined organizational envir-onments or institutional frameworks, it will be necessary to set these out and the degree to which they have changed over the years. The rate at which such contexts have been changing since 1949 is another interesting dimen-sion to explore. Since China's economy, the main setting for such institu-tional adaptation, has been expanding at an almost unprecedented rate in modern economic history, it is not surprising that there may be a relative lack of organizational adaptation or even inertia in the circumstances. Trade unions are not the only example of organizational inertia in the Chinese organizational life. Even so, many parts of Chinese society which affect the ACFTU have acquired greater autonomy (see Davis *et al.*, 1995).

As Chan (1995) points out:

In sum, the reforms that originally were initiated from above have eroded the power of the Party-state. A labour market has emerged, and the State's encroachment on personal space has diminished. Individuals can privately, and more curiously in public, criticize the Party and the government without fear of being thrown into jail. The once-direct relationship between State and workers is now mediated by the State's surrogates, bureaucracies and regional power brokers and capital. (Ibid., p. 41)

An implicit conjecture here is that the present ACFTU organizational structure is problematic, and that it is now under pressure both internally and externally (see Fang and Lin, 1990; Walder, 1991; Wang, 1993). Built into this argument is the assumption that such economic and social changes are shaping the environments in which labour organizations operate. Assuming that structure follows strategy, then we must look to a change in the latter to inaugurate any organizational innovation. Since the ACFTU's strategy has always been constrained by the Party and the state, it therefore follows that either it has to have a new strategic direction imposed from above, or it moves, albeit slowly, to a more autonomous role in Chinese economy and society under increasing pressures from below – a point to be taken up later in Chapter 8 – a somewhat optimistic scenario in the short-term at least.

To sum up, we have set out the basic issues in this opening chapter which are shaping the current relationship between Chinese trade unions and management, as well as their relationship to the broader political arena of Party–state collaboration. We have examined the way in which current changes in the economic, political and social environments may potentially lead to organizational change in the Chinese institutionalized industrial relations setting, given the way in which 'market socialism with Chinese characteristics' is taking even deeper roots in the PRC. We now turn, in the next chapter, to the recent historical development of the Chinese labour management since the Liberation in 1949 and its emergence in its modern form.

2 The Chinese Labour Movement After 1949

2.1 INTRODUCTION

The organized labour movement in China had come into existence prior to the establishment of the Communist Party in 1921 and unions had been active even before the turn of the century (see Chesneaux, 1969). As industrialization had been confined to the coastal areas and especially the large cities such as Canton (now Guangzhou), Hong Kong, Shanghai and Tientsin (now Tianjin), it is not surprising that the early workers' organizations had started their life there (see Guillermaz, 1972; Chan 1981; Chen 1985 for further details).[1]

In China, the formal national union structure goes back to the early 1920s (see Littler and Lockett, 1983) with the setting up of the All-China Federation of Trade Unions (ACFTU) in 1925 in Canton.[2] The dominance of the Communist Party was established from the outset, with rule from above rather than below, although collaborating with the 'yellow' unions of the Kuomintang (now referred to as the Guomindang) Nationalist Party (KMT) and 'grey' unions of the politically unaligned workers (Leung, 1988, p. 10). The Right within the KMT came to power in 1927 when Chiang Kai-shek organized a coup against the Communists. As many as 13 000 activists were executed in the struggle for political ascendancy and over 25 000 died in combat (Guillermaz, 1972, p. 226); labour unions were savagely treated, particularly where they could not be taken over by the KMT (Wilson, 1987, p. 221). The struggle for power (see Brandt, 1958) resulted in the disappearance of leftist unions. As a result of this, the KMT prevented the ACFTU establishing unions all over China, as the CCP could not organize all the industries on a national level (Lee, 1986, p. 14). Some occupational groups could be recruited, however, and seamen, mechanics, railway-workers, print-workers, and miscellaneous unskilled operatives began to play an important role in the leadership of the unions (Chesneaux, 1969, pp. 400–2). By and large, however, the ACFTU worked in the agrarian areas between 1927 and 1949. Unions were set up hurriedly and often only existed on paper. The 'industrial' logic was never fully pursued and the number of experienced union cadres was very thinly distributed across the country (Wilson, 1987, p. 219).

As a consequence, the unions had a skimpy industrial spread and a limited 'proletarian' base before 1949. This 'weakened their ability to make demands on the party' (Lee, 1986, p. 30). A new organizational basis was established by the Constitution of the Sixth Labour Congress in 1948 and the Trade Union Law of 1950. From these, the principle of 'democratic centralism' was consolidated, and the industrial sector basis became pre-eminent, in harness with geographically established trade union councils, in a 'dual system' of authority (Littler and Lockett, 1983). The historical legacy of the pre-1949 period and the difficulties of organizing nationally led the CCP to use the ACFTU essentially as a one-way link between Party and 'masses'. The problems faced by the regime in terms of grass-roots support in the cities were not however always clear-cut (see Perry, 1993; 1994).

The 'Liberation' and inception of the People's Republic under a Chinese government led by the Chinese Communist Party (CCP) in 1949 provided the context for the consolidation of a monolithic union structure which has since characterized the mass organization of the Chinese workers. Trade unions in the PRC have subsequently functioned and indeed been fashioned as the state's transmission-belts within the organizational umbrella of the nation's mainstream and unitary trade union centre, the All-China Federation of Trade Unions (ACFTU) (see Warner, 1995). Since its early days, the ACFTU has been and still is reminiscent of the notion of 'socialist' trade unionism coined in the doctrinal orthodoxy of Marxist–Leninist ideology as described in Chapter 1. The 'socialist' character of the ACFTU extends from the logic of 'democratic centralism' and the subordination of the unions to the revolutionary political party as one of its popular organs for organizing the masses. It is still considered as sacrosanct today, in spite of the growing need and pressure upon the ACFTU to restructure its philosophy, strategy and organization in order to harmonize with the current 'marketplace' reforms in the economy and to reconcile the role of the Chinese trade unions with these new imperatives.

2.2   THE ACFTU AFTER THE LIBERATION

The All-China Federation of Trade Unions (ACFTU) was revived by the CCP in 1948 at the convention of the Sixth National Labour Congress in Harbin, a year before its assumption of government in Peking (later to be Beijing) in 1949. The National Labour Congress adopted a new constitution for the ACFTU which defined its membership to be drawn from all waged workers (including manual and non-manual workers and staff members in enterprises, institutions and schools) and prescribed a basic framework for structuring the subsequent system of trade union organizations in China. Understandably, the immediate mission of the ACFTU upon its renewal was to forge a 'united front' across all social classes, including the 'progressive' factory owners, in combating the Nationalists (Lee, 1984, pp. 4–6).

In 1949, the ACFTU made explicit its internal principle of organizing its member unions in the nation – that unions be structured on the basis of industry and not along occupational lines. As stated officially by the ACFTU, 'All trade union members in the same enterprise or institution are organized in one single basic organization: all trade union members in the same industrial branch of the national economy are organized in the same national industrial union' (ACFTU, 1953, pp. 131–2). The notion of 'industrial' unionism was not only consistent doctrinally with the Marxist–Leninist ideology of 'socialist' unionism, but also seen as instrumental by the ACFTU leadership for consolidating the organization (and solidarity) of the Chinese workers in the 'grass-roots' unit of the workplace, especially in the wake of the 1949 Liberation. It also gave unions, as the state's mass organization, the additional roles of agitating against the so-called 'unrepentant' capitalists and supporting the established order, that is the PRC, in order to industrialize China (see Lee, 1984, p. 9).

Otherwise, the ACFTU and its monolithic body of Chinese trade unions had adhered closely to the Soviet model (see Howe, 1971; Littler and Palmer, 1987; Kaple, 1994). Similar to the integration of the trade unions into the Soviet system, unions inside China were ideologically conceived as 'mass organizations of the working class' led by the Party. In the aftermath of the 1949 Liberation, economic recovery was a central concern of the Party leadership's national agenda. Commensurate with such a priority authorized by the State, the Chinese trade unions were observed to be 'conciliatory' towards managements, often siding with them against striking workers and approving reductions in wages and welfare benefits (Hearn, 1977, pp. 161–2). Literally, from the beginning of the People's Republic, the Chinese labour movement, in becoming the 'mass' agency of the state, consistently exhibited a paradoxical character of assuming an ambassadorial role in appeasing and, where necessary, accommodating capital for 'mutual non-conflictual co-operation' (Ng, 1994, p. 25). Again, back in 1949 and 1950, the Chinese trade unions were allegedly enmeshed in such tasks of 'comforting' private businessmen. They were, according to Lee (1984), instructed to seek settlement of labour disputes with managements by negotiation and to enter into 'labour–capital' consultative conferences for collective decision-making at the enterprise level on workplace issues like 'collective contracts, production plans, production organization, technology, management, personnel policy, wage, work hours, and various welfare policies' (ibid., p. 12).

In the decade after the 'Liberation', the Chinese trade unions as centrally coordinated by the ACFTU had consolidated so monistic an image of 'socialist' trade unionism, aligned in subordination to the policies of the State and the CCP, that Hearn (1977) portrayed them as being 'reduced to little more than agencies responsible for ensuring enterprise control by the State's representatives', enforcing labour discipline, regulations and organizing contest or emulation campaigns (*laodong jingsai*) to increase productivity (Hearn, 1977, pp. 162–3). As early as 1950, a new Trade Union Law legitimated the ACFTU as an integral part of the newly established system of 'democratic centralism' under the socialist administration of the CCP. The legislation enabled the ACFTU to legitimize its new organizational structure which was to crystallize both at the central bureaucracy and at the myriad of provincial, local primary ('grass-roots') levels. It also equipped the ACFTU with the necessary resources (including, notably, human resources) to pursue its designated tasks as the State's 'transmission-belts' (Lee, 1984, p. 33).

At the end of 1951, the ACFTU umbrella already covered a sizeable fringe of as many as 100 000 primary unions in enterprises. This strength at the 'grass-roots' level ascended to over 160 000 unions in 1952 and again to over 180 000 unions in May 1953, by the time the nation convened its Seventh Trade Union Congress. The 1950 Trade Union Law prescribed that any work-unit with a workforce strength of 25 or more could be organized by a trade union committee staffed by a full-time union cadre(s). In 1952, a nationwide conference on the building of primary trade unions as the basic union organ (that is grass-roots labour organization), exalted the Wusan Factory in North East China as a model plant for nationwide emulation. The 'Wusan' model featured daily joint meetings of the union together with the Party, the management and the Youth League in the workplace in order to 'review work of the previous day and decide on the day's work as directed by the upper level' (ibid., p. 27). The practice was apparently later consolidated into the 'dualistic' institutions of first, the Factory Management Committee; and second, the Workers' Congress.

Such a 'dual system' of the Factory Management Committee and the Workers' Congress owed, of course, its *raison d'être* to the primary dictate of the socialist logic of managing the economy's production activities –

that 'Party hegemony' was (and should be) complemented at the work-place by an ancillary arrangement of 'democratic management'. The history of the dual system, which dated back to the insurgent days of the CCP in China during the 1920s, can be narrated briefly as follows:-

> In the Communist 'liberated' zone, economic enterprises were organ-ized under the pseudo-orthodox notion of 'director's accountability under the leadership of the party's branch secretary' ... [Later] this [became] the dual system of the factory management committee (*gongchang guanli weiyuanhui*) and the workers' congress (*zhigong daihiao dahui*) introduced to the public enterprises on a universal basis under a 1948 resolution adopted by the Sixth National Labour Congress. In May 1949 the First National Congress of Workers' Delegates convened in Northern China, leading to the promulgation in February 1950 of a Regulation of Application (1948). By virtue of the 'Instruction Concerning Management Committees in State Factories' thus decreed, every state industrial enterprise was required to institute the consultative organ of workers' congress. (Ng, 1984, pp. 57–8)

As is to be noted in greater detail later, the trade union organ has been put forward at various points in time, as an entrusted agency designed to prac-tise and experiment with 'democratic management' in the workplace and to deputize administratively for the Workers' Congress when it was not in session. Otherwise, the workplace union itself, according to the early prac-tice preached in the Wusan-inspired arrangement, was known to meet in plenary sessions for its membership twice a month, while its standing committee would normally handle its affairs on its behalf during the inter-vals between sessions and report to the Party, management, trade union and the Youth League in the workplace.

Parallel to the 'grass-roots' labour organizations at the primary level, the trade union councils at the local level of the province or municipality (that is, the city) have, in addition, played a strategic role in assisting the local gov-ernment to consolidate political control and economic order since the found-ing of the People's Republic. Noticeable, for example, were the Shanghai Trade Union Council and the General Trade Union Council of Canton (later, Guangzhou) which, together with other provincial/municipal union councils, were instrumental in buttressing the local party bureaucracy, weeding out the Nationalist-controlled 'Yellow' unions as well as purging the nation of the 'ill' and 'corrupted' influences of the bourgeoise in the 'Three-anti' and 'Five-anti' campaigns. Such a political partnership between the Party and the union organ in the post-Liberation days was reminiscent of the 'solidaristic' agitation of the intellectuals and workers in the earlier period of the insurgent Chinese labour movement in the 1920s.[3] By 1951, the ACFTU had integrated all local trade union councils in North China under its direct jurisdiction. But, outside the scope of its direct prerogative, there were still 47 provincial municipal trade union councils under the aegis of the great administrative regions, 176 municipal trade union councils under the jurisdiction of provinces and 1684 trade union councils and 173 sub-offices under the jurisdiction of administrative districts (Lee, 1984, p. 21).

The ACFTU and its umbrella system of Chinese trade unions steered through a period of adjustments after its renewal and vindication as the nation's mainstream labour movement from the inception of the People's Republic in 1949. The gestational experiences and accommodating strategy of the early 1950s were followed by the adjustments and policy re-alignments of the union bureaucracy which punctuated the period preceding the outbreak of the Cultural Revolution in the late 1960s. Two significant national trade union congresses convened in this period, the Seventh All-China Congress of Trade Unions held in May 1953 and the Eighth Congress in 1957 – the former coalesced with the early advents of the 'Three-anti' and 'Five-anti' campaigns, and the latter announced the arrival of the 'Great Leap Forward'.

As Lee (1984) observed, the Seventh ACFTU Nationalist Congress strengthened the political grip of the CCP leadership over the unions' government and amended the national trade union centre's constitution in order to rationalize its organizational structure and strategy. As a result, the unions' role could be harmonized better with the state's anxiety to hasten the nation's industrial growth under the new government which had just buttressed the reign of 'socialist democracy' following the Liberation (Lee, 1984, pp. 36–7; 1986, pp. 48–9). As declared by the ACFTU at this convention, 'the historic task of the Chinese working class movement set forth by the Sixth All-China Labour Congress had been fulfilled. The Constitution of the All-China Federation of Trade Unions adopted by the Sixth Labour Congress is no longer in conformity with the changed and developed situation today' (ACFTU, 1953, p. 84). Reflecting the shifting political mood, the 1953 amended Constitution of the ACFTU was preambled with a reference to the newly enshrined mission of the national trade union centre which was to help improve and increase productivity in the socialist enterprise and in the nation (ibid., p. 128). Concomitantly, union members were also exalted to advance not only their class consciousness but also their technical capabilities at work (ibid., p. 130). The most recent version of the Constitution (ACFTU, 1993) is set out later, in the Appendix.

In terms of organizational reforms, notable measures adopted by the ACFTU in streamlining its internal bureaucracy included: the creation of the Presidium as the governing body in place of the Standing Committee, to be supported by a full-time and high-powered Secretariat; the enhancement of its administrative and welfare-handling capabilities through the addition of new departments; and the appointment of an independent Auditing Commission. However, the most strategic piece of structural reform aimed at rationalizing control and complementing a centrally-planned 'command' economy (as the 'Five Year Plan' cycle was launched) was the strengthening and centralization of the national industrial unions in a design which was also in part to contain the nation's imminent drift towards regionalism. The organizational logic was reaffirmed as imperative that 'trade union members of the same industrial branch of national economy should be organized on a national scale into a national industrial union, with the aim of ensuring the fulfilment of state production plans in accordance with the special features of the various industries and the needs of national construction' (ACFTU, 1953, p. 97). Such a shifted priority was evidenced by the spectacular growth in number of the nation's industrial unions during this period, from 11 in 1954–5 to 25 in 1957–8. Correspondingly, there were important and conscious efforts directed from the central bureaucracy aimed at curbing the otherwise excessive influences of the regional and city union councils.

At the 'grass-roots' level of labour organization, the ACFTU's 1953 constitutional amendments also made explicit the 'normative' configuration of the primary union structure, to be three-tier comprising 'the primary organ (that is, the enterprise), workshop and group'. Such structural stipulations were apparently designed to enhance the ACFTU's role to serve as the state's transmission-belt in mobilizing and organizing the workers at the basic union level in industry (see Warner, 1995, pp. 21ff).

When the CCP-led government was about to complete its nationalization of the economy by the mid-1950s, it was obvious that the Chinese trade unions were increasingly and overtly purged of the Western-style role of challenging enterprise management in the workplace. In contrast to their evangelistic character in the 1920s, unions in China became socialized inasmuch as they ceased to be adversarial but in effect became agencies and partners to management. Such a role arose because in the 'People's Republic' before the present market-oriented reforms, the workers and staff members were, as noted earlier, the 'masters' (*zhuren*) of the enterprise.

In 1957, the ACFTU held its Eighth National Congress when the first Five Year Plan was satisfactorily concluded, while the quasi-syndicalist utterances of the 'Hundred Flowers Campaign' started to be critical about the pathos of 'bureaucratism'. Unsurprisingly, neither was the trade union system exempt from criticism by sceptics that 'not enough attention had been given to the fact that as an organization of the masses, a trade union, apart from submitting to the leadership of the Party in policy and thought, must unfold its own independent activities' (cited in Lee, 1984, p. 51). However, such a spirit of 'political liberalism' proved transient and was soon aborted – corrected by the subsequent imperative of hastily ushering the Great Leap Forward on to the nation's agenda. However, the novel idea of a devolved union system hinted at in the 'Hundred Flowers' episode was sufficient to alert the state to the propensity of unions to drift into syndicalist opposition against authority. The trauma of such a shock caused an apprehensive leadership to tighten its grip by amending the ACFTU's Constitution in the Eighth National Congress. The amended Constitution reaffirmed the labour movement's unequivocal commitment to subscribe to the direction of the state and its industrial and economic policies, and remembered the rhetorical pledge that it would help regimentalize the socialist workforce to 'safeguard the socialist system and protect public property; to fight against all anti-socialist views and acts ... violation of law and social and work discipline and all acts of corruption and waste' (ACFTU, 1958, p. 112). At the same time, the ACFTU accentuated its activities in ideological education and indoctrination.

Nevertheless, the organizational structure of the ACFTU at the lower levels of the industry and locality was again revamped – this time apparently in order 'to facilitate the decentralization required by the "Great Leap Forward"' (see Turner *et al.*, 1980, p. 48). The earlier logic of placing the local councils under the industrial unions (as was ratified in the Seventh Congress of 1953) was literally reversed when the Chinese unions 'were reorganized on a regional basis with industrial branches' as a sequel to the Eighth National Congress. In recognition of the fallacy of its earlier policy to rely upon the weak national industrial unions, the ACFTU declared its reoriented organizational strategy in the 1957 National Congress that:

> with the exception of a few industrial unions ... the daily work of the local organizations and primary units of all other industrial unions should be carried out mainly under the leadership of the related local trade union council. (ACFTU, 1958, p. 99)

There were simultaneous endeavours to revamp the organization of the workplace, stemming from the ACFTU's constitutional amendments in

1957, which relaxed the threshold size of the workplace from 25 members to a considerably lowered level of ten, in order to qualify the appointment of a grass-roots trade union committee (Lee, 1986, p. 59). The Eighth Congress of the CCP held a year earlier endorsed, in parallel, the system of the Workers and Staff Congress to be established under the leadership of the Party branch secretary in the works. Before that, the Workers' Congress as a workplace institution for 'democratic management' and 'worker participation' used to perform as an adjunct to the Factory Management Committee which was, however, itself restrained because the Plant Manager was answerable only to the Party secretary in the enterprise and, as such, was not bound by any resolutions made by the Management Committee. The role and activities of the Factory Management Committee became consistently eroded and diminished under the impact of the 'Three-anti' and 'Five-anti' movements, until the state leadership decided, in the late 1950s, to detach the Workers' Congresses from such a withering system of Workplace Management Committees and instead place them directly under the prerogative of the party, with a view of involving the grass-roots union to serve as administrative agency and secretariat.

As was noted at the time:

> Methods of running factories and enterprises democratically have been experimented with ever since the People's Republic was founded in 1949. In 1957, the Party Central Committee decided to introduce, on a trial basis, the system of Workers' Congresses under the leadership of Party Committees. (Cited in Zhou, 1981, pp. 14–16)

This blueprint for the Worker Congress-cum-Trade Unions which devised a nominally 'participative' arrangement in the workplace was codified by the adoption of 'The (Drafted) Operational Regulations for State Enterprises' in 1961 at the Third Plenary Session of the Central Committee of the Eighth Party Congress. This step authorized the Workers' Congress to formally discuss and resolve any central problems of enterprise management deemed relevant to the workers' interests. The 1961 regulations were amended in 1965 in order to streamline the structure and prerogative of this workplace arrangement. During 1962 to 1966, the Workers' Congresses were used for airing grievances and, in a limited way, proved instrumental to the grass-roots union committees in wielding a degree of workplace influence in matters of factory management. According to Andors (1977), before the Cultural Revolution, the twin institutions of the basic union and the Workers' Congress complemented 'the two participation, triple combination system' as the 'management tools for smoothing over human conflict and making communications more effectively' (ibid., p. 136).

Subsequently, the austere and fundamentalist overtone of the 'Great Leap Forward' began to anticipate a nationwide 'leftist' drift towards radicalism – a 'chiliastic' mood which was soon to erupt into the open in a new drama.

2.3   THE ACFTU DURING THE CULTURAL REVOLUTION

The Cultural Revolution in its wake inflicted great damage to the development of the Chinese labour movement, because of the suspension of the ACFTU at the height of the sociopolitical upheavals which this traumatic movement engendered. 'During the Cultural Revolution, the position of the unions became increasingly dubious and later suppressed when suspended in 1967–68' (Ng, 1984, p. 64). The huge bureaucracy which the ACFTU epitomized in terms of organized labour as a 'popular' mass organization was seen by some as both a blessing as well as a threat of a potentially antagonistic and alternative influence to the 'authoritarian' claims of the ruling socialist party. The mid-1950s, for example, had seen tensions between the Party and the unions (see Perry 1994). The extremism of the Cultural Revolution unmasked the ambivalence and latent suspicions (if not hostilities) of the political ideologies against the ACFTU. Its purge by the vanguards of the revolution henceforth revealed a perennial feature of the Chinese labour movement, namely the Party's fears that the trade unions were establishing their own bureaucratic power-base, which has always strained the relationship between the political and the union movements. Indeed, the Party's distrust of the trade unions even after the Liberation, given their organized strength in the cities and industrial areas, was historically ingrained in its political struggles of the late 1920s.[4] Recreated in the Cultural Revolution was hence:

(a) reliance on the peasantry after 1927 ... [which] was an adaptation to a rural environment forced upon the communists by the annihilation of their numbers in the industrial centres by the Kuomintang Nationalists; ... isolation from urban environments and from the working class did, however, leave an undeniable stamp of primary reliance on revolutionary peasant consciousness and a consequent implicit denigration of the urban proletariat. (Hearn, 1977, pp. 160–1)

The impact of the Cultural Revolution was not just political and ideological; it also seriously disrupted the function of the economy and production in the enterprise. The twin machinery of the Factory Management Committee and

Workers' Congress was suspended throughout the country, and enterprise management fell into the control of revolutionary committees at the workplace (Andors, 1977, pp. 214–16). However, as the rigour of the Cultural Revolution escalated, there was a consistent and creeping growth of 'hegemonic' control by the Party. When celebrating its fortieth anniversary in 1965, the ACFTU acclimatized itself by canvassing the political imperative that 'professional work serves politics. That if politics is neglected, a wrong direction is taken ... Some say a good achievement in production expresses correct political thoughts' ('Editorial', *Gongren Ribao/Workers' Daily*, 19 September 1965, cited in *China News Analysis*, 1965, no. 627, p. 3). It subsequently declared that 'in the spirit of the instruction of the Party Central, all discussed and agreed to *lift high the great red banner of the thought of Mao Zedong*' (*China News Analysis*, 1965, no. 627, p. 5).

In their anti-establishment zeal to dismantle the institutional order, however, the recalcitrant Red Guards and their revolutionary worker--comrades soon launched a radical offensive against the ACFTU bureaucracy and purged it out of existence. In December 1966, the All-China Red Worker Rebels General Corps was organized 'with the support of the Cultural Revolution Group to seize power from the Ministry of Labour and ACFTU' (Lee, 1986, p. 110). At the height of the upheavals, Liu Shao-Ch'i, the State President whose power-base was rooted in his organization of the urban proletariat into unions before the Liberation, was denounced. His purge coincided with the suspension of the Chinese trade unions in 1967–8. Liu was condemned for 'promoting "counter-revolutionary economism" in the trade movement' and contesting the control of the party authority: that is, 'opposing Party leadership of the unions and supporting ... the unions' periodic attempts to gain independence from the Party' (Hearn, 1977, p. 161). As a sequel, the ACFTU, as an organ cradled under Liu's patronage since the Liberation, was accused of betraying the goal of 'class struggle' in production and advocating the supremacy of the technocrats over the party ideologues – that is, by unduly placing priority on the 'expert' to the 'red' criteria in production. Unwittingly, the ACFTU encountered its annihilation by failing the sacrosanct test that 'acceptance by the trade unions of Party leadership means acceptance of the leadership of Mao Zedong's thought' (*Beijing Review*, 8 December 1967, p. 31).

2.4   THE CHINESE TRADE UNIONS AFTER 1978

As the trauma of the Cultural Revolution subsided and waned in the late 1970s, the ACFTU was re-instated at the helm of the Chinese labour movement when the Ninth Trade Union Congress was convened in October 1978. The Congress, by revising substantially the Constitution of the national trade union centre, signalled the reconstruction of this organ of workers' organization. Under the blueprint of the reconstruction, some of the pre-1957 properties of the ACFTU were restored – such as redefining the size of a primary union again by the minimum of 25 members (instead of ten) and reviving the organizational strategy of focusing upon the regional and local labour union organs, so that there 'were again regionally based organizations with industrial or trade branches' (Turner *et al.*, 1980, p. 148).

The restored structure of the ACFTU has, since then, been fashioned as a complex hierarchy that is constituted at the upper tier of regional federations to 'link with the Party structure organized on a geographical basis'. Below it are further divisions based upon 'vertically organized industrial unions to parallel government ministries responsible for particular industries' – that is, industrial bureaux in the district (see Henley and Chen, 1981, p. 90; Hoffmann, 1974, pp. 127–34). It has been suggested that although the ACFTU was redeemed in 1978, the suspicion of the Party bureaucracy towards unionism as a rival political force persisted. As observed by Hearn (1977), 'the re-birth of the trade unions must surely be interpreted as rather more symbolic than substantial despite any merits in claims that the present union structure is part of an overall pattern of industrial democracy, Chinese style' (ibid., p. 168). In this context, it has been argued that the concurrent resurrection of the trade union structure and the Workers' Congress system could be interpreted in Chinese eyes as a purposive strategy to pre-empt the undue concentration of organized labour's power – otherwise feared by the Party if the labour movement were allowed to evolve its centralized bureaucratic strength on its own.

Even so, it appears that, in the aftermath of the Cultural Revolution, the official search for economic vitality under the ensuing 'modernization' drive encouraged the state to foster enterprise autonomy and to do so by restoring a system of workplace democracy. In the reformers' view, this was in partial emulation of the arrangements before the Cultural Revolution. Consequently, in place of the 'dual structure' enshrined in the mid-1950s, the Workers' Congress was revived but not the Factory Management Committee. In 1978, Deng Xiaoping declared before a national conference of trade unions that 'democratic management should be put into effect and the system of workers' congress should be established and perfected in all enterprises' (Ng, 1984, p. 59). Three years later, in 1981, the Central Committee of the Chinese Communist Party and the State Council promulgated the 'Provisional Regulations

Concerning Congress of Workers and Staff Members in state-owned Industrial Enterprises'. Parallel to the principle of 'directors assuming responsibilities for production and administration under the leadership of the Party Committees', all enterprises were called upon to set up 'Congresses of Workers and Staff members under the leadership of their Party committees' (see ibid.).

Since the beginning of the 1980s, as part of its national strategy to promote democratic management of the workplace, it became the state's policy to appear to devolve the Chinese trade union organization to the grass-roots level and make its presence and activities more conspicuous at the workplace in support of the Workers' Congress system in the enterprise. Such an idea has been hinted as early as in 1978 by Deng Xiaoping at the Ninth National Trade Union Congress at that the responsibility to establish and propagate the Workers' Congress among the Chinese workers would be incumbent upon the Chinese trade unions. After the pledge of the ACFTU in its Ninth National Congress to commit itself to improving production relations in the enterprises in order to support the 'Four Modernizations', the nation's trade union centre placed as the top priority on its agenda of five tasks in 1981, to 'mobilize' and 'organize' the workers and staff members to carry out reforms in the enterprise. In the wake of the above institutional adjustments, the theme of the post-Cultural Revolution reforms – aimed to decentralize the economy by sponsoring enterprise autonomy as well as to pragmatize the unions and democratize the workplace in order to make management more responsive to the managed – began to consolidate at the turn of the decade into the 1980s. Workers' demands were again at least formally enshrined as important criteria for determining the performance of the Chinese trade unions as their representative mass organizations.

The ACFTU attempted to vindicate its resurrected role and image amidst the euphoria of the 'Four Modernizations' ordained by the party at the Tenth All-China Trade Union Congress which was held in October 1983. Its Chairman, Ni Zhifu, laid out the agenda of the Chinese unions' newly pragmatized mission by appealing to them, in this session, to follow the Party's directions of practising the three 'musts' in order to articulate the workers' interests and authenticate their tasks by serving with dedication such interests. The 'three musts' canvassed hence the prescriptions that:

(i)   Trade unions, as mass organizations under the leadership of the CCP, must honestly serve the workers' needs, do more for workers and arouse the activism of workers;

(ii)   Trade unions must protect the legitimate rights and interests of workers, support what is right and oppose what is wrong in order to play a positive role in society and the country; and

(iii) Trade unions much face workers at the basic level squarely, forge close ties with them, voice their opinions and demands, and become truly 'home of workers'. (*Renmin Ribao/People's Daily*, 27 October 1983, p. 1)

It was evident that the ACFTU was determined to re-align its strategy in order to dilute its image of bureaucratic officialdom and instead to cultivate its popular appeal as the representative agent of the Chinese workers, now destined to embrace the dynamics of the 'Four Modernizations': 'Such recognition would provide an important corrective to the former over-emphasis upon the State's interest without commensurate and sufficient attention to safeguard the individual interests of workers' (Ng, 1985, p. 7). Given such an intent to rationalize and pragmatize its programme of activities, it was little surprise that the ACFTU at its Tenth National Congress had given emphasis to the harmonization of the State's policies and workers' interests, as well as its role in organizing and mobilizing the general workforce in the 'Four Modernizations', as the interrelated themes of its anticipated tasks. Specifically, the priorities of work prescribed for the Chinese trade unions at this 1983 National Congress appeared to be:

(i)   popularizing, strengthening and consolidating the Workers' Congress system and their grass-roots union organizations;

(ii)   safeguarding the welfare of workers and staff members in enterprises through labour legislation improvements;

(iii) organizing, promoting and performing extensive education activities among workers and staff members in order to enhance their political, cultural, spiritual and technical standards which help ensure their 'moral high-mindedness, discipline, dedication and competence' (for instance, the 'Worker Spare-time Committee' system was created to plan spare-time cultural and sports activities, as well as to develop the relevant facilities, premises and undertakings run by the ACFTU and its unions at all levels and to foster mass cultural work in cities, factories and mines); and

(iv)   strengthening the internal organization work of the trade unions themselves and gearing the trade union work to the needs of the rank-and-file at the grassroots so as to keep close ties with the 'broad masses' needs and aspirations of the workers and staff members (Ng, 1985, pp. 7–8).

It appears that the rigours of the 'Four Modernization' reforms were focused by the Chinese trade unions upon the 'dualistic' aspects of, first, democratic management of the workplace; and, second, labour market reforms and liberalization during the 1980s up – to June 1989 – which temporarily halted the stamina of the reformers. In a move to enhance their workplace role, the Chinese unions sought to merge the union branch in the same plant with the Congress into a twin machinery of worker representation. Like the Workers' Congress, each enterprise was to set up its trade union under the relevant industrial union of the district, with its chairman, vice-chairman and the trade union committee members 'democratically elected by the workers' (Xiang, 1980, p. 22). In this context, the production-unit itself has now been highlighted as the refocused centre of work for the union movement. However, what seemed to be a landmark was 'the changeover from the system of "party committee leadership" to that of "factory manager responsibility", as a sequel to the "nation-wide economic reform programme" promulgated by the Party's Central Committee in 1984' (Ng, 1986, p. 7).

As the Party withdrew steadily into an advisory capacity, while rescinding its direct control of the daily operations of the Chinese enterprises, it appears that the nexus of the latters' governance – at least in terms of the state's blueprint of workplace reforms that predated June 1989 – had been shifting consistently towards the workplace assembly, using the Workers' Congress as the principal organ of allegedly realizing 'democratic management'. Such a logic of enterprise governance was later developed further and consolidated into the relatively novel idea of the 'Factory Manager Responsibility and Workers' Congress Decision' principle. In the autumn of 1985, such an enhanced system was set up in Shanghai to formally vest the Workers' Congress formally with a three-fold power to:

(i)   check and inspect important decisions of management in the enterprise;
(ii) protect workers' legal rights in the enterprise; and
(iii) supervise, evaluate and elect members of the enterprise's management.

The Shanghai Municipal Trade Union Council, at its Seventh Municipal Congress of Trade Unions held in Shanghai in 1985, recognized as the top priorities on its agenda the policies to first, participate in economic reforms and mobilize workers to contribute towards this process (by involving, specifically, the Chinese workers in the 'democratic management' of the enterprise); and second, mobilize workers to contribute towards the improvement of the enterprise's efficiency and productivity;

as well as to third, promote 'democratic management' and 'worker participation' through the vehicle of the Workers' Congress (see Ng, 1985, p. 27).

In the mid-1980s, the ACFTU also launched a nationwide and comprehensive programme of worker education in order to promote the grass-roots' participation in the activities of 'democratic management' of the Workers' Congress. In Shanghai, its Municipal Trade Union Council created the office of 'Director of Democratic Management' in assisting enterprises and their union committees to set up their arrangements in the Workers Congress system. In Guangzhou in 1986, the endeavours by the Guangdong Provincial Trade Union Council and the Guangzhou Municipal Trade Union Council to advance democratic management in the workplace enabled these twin trade union organs to report a profile of their achievements that:

 (i)   5383 grass-roots union organizations had been established;
 (ii)   3813 of the 4690 enterprises in the city had instituted the Workers' Congress (i.e. 81 per cent);
 (iii) 1997 enterprises had introduced the system of 'Workers' Congress and Factory Manager responsibility';
 (iv)   2132 enterprises had instituted the system of 'Workers' Congress and democratic appraisal of the factory cadres';
 (v)   958 enterprises had introduced electoral procedures for the selection of the Enterprise Director; and
 (vi)   53 enterprises had been designated as the test points to experiment with the pilot scheme of merging the Worker Congress representative committee with the Trade Union representative committee (Ng, 1986, pp. 13–14).

In retrospect, all these drastic changes occurring in the mid- and late 1980s to the Chinese enterprises were apparently suggestive of a new role for trade unionism in China. The structural intricacy involved in rebuilding the augmented Workers' Congress system may be interpreted as a reform strategy to reinforce the influence of the centrally administered Chinese union bureaucracy by strengthening its 'grass-roots' organization in the enterprise, where its presence used to be feeble. The union had thus become more visible now in the workplace, inasmuch as it has been made to deputize for the Workers' Congress during its recess. Such processes enabled the Chinese union to appear to enjoy the prerogative of the Congress over plant-wide management, with its mandate derived vicariously by virtue of its 'agency' role for the Congress. In the late 1980s, when the state was about to free the nation from the grip of its historical vestiges owed to the Soviet model, and to evolve its own management system with 'Chinese characteristics' (see Warner 1993; 1995), such a *hybrid* arrangement apparently aroused promises of a more pragmatic approach by giving scope to members to participate in, for example production conferences. However, for the newly reconstituted union structure in China, the odds were that the adjusted workplace terrain was liable yet again to implicate it in new areas of potential role conflicts and ambiguities. For instance, it became incumbent upon the Chinese trade unions to monitor the Workers' Congress in the workshop carefully and successfully (Xiang, 1980, p. 22) 'lest the paradox of uncontrolled drifts towards workplace "syndicalism" contrary to doctrinal "democratic centralism" might result' (Ng, 1984, p. 67). The dilemma of these enlightening reforms to enhance the 'socialist' unions in China and to convert them into the more authentic workplace agencies of the Chinese 'labouring mass', which still haunts the conscience of the ACFTU leadership today, was already emergent over a decade ago.

Parallel to these reforms of workplace representation and their problematic ramifications for the Chinese trade unions was the concomitant, and perhaps more ambitious, endeavour of the state to engineer labour market reforms as the key to fostering enterprise autonomy and dismantling the 'socialist command economy' and 'iron rice bowl' (see Warner, 1986; 1987a; 1987b; 1989; 1992; 1993). Foremost amongst these labour market advances were the 'core' activities to liberalize the formerly rigid and highly-structured central wage system (see Takahara, 1992; Warner, 1995). The state's strategy was to devolve its highly-centralized, wage-determining prerogative to the enterprises, by virtue of these wage sector reforms, in order to enable them 'to decide on their wage levels and to choose the forms of wages according to their own needs and possibilities' (Sun, 1990, p. 255). The authority vested in the enterprises which enabled them to determine and negotiate their own wage arrangements, and which is now ideologically justified for giving scope to the doctrinal principle of 'each according to his work', was apparently intended to help the individual enterprises to prepare better for competition in the 'commodity exchange market', because they could now vary the wage bill according to their abilities to pay. In 1985, China adopted on a nationwide basis a drastically revamped wage system – being itself made up of 'a basic wage, post wage, seniority wage and incentive wage', with a 'post wage' (that is pay for responsibility) item as the principal component (see Sun, 1990, pp. 270–1; Warner, 1995, p. 133).

In spite of the official zeal to propagate the individualistic notion of 'egalitarian' pay determined at the plant level and the support given by the union agencies to buttress its application, it appears that the transformation of China's once heavily-centralized system of wage administration was probably trapped, at best, in a 'half-way' house under the pre-1989 reforms. The wage reforms were associated with the creeping inflation which was to beset the Chinese economy on the eve of the students' democratic demands that erupted later into the events of June 1989. A critique of that time summed up the disarray of disturbed disequilibrium in the wage economy:

> The old wage administration system has been broken and enterprises begin to wield powers in wage distribution in varying degrees. But interference in wage distribution by administrative departments at different levels is still quite common. So there is a long way to go to attain the goal of enterprises having full responsibility for their own profit and loss and full autonomy in distribution. (Sun, 1990, p. 274)

In addition to the highly-intricate wage reforms ushered to the Chinese workers, other key features of this mixed-bag of labour market reforms introduced by the state in its ambitious, yet ill-coordinated restructuring strategies in the 1980s included: interrelated measures to enhance the manpower utilization flexibility of the individual enterprise by, first, devolving to it an ability of discretion almost analogous to a crucial personnel function otherwise assumed in a capitalist enterprise – namely, recruitment, transfer and firing (as the once sacrosanct socialist norm of the worker's permanent membership and employment in the enterprise was steadily rescinded); and, second, propagating the newly instituted device of 'contract labour', to be adopted by the enterprises in hiring new workers and staff members – as a preferred and more flexible option to the older practices of either 'permanent employment' or 'temporary employment'.[5] These innovative arrangements, reminiscent of Western-style labour market practices, engendered a new risk of precipitating mass unemployment and impeding the job security of the Chinese worker – which had been hitherto taken for granted. Such new labour market threats to the individual's securities (in terms of employment and wage entitlement, and so on) in spite of their promises of bettering production efficiencies and flexibilities, presented again to the Chinese trade unions a new challenge in their newly enhanced agenda to safeguard the workers' occupational and workplace interests (see Warner, 1995).

Inasmuch as the trade union has been made the *de facto* agency in deputizing for the Workers' Congress, the Chinese trade unions were not immune (even if they were just the reluctant partners to the factory management) from the criticism about their tendencies to drift into lay intervention in managerial decision-making which could be not only detrimental to their image and identity as the authentic representatives of workers' interests, but also unprofessional and hence inadvertently impairing the efficiencies of production.

2.5   CONCLUDING REMARKS

To sum up, as 'market socialism' began to emerge, the national trade union centre, as a quasi-official agency organizing the Chinese working class, was probably trapped in new ways that stemmed from such sources as the creation of new (economic, business and occupational) opportunities, proliferation of sectional interests, haggling over conflicts between the managers and managed, as well as the subsequent generation of grievances in the workplace. A major theme of China's 'Four Modernizations' movement has been and is still centred upon reforming enterprise management with an associated concern to instil into the labour and wage domain, a 'market economy' orientation. There were even moves within the ACFTU to reform itself (see White *et al.*, 1996). However, in hindsight, these reform endeavours before mid-1989 were perhaps overly ambitious, as well as merely unsystematic, directed simultaneously at the enterprise and the wider economy, yet with no more than lukewarm intentions to revitalize a basically 'socialist' economic system.[6] As a result, these efforts fell short of a coherent approach and frequently lapsed into mere rhetoric. What has emerged from this hybrid approach has been an impasse, inheriting strong vestiges of a 'socialist' command economy, but interwoven with some 'half-way' innovations adapted from Western capitalist institutions. For the ACFTU, its uncertainties have been accumulating, for example over its apprehension about the foreign-funded business sector, as illustrated by the highly-restrained or ambivalent stance of the Chinese trade unions in dealing with joint venture enterprises. However, elsewhere, as in the state-owned sector, the euphoria of affluence, as well as the associated strains and imbalances emanating from the labour market and other economic reforms have coalesced to present a rapidly shifting terrain of industrial relations for Chinese workers and their managers. Indeed, '[I]n this context, with the transition to the "socialist market economy" officially proclaimed in October 1992, different ownership bases may coexist and hybrid organizational forms may result ... As in previous phases of economic and organizational development, the position is far from neat and systematic' (Warner, 1995, p. 162). These changes have implied, in turn, a formidable challenge to the ACFTU. However, the events of June 1989 put all these initiatives into a transient 'freeze', despite their revival in 1992 after Deng Xiaoping's 'Southern Tour'. In retrospect, what transpired 'has itself been interpreted as a syndrome of the institutional incapacity of China's mammoth state bureaucracy to cope with the frustrated and alienated expectations in the populace which its spectacular economic reforms have ironically inspired' (Ng, 1995, pp. 65–6). We now turn, in the next chapter, to the ACFTU's evolving role in its near-present and contemporary setting.

3 The ACFTU's Evolving Role

3.1 INTRODUCTION

As we have seen in the previous chapter, the legacy of the past weighs very heavily on the present strategy and structure of Chinese trade unions. Therefore, the direction and shape of the ACFTU cannot be fully seen in isolation from its origins and historical context, the most recent, post-1949 background having been set out in detail in Chapter 2. The historical dimension is built into not only their strategic goals but also their structure and function.[1] As Leung (1988) observes:

> The current function and importance of Chinese trade unions can only be understood in the context of the development of the Chinese labour movement. Trade unions evolved in the midst of the immense social upheavals which shaped modern China. The unions' present status, self-image and power reflects their role in these revolutions, regressions and reversals. Their historical development will continue to influence their future role in the changes still sweeping China. (p. 7)

It is perhaps the above link to past societal turbulence which may have given Chinese trade unions their distinct character, although many other labour movements have also emerged from very long periods of struggle. Even so, the ACFTU's past was particularly tumultous.

3.2 STRATEGY AND GOALS OF THE CHINESE TRADE UNIONS

The strategy and goals of the ACFTU were, from the early years, closely linked, and often identical to those of the CCP. However, they were also distinctive in order to be appropriate for a trade union and its specific activities. The CCP had attempted to organize workers before the formation of its Labour Secretariat in 1921 (Lee, 1986, p. 1). The First All-China Labour Congress had been convened in 1922, but it was not until 1925 at the Second Congress that a Marxist resolution on 'class struggle' was adopted (ibid., p. 8).

'Class struggle' required a 'working class' – as a leading scholar of the Chinese labour movement points out:

> Political leaders in twentieth-century China have accorded the working class a prominent place in their vision of a new society, modernization was seen as virtually synonymous with industrialization and workers were esteemed as the agents of development. A party claiming to represent the forces of progress thus needed a working-class constituency. The labour movement's ideological significance gave it a far greater political voice than the relatively small size of the Chinese work force might otherwise warrant. But ideology was not the only explanation for the key role that workers came to play in political events. (Perry, 1993, p. 4)

Indeed, the industrial damage that organized workers could wreak gave them an importance disproportionate to their actual numbers. Both Nationalist and Communist parties tried to actively channel this resource to their own ends and harness it to their political agendas. Labour thus became a potent force in Chinese politics both prior to and during industrialization. It is clear that the origins of its subsequent political role pre-date both Guomindang and CCP formal associations, as one writer has clearly spelled out (see ibid., pp. 4–9).

The formal goals of the ACFTU were, from the very start, 'to unite all workers and promote the welfare of workers' (Lee, 1986, p. 9). It thus set out from 1925 onwards to (1) develop workers' unions in China; (2) unify the labour movement; (3) set up an organization system; (4) direct union activities; (5) adjudicate inter-union disputes; (6) propagate the aims of class struggle; (7) represent the Chinese workers in relations with outside countries; (8) raise workers' educational levels; and (9) protect workers' benefits (ibid.).

Many decades later little had changed, as the *ACFTU Constitution* (1993) proclaims:

> 'The trade unions of China are mass organizations of the Chinese working class led by the Chinese Communist Party and formed by workers and staff members voluntarily, and the bridges and bonds linking the Party and the masses of the workers and staff members, are the important social pillar of the State power and are the representatives of the interests of trade union members and workers and staff. (*ACFTU Constitution*, 1993, p. 1; see Appendix)

A typical example of official rhetoric can be seen in an editorial of the official CCP newspaper – the *Renmin Ribao/Peoples' Daily* – entitled 'Back-bone of China Today', to celebrate May Day 1995 and the Seventieth Anniversary of the founding of the ACFTU. It contains one of the clearest examples of such rhetoric in the Chinese context:

> In the great transformation to the development of the socialist market economy, trade unions of various levels should inherit and develop the fine traditions, fully play the safeguarding functions of trade unions, diligently raise trade unions' work to a new level, shoulder the duties which are more difficult and play a more important role. They should organize staff and workers to seriously learn from Comrade Deng Xiaoping's theory of building socialism with Chinese characteristics and arm their minds with scientific theories. They should take care of the staff and workers in and workers in a better manner; safeguard their labour rights and interests, material interests and democratic rights and interests; and do more solid things for them, solve difficulties for them and reflect their wills, desires, demands and voices. They should strengthen and improve their ideological and political work, be skilful in addressing grievances and solving conflicts, and properly guide, protect and develop the enthusiasm among the staff and workers. (*Renmin Ribao/People's Daily* editorial, 29 April 1995, p. 1; *SWB*, 5 May 1995)

Apart from the genuflection to Comrade Deng, as opposed to Chairman Mao, the erstwhile 'Great Helmsman', and the reference to the new 'socialist market economy' this tribute could have been penned in the mid-1950s. Otherwise, not a great deal appears to have changed (cf. Wilson, 1990b). The example above is, indeed, resonant of yesteryear's phraseology. The Party-line is consistent throughout these declarations, whether of editorials of Party newspapers, Party leaders, union chiefs or senior government ministers. Reading between the lines and behind the rhetoric, there are new anxieties that are often revealed in such utterances these days.

The top Chinese trade union leader, Wei Jianxing, a member of the Political Bureau of the CCP Central Committee and chairperson of the ACFTU, stressed the union's goals of protecting the legal rights of workers in the light of changing economic times:

> Workers ask more consideration from trade unions to safeguard their labour rights, material gains and democratic rights, under the situation that economic relations and labour relations in China have undergone

profound changes when the country is developing a socialist market economy ... Work of trade unions must be linked with economic development. Rights and interests of workers can never be protected and workers' initiative cannot be brought into play if trade unions do not focus on economy ... At present time, ... trade unions should work in new ways and new systems, such as signing collective contracts on equal consultation. (*Xinhua News Agency*, 30 April 1995; *SWB*, 3 May 1995)

A year later, a *People's Daily* editorial further underscored the problems encountered in the deepening of the economic reforms:

because of the diversity of interests at stake and the readjustment of the relationship of interests among the parties concerned, and since this is an unprecedented undertaking, the interests of some people, including some of the workers, may be somewhat affected in the course of realising the ... changes and they will face some difficulties in their work and lives. This is a problem that the party and the government are doing their utmost to avoid but find it hard to eliminate. In this regard, the understanding and support of the workers and the masses is needed. As for some workers who have actual difficulties and ideological problems, party and government leaders and trade union organizations at all levels must show great concern and care for them and make every effort to relieve their difficulties, solve their problems, give a clear explanation to them and send them warmth. Never should we ignore problems and only try to solve them when they have been aggravated. (*Renmin Ribao/People's Daily,* 30 April 1996; SWB, 2 May 1996)

In a nut-shell, trade unions in China are currently organized around four main functions, according to the most recent official (and legal) definition. First, they claim they must protect the interest of the whole country, but at the same time safeguard the legitimate rights and interests of the workers. Second, they must help their members participate in the management of their own work units. Third, they should mobilize the labour force to raise productivity and the economy's performance. Fourth, they should educate the workers to be better members of society. These functions are clearly set out in the Trade Union Law, which was revised in 1992. Whether their rank-order is significant is moot, but it may well be. The union spokespersons who formulate such phrases may be readier to put the rights' 'safeguard' and 'participation' function before the 'mobilization' (and 'education') priority of earlier times, although the managers and Labour Ministry bureaucrats may arrange them otherwise (Interviews at ACFTU Headquarters, July 1993). The ACFTU has also evolved many other activities, such as revenue-raising, for example by running its own enterprises to bolster union finances to support welfare activities (see White *et al.*, 1996, pp. 56–7). By the end of 1995, it had launched 139 000 enterprises, of which 67 000 were economic entities, with a business income of 45 million, RMB; most are in the service-sector, take the form of 'collective ownership, and now employ over one million employees. (ACFTU statistics, 1996).

The first articles of the most recent Trade Union Law (PRC, 1992) set out the initial terms of reference:

Article 1   This Law is formulated in accordance with the Constitution of the People's Republic of China with a view to ensuring the status of trade unions in the political, economic and social life of the state, defining their rights and obligations and bringing into play their role in the cause of socialist modernization.

Article 2   Trade unions are mass organizations of the working class formed by the workers and staff members on a voluntary basis.

Article 3   All manual or mental workers in enterprises, institutions or state organs within the territory of China who rely on wages or salaries as their main source of income, irrespective of their nationality, race, sex, occupation, religious belief or educational background, have the right to organize and join trade unions according to law. (see Appendix 1 in Warner, 1995, p. 167)

Key words, like 'mass organizations', 'working-class', 'masters of the country', 'socialist labour emulation', 'collectivism and socialism', 'democratic centralism', and so on, set the tone of the document. The 1992 revised law does not differ very much, in its essentials, however, from the 1950 version, and contains similar *ideological* terminology. Rights and obligations are stressed, but the right to work and the right to strike do not feature. The latter, which featured in the 1975 Chinese Constitution, was removed by constitutional amendments in 1982, as noted earlier. There are also no rights regarding dispute-resolution. Rights are also qualified by the term 'legitimate' and 'democratic'. The phrase 'voluntary basis' also appears, as does 'work in an independent and autonomous way'. Thus:

Article 4 Trade unions shall observe and safeguard the Constitution, take it as the fundamental criterion for their activities and conduct their work in an independent and autonomous way in accordance with the Constitution of Trade Unions of the People's Republic of China. (Ibid., p. 168)

The term 'workers' is normally expressed as 'workers and staff members', linked to 'alliance of workers and peasants'. The ultimate goal is to 'turn them into well-educated and self-disciplined labourers with lofty ideals and moral integrity'. All actions must conform to the 'Constitution', the 'law', and 'patriotism'. There is obeisance to other countries' trade unions on the basis of 'non-interference' in 'each others' internal affairs'. Much is included; very little is excluded.

While 'Socialist Modernization' is set out as a goal, the terms 'Economic Reform', 'Four Modernizations' or 'Open Door' are not noted. Nor is the 'Liberation' even mentioned. Previous clauses about representing and protecting employees in private firms have been deleted. However, 'labour-contracts', 'joint-ventures', and 'foreign-capital enterprises' enter the scene, but not 'Special Economic Zones' and 'Open Cities'. The tone of the document still remains in the 1950s, but the detail has been extended to cover the economic and political realities of the 1990s – to a degree, at least. Paradoxically, labour legislation in the PRC was weak for many years (see Josephs, 1990; Xia, 1991; Korzec, 1992; Leung, 1993) and most laws mainly protected the employees of SOEs. Even in early 1994, there was still inadequate legislation setting out minimum wages, working hours, industrial safety and so on. The eventual national Labour Law was published on 6 July of that year, to be effective 1 January 1995, details of which are set out in the next chapter.

3.3   STRUCTURE OF THE ACFTU

Structural characteristics of trade unions have been linked to two broad sets of functions: first, their administrative rationale and second, their representative rationale (see Child *et al.*, 1973; Warner, 1995).[2] Many industrial relations writers have stressed the importance of structural characteristics (see Barling *et al.*, 1992, pp. 10 ff). Trade unions are, however, clearly different from business organizations, largely because of their membership characteristics.

Trade union structure is, more often than not, as noted earlier, a product of its history. Chinese unions are no exception to this axiom, therefore, we must take note of their fundamental rationales in the years prior to the 'Liberation' in 1949 that played such a major role in shaping their present state. These rationales represent a variant on the cases noted in Western industrial relations' systems as there was always a strong ideological and political dimension to unions to be found in what are now or were Communist states. The goals and structures of their collective organizations were affected by both state socialist theory and practice, most notably stemming from Leninist influences.

Trade unions in such economies were dramatically different from those found in Western contexts, for example the specifically Leninist concept of trade unions in communist societies based on what was called 'democratic centralism' (see Poole, 1986, p. 92). Accordingly, the Soviet model which had high levels of formal unionization, industrial unions and an apex-governing structure, dutifully implementing party policy in 'ideal-typical' terms, greatly influenced the emergence of Chinese organized labour after 1949 (Wilson, 1987, p. 221). The trade unions soon became an intrinsic part of the Soviet-influenced model introduced by Mao and colleagues during the First Five-Year Plan (1953–7) (see Littler and Palmer, 1987, p. 268). Their 'transmission-belt' role was to translate policy decided above into action at workplace level. Lenin believed that 'consciousness could not occur amongst workers themselves and "would have to be brought to them from above"' (cited in Poole, 1981, p. 13)

Trade unions in the People's Republic of China had been organized on two principles, namely vertical and horizontal, the former in keeping with Soviet 'industrial' principles of organization (see Brown, 1966; Poole, 1986; Pravda and Ruble, 1987; Chiang, 1990; Kaple, 1994). Craft and occupational structures represented the horizontal principle and were based on an older 'guild' tradition which had traditionally characterized master–apprentice relations in pre-industrialized China (see Ma, 1955; Chesneaux, 1969). The organizational rationale of post-revolutionary Chinese unions was therefore to set them up along industrial and craft lines, but a geographical principle was later introduced when local union councils were given the power to run all local industrial unions except those already under national industrial unions (see Figure 3.1). The above move was spurred by the small percentage of industrial workers in the PRC's labour force, political considerations and emulation of the Soviet model (see Brown, 1966; Littler and Palmer, 1987) rather than any logic of union organization based on 'trades' (see Lee, 1984; 1986).

43

Figure 3.1   ACFTU dual-structure of organization after 1949

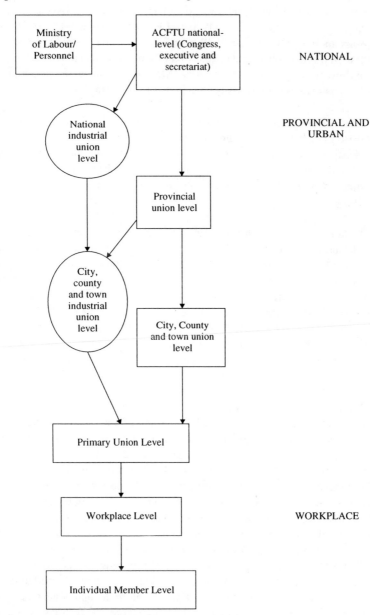

Source   Adapted from various ACFTU publications.

The present structure of Chinese labour organization as set out in the ACFTU Constitution, (see Appendix) has not dramatically changed in nearly five decades, since 1949 (see Lee, 1984; 1986). The model of unions in the PRC, as we shall see, has remained roughly the same, although there had been vast expansion of union membership as urbanization drew more workers into industry. After the unions were reconstituted in the post-Maoist era, it has been said that Deng Xiaoping:

> sought to rationalize the state planning system and the productive enter-
> prise in order to achieve greater efficiency ... The labour movement ...
> [was] ... also ... restructured to harmonize with government ministeries
> on industry lines, while regional federations of unions ... [were] ...
> linked with the Party structure on a geographical basis. (Lansbury *et al.*,
> 1984, p. 57)

If there were only just under two and a half million union members at the Liberation when they were probably more of an 'industrial elite' than today, there were (on paper, at least) just over 100 million by 1995 (see Table 3.1) by the end of the 1980s, with around half a million full-time worker representatives by the latter date (see Table 3.2). There were only around 100 000 primary trade union units in 1951, but this had risen to about 600 000 by the early 1990s. There has in turn been a growth in the degree of nominal unionization of urban industrial workers from just over one in four, to over nine out of ten in the state-sector by then (*Beijing Review*, 13 February 1989, pp. 27–31), a figure still unchanged. We shall return to this point a little later.

By early 1997, there were six industrial unions and 30 provincial trade union federations. The ACFTU remained the 'apex' organization which integrated the constituent parts (for details, see Appendix. As its Constitution states: 'The highest leading bodies over the trade unions are the National Congress of Trade Unions and the Executive Committee of the All-China Federation of Trade Unions as elected by the National Congress' (1993, p. 6). The National Congress meets normally every five years. The 16 national unions were organized respectively by trade in the among following industries: railways, civil aviation, seamen, road transport, post and telecommunications, engineering and metallurgy, petrochemicals, coal mining and geology, water and electricity, textiles, light industry, urban development and building materials, agriculture and forestry, finance and trade, and education. The federation's eight departments were organized as follows: namely economy, technology and labour protection, labour and wages, women workers, propaganda and education, international liaison, organization,

Table 3.1 Distribution of Chinese trade union membership (geographical division by the end of 1995)

Geographical distribution	Members of trade union	Female worker membership	Labour contract worker membership	Minority nationality membership
National Total	103 996 341	41 164 778	44 838 227	4 552 195
(1) Beijing	2 702 171	1 236 104	1 516 835	93 568
(2) Tianjin	2 254 530	1 023 819	740 760	80 404
(3) Hebei	5 205 115	1 977 346	2 971 711	164 526
(4) Shanxi	3 086 897	1 063 165	1 800 762	17 931
(5) Inner Mongolia	2 260 891	892 208	497 245	297 264
(6) Liaoning	9 234 588	3 796 173	4 206 770	490 326
(7) Jilin	3 497 799	1 492 020	1 516 699	246 294
(8) Heilongjiang	5 582 259	2 142 157	1 353 253	151 959
(9) Shanghai	3 962 784	1 736 653	2 728 480	22 083
(10) Jiangsu	6 697 435	2 790 716	3 861 281	43 492
(11) Zhejiang	3 568 469	1 465 963	1 704 878	9 825
(12) Anhui	3 141 831	1 164 309	913 323	40 304
(13) Fujian	2 569 606	970 310	933 613	13 682
(14) Jiangxi	2 817 659	1 001 493	863 476	6 078
(15) Shandong	5 929 556	2 256 550	3 134 189	69 174
(16) Henan	5 438 003	2 068 654	2 647 224	108 626
(17) Hubei	5 111 157	2 074 952	1 756 899	85 142
(18) Hunan	4 033 918	1 618 200	1 287 503	214 813
(19) Guangdong	4 401 306	1 850 645	2 139 975	23 297
(20) Guangxi	2 551 688	990 617	849 094	600 362
(21) Hainan	736 464	299 097	338 339	56 977
(22) Sichuan	6 889 060	2 604 428	3 135 003	162 190
(23) Guizhou	1 514 610	546 286	392 871	247 002
(24) Yunnan	2 576 557	983 357	827 086	400 845
(25) Tibet	111 290	40 530	13 279	75 950
(26) Shaanxi	2 427 006	866 918	1 252 489	27 185
(27) Gansu	1 741 046	623 487	548 346	71 394
(28) Qinghai	512 539	191 872	113 038	65 634
(29) Ningxia	460 334	176 734	178 683	69 498
(30) Xinjiang	2 544 883	1 049 735	552 771	584 045
State Government Offices	393 339	154 034	59 740	11 310
Organs. responsible to the Party Central Committee	41 551	16 246	2 612	1 015

Source: Adapted from ACFTU statistics, 1996.

Table 3.2 Distribution of Chinese trade union committees (by scale of unit and economic type, by end of 1995)

Sub-division	Number of basic trade union committees	Number of workshop trade union committees	Number of small groups
National Total	593 113	940 088	6 130 799
1. Categorized according to scale of unit (employees)			
(1) 1–10	14 490	666	7 413
(2) 11–50	209 964	41 235	305 111
(3) 51–100	143 022	69 128	538 648
(4) 101–200	109 299	91 963	759 005
(5) 201–300	40 414	71 818	471 909
(6) 301–500	33 427	120 471	618 314
(7) 501–800	19 718	131 885	658 582
(8) 801–2999	19 635	270 920	1 589 282
(9) 3000	3 144	142 002	1 192 535
2. Categorized according to economic type			
(1) State-owned	456 588	755 323	5 217 522
(2) Collective	117 582	136 418	678 179
(3) Privately operated	1 346	2 563	11 031
(4) Individual	541	933	6 206
(5) Collaboratively operated	922	1 711	0 157
(6) Joint-stock	4 632	17 292	120 353
(7) Foreign invested	6 822	22 517	76 814
(8) Hong Kong, Macau and Taiwan invested	2 572	2 381	12 863
(9) Others	2 108	950	7 674

Source: Adapted from ACFTU statistics, 1996.

finance and accounts auditing. The ACFTU – it has been said – 'advises' the government and the party on new legislation and then helps to interpret their application (Interviews at ACFTU Headquarters, November 1995 and March 1997).

The leadership-structure of the ACFTU (and the actual incumbents in 1993–4) is set out in Table 3.3. There was one chairman, nine vice-chairmen, 25 members of the Praesidium, 10 members of the Secretariat, 241 members of the Executive Committee (plus eight members of the Auditing Commission). There was a sprinkling of women top officials (many fewer than their proportionate share of members) plus provision for minority people representation, who were similarly sparse.

It can be seen from Table 3.1 that out of nearly 104 million ACFTU members at the end of 1995, there were over 41 million female members and over four million minority people members. It is clear from Table 3.3 that there is chronic under-representation of women in the top policy-making bodies of the trade union federation.

Table 3.3   Leading members of the All-China Federation of Trade Unions, 1993

Chairman:
> Wei Jianzing

Vice-Chairmen:
> Zhang Dinghua, Yang Xingfu, Li Qisheng, Liu Heng, Jiang Hiafu(m), Zhang Guoxing, Fang Jiade, Xue Zhaoyun(f), Teng Yilong

Members of the Praesidium (listed in order of the number of strokes in their surnames in Chinese):
> You Ren(m), Feng Zuchun, Liu Zhifeng, Liu Hongren, Guan Huan, Sun Lianjie, Sun Xiangyan, Memet Nur(m), Li Yongan, Li Guozhong, Yang Jingyu, Xiao Zhenbang, Dong Baifen(f/m), Zhang Shaofeng, Chen Bing, Luo Shuzhen(f), Shan Yihe, Zhao Di(f), Shi Yi(m), Gao Zhongquian, Shang Baokum, Jiang Wenliang, Pan Yiqing, Qu Zugeng

Members of the Secretariat:
First Secretary of the Secretariat: Zhang Dinghua
Other Members of the Secretariat: Yang Xingfu, Li Qisheng, Zhang Guoxiang, Fang Jiade, Xue Zhaoyun(f), Teng Yilong, Xiao Zhenbang, Li Yongan, Shan Yihe

Members of the Executive Committee: 241

Members of the Auditing Commission:
> Chairman: Zhang Fuyou
> Vice-Chairman: Jiang Yongqing
> Standing Members: 6

Note: female members are indicated by the suffix (f) and minority people members by the suffix (m)

Source: Adapted from Proceedings of ACFTU Twelfth National Congress, 1993, p. 79.

3.4   GRASS-ROOTS MEMBERSHIP AND UNIONIZATION

Membership of an ACFTU-affiliated union is *prima facie* not much different from belonging to a similar kind of organization elsewhere in China. However, there were specific conditions involved. The composition of the

ACFTU membership has resulted from a somewhat 'elastic' definition of the term 'worker' and 'workers' organizations'. Those who were involved in 'mental' as well as 'physical' labour were deemed to be eligible, but 'permanent' workers were favoured. Apprentices and trainees, as well as temporary workers, were not normally enroled. As the ACFTU Constitution (1994, p. 4) states: 'Membership in trade unions is open to all manual and mental workers in enterprises, undertakings and offices within the territory of China, who live on wages or salaries as their main source of income,' (see Appendix later). As most of the Chinese labour force worked on the land as peasants, with a minority in industrial employment, with an even smaller group in large enterprises, the ACFTU tended to be 'generous' in its categorization of who was eligible and who was excluded in order to expand its membership, although union members were attacked as a 'labour aristocracy' during the Cultural Revolution.

Who did the ACFTU speak for? Any 'representative' function of its trade unions for the labour-force was mitigated by their 'exclusive' membership requirement, as 'only permanent workers could join unions and were eligible to the medical care, unemployment, housing and other welfare benefits administered by trade unions' (Lee, 1986, p. 115). A smaller and smaller percentage of the total Chinese industrial labour force were eventually able to join up, as other sectors of the economy expanded.[3]

In the early phase of the post-Mao economic reforms, the unions had asked local committees to help recruit contract (as distinct from temporary) workers (Wilson, 1987, p. 229). Clearly, the growing use of such labour contracts has fuelled dissatisfaction with official trade unions as the contract system has been extended nationally (see Leung, 1988; Warner, 1995). The failure of Chinese trade unions to cater for *all* workers had been a weakness which represented a grievance which periodically surfaced during the Great Leap Forward in the late 1950s and again in the early 1960s when the labour contract system was initially used. Temporary and contract workers had been kept out of union protection, which was one reason behind the 'fall' of the ACFTU during the Cultural Revolution. Temporary contract labour had originally been a 'socialist' idea imported earlier from the Soviet Union when top officials had been sent there to study its contract system in order to reduce overhead costs and to gain greater labour flexibility (Lee, 1986, p. 115).

Unionization in China is at a high level but in a sense which is different from other advanced country-examples. If the state-owned sector is taken in isolation, then the estimated rates of union membership are in the lower 90 per cents. For example, the SOEs and the larger collectives employed the bulk of the urban workforce before 1979. The SOE employees rose from 76.9 million in 1979 to 110.9 million in 1993, with urban collectives rising from 22.7 to 36 million in 1991 (cited in White, 1996, p. 7). Further increases in non-state sector employment have taken place since then.[4]

The rate of unionization in SOEs rose from 84.7 per cent in 1981 to 92 per cent in 1992, based on the ACFTU estimates using lower aggregates of numbers employed; and approximately the same figure using SSB estimates. There was a high percentage of basic trade union organs in the state-owned sector. In many SOEs investigated by the present writer, almost complete unionization had been claimed in the North-East (see Warner, 1995) and in the upper 90 per cents in several Beijing enterprises visited depending on the number of temporary workers or apprentices (see Warner, 1996b). As a generalization, state-ownership and high union density probably still go hand in hand. Since unionization was much lower in other sectors, the overall rate remains problematic. In the fast-expanding TVEs, the rate was very low, around 3 per cent of workers according to one estimate (*Renmin Ribao/People's Daily*, 28 April 1992, p. 1). In FFEs, for example, the estimates of the number of firms unionized varies from as low as one in ten to around half of their total workforce, but in some cases an even higher share, especially in the larger joint-ventures (for further details see Chapter 6). The larger the city in which the JV is located and the larger the original state-owned core out of which the JV developed, the higher the degree of union representation claimed. (Interviews at ACFTU headquarters, March 1997).

If we try to calculate the unionization for the whole workforce including agriculture, we arrive at a figure of over one in six, based on the official total labour force statistic of around 615 million workers and peasants (SSB, 1995, p. 20). If we take the percentage for the urban industrial working population only, then this would be approximately two in three, that is to say just over 100 million ACFTU members out of an urban workforce of around 150 million (ibid.). However, since there is only one official union federation and since membership is quasi-obligatory, then the rate of nominal unionization is a rather artificial one. It is probably comparable with examples found in some Western 'closed-shop' cases.

The size of the agricultural population in China makes overall comparisons with other advanced (or even less advanced East and South-East Asian economies) rather unfair. On the other hand, the 'closed-shop' nature of ACFTU membership in the state-sector renders the figures difficult to render comparable. If nominal membership for the whole workforce in China is, say, 15 per cent, then this places China in the lightly unionized group of countries. However, if the figure of 65 per cent is accepted for the state-owned industrial sector as a whole including urban collectives, then this puts the country in the high-unionization category, on paper at least (see Table 3.3). By comparison, the rate of Hong Kong is over 20 per cent, for Singapore over 25 per cent and for Taiwan over 30 per cent – see Chapter 7.

Taking the high nominal unionization rate at its face value, we find that empirical studies of Chinese workers' attitudes to their unions indicates low degrees of member-involvement. For example, an internal ACFTU survey in early 1990s revealed not surprisingly that over one-in-three (36.3 per cent) thought they were no longer 'masters' and just over half (51.5 per cent) thought workers' status overall unduly low. Low motivation was reflected in minimal enthusiasm both at work and outside, such as in political and union activities (SWB, 21 March 1992). In spite of the stability of union membership in the state-owned sector in China, 'closed-shop' as it may be, unionization as we have seen has been falling as a percentage of both the total industrial (and aggregate) labour force. China now has a 'dual' labour market with the non-unionized sector outstripping the unionized one, particularly if the migrant worker population is taken into account.[5] The number of such transient workers may now even outnumber the total union membership of the ACFTU.

Table 3.4   Union density in selected countries (in the early 1990s)

Country	%
Sweden	83
China	65 (industry)[*]
	15 (industry plus agriculture)[**]
Denmark	73
Italy	39
UK	39
Germany	32
Taiwan	30
Japan	23
Hong Kong	21
USA	15
Singapore	25
Spain	11
France	10

[*]   As a percentage of the industrial workforce including urban collectives
[**]   As a percentage of total working population (including agriculture)
Sources: *OECD Employment Outlook* (1994, p. 173) and various ILO statistics.

Numbers of transient workers (*mingong*) are now officially reckoned to be between 50 to 70 million (Solinger, 1995, p. 113) even over 80 million (*Beijing Review* 3 June 1996, p. 20) but may be in excess of this total. Nobody knows for sure but official estimates are usually on the low side. Statistics from the Ministry of Public Security claim there are 3 million in Beijing, 3.2 million in Shanghai and 6.5 million in Guangzhou alone (ibid., p. 21). There are several categories of non-unionized workers here. First, there are *full-time* employees, largely in the non-state sector, for example in joint ventures, who are not in unions. Second, there are *temporary contract workers* as well as part-timers in all sectors, but particularly in FFEs. Third, there are *migrant* casual workers seeking employment. Fourth, there are *unemployed* workers who have never found a job, or who were in the second and the third categories above. There are, therefore, as in other countries, two systems: one for the organized and the other for the unorganized. Rights and conditions of work are very different in the two sectors. In China, however, there is a major difference, even the organized workers do not enjoy comparable collective bargaining and associated rights compared, for example, with many Western or Japanese workers.

There are, however, some 'family-resemblances' between organized workers in China and elsewhere, such as relative protection in terms of comparatively higher pay and 'perks', social security and so on *vis-à-vis* the unorganized (ibid., p. 98). Even with the gradual demise of the 'iron rice bowl' system, shelter from dismissal is still more or less assured for many ACFTU members.[6] By contrast, unorganized workers suffer greater relative deprivation than elsewhere because they are debarred from urban residency and its basic benefits. More recently Western researchers (White, 1996, for example) have pointed to relatively low levels of trust and involvement by the membership of the official union machinery in the individual plants they studied in the North-East. White (1996) found that only a very few (12.8 per cent) saw their unions in the early 1990s as representing their interest and opinions and many more (41.1 per cent) saw them as mostly instruments for ensuring obedience and compliance in the workplace (1996). Another survey, by the Hebei Federation of Trade Unions in the mid-1990s, found that half the number interviewed voiced the grievance that they were no longer 'masters of the enterprise' and that 40 per cent believed they were 'employees' and were even upset by the formula of 'wholeheartedly relying upon the working class' (see *SWB*, 1 February 1995). In short, the unions are not gaining many points as 'intermediaries' (see Zhang, 1997).

Union officials themselves, as well as managers, interviewed in other empirical studies showed the degree to which unions had become marginalized by the early 1990s. For example, one study (Verma and Yan, 1995) compared the role of the union in both SOE and JV sectors (ibid, p. 333): 'Their primary role was one of workers' welfare in general off-work situations and no presence on the shop-floor. A related practice in both sectors is the absence of a formal grievance procedure. Workers' Congresses were seen as a major voice for workers in the state enterprises but there were no such requirements on the joint ventures. Lastly, neither sector seemed very keen on employment involvement in any form' (ibid., p. 333).

In spite of the rhetoric of union leaders at May Day celebrations as late as the mid-1990s, there was evidence of a growing 'credibility-gap' that revealed the anxiety-level of the party as well as unions. Conflicts of interest between the state, enterprises and workers have surfaced as the following report suggests:

> Since the beginning of the 1990s the pattern of interests between the state, enterprises and workers has gradually changed. Workers' employment, distributions, labour protection, collective welfare and other tangible interests, which used to be issues between workers and the state, have gradually become issues between workers and enterprises, and have become increasingly market- and contract-based. In addition, workers have come from more diverse sources – the 20 million once-peasants working for town and township enterprises have become new members of the working class, and the 15 million people working for foreign-funded and private enterprises also have become a new source of supply of workers. These new realities call for trade unions to strengthen their and to open up a new way for carrying our trade union work in Chinese style. (*Xinhua News Agency*, 27 April 1995; *SWB*, 5 May 1995)

Yet, there are shifting priorities that are often revealed in official policy statements. In the mid-1990s, for example, the limitations of the trade unions in terms of their existing roles and domains are clearly expressed in such speeches and documents. While a major section of the 'working class', that is, those in the state sector, must have their interests promoted, the needs of the residual sets outside in the non-state sectors must also be catered for. Collective contracts are now seen as one way to promote the former, whereas extending unionization to the latter is seen as necessary, if not sufficient.

There is little risk in the short-term at least that the predominance of the official unions will be displaced in the SOE sector. However, if in the medium- and long-term, the moves to 'corporatization' (that is to say, a 'quasi-privatization' involving the sale of the SOEs' shares to 'stake-holders') takes place, then their official position may well be questioned unless we see 'micro-corporatism' effectively introduced into many such large enterprises, with a German-style format of supervisory boards and workers' councils in place. The main shopfloor problems arise from the widespread absence of unions in the TVEs and patchy representation in the JVs (for further details, see Chapter 6). Since both sectors are growing rapidly in the number of workers employed as well as the share of GDP (and exports) produced, the authorities fear the threat of industrial disorder (*luan*) if grievances were to be articulated by rival worker organizations or by *ad hoc* unofficial shopfloor groups.[7] Since many large JVs are in major urban conurbations such as Beijing, Guangzhou, Shanghai and so on, the political risks of weak union organizations must be apparent to the union and party leaderships. The potential for political instability is evident, especially if the history of the Chinese labour movement is taken into account (see, for example, the role of the Shanghai workers in the interwar years and after). As Perry put it: 'Labour unrest has played a central role in the political transformations that have swept twentieth-century China' (Perry, 1993, p. 2).

The 1994 Labour Law and the associated amended 'Regulations for Foreign-Owned Enterprises' both reflect the anxiety of the authorities *vis-à-vis* the above problem. Moreover, there is also the intention to have such a Labour Code applicable to all enterprises, indicating that the state does not condone weak union organization in the non-state sector. China's labour legislation on the one hand, expresses 'a commitment to equality for all workers. At the same time, the laws accommodate differential treatment of particular classes of workers' (Josephs, 1995, p. 565). Both the revised 1992 Trade Union Law and the new 1994 Labour Law to a degree reflect concern with the new ownership-pattern in the Chinese economy in varying degrees. As Josephs points out: 'A positive effect of the [1994] Law is to reinforce the authority of government agencies in requiring standards for those employed in 'private' and 'foreign' enterprises to meet the same level enjoyed by those employed in state enterprises' (ibid., pp. 566–7). Such attempts at legal parity are not surprising given the massive structural changes in the economy, particularly over the last decade.

The difficulty the critical observer of industrial relations may have, however, relates to the gap between the stated goals of such legislation and the *de facto* realities on the ground. The laws do enhance the role of unions and other labour agencies in their regulatory capacity but at the same time implicitly reflect a diminution of union influence in that whatever is said at the level of ideology and rhetoric, the 'working-class' and their representatives are increasingly seen to be less and less 'masters' in their workplaces.

Since there is only one official union body, the ACFTU – too large and bureaucratic to cover all contingencies – and since to date it has come down heavily upon independent unions, there are clearly weak points in the system where labour unrest could flare up to the potential inconvenience of foreign-invested managements. Clandestine labour activists operate in the shadows. For the most part, unofficial structures remain suppressed and therefore out of sight (see Goldman, 1989; 1994). Repeated reports of such clandestine and presumably loose unofficial union structures surface regularly in the foreign news-service reports and Hong Kong-based newspapers and magazines (for example, recent issues of the *China Labour Bulletin*). They normally describe reported activities of such labour groups or trials of union activists. Some are rather general, often based on second-hand sources; others are specific, dealing with individual incidents. Many of these accounts follow on the heels of reasonably well-documented accounts of 'autonomous workers' associations' involved in or immediately after the 1989 Tiananmen Square events (see Warner, 1993; Walder and Gong, 1993, for example). Noted amongst the Tiananmen Square protesters in the early summer had been the presence of the Beijing Workers' Autonomous Federation (BWAF), set up 19 May 1989. Its features have been well-documented (Fathers and Higgins, 1989; Lu, 1991; Walder and Góng, 1993; Schell, 1994) as were examples elsewhere in other large cities in China. Its leaders were prominently featured in the subsequent official crackdown, and were severely sentenced for their apparent audacity. Workers from large enterprises such as the *Shougang* Steel-works were seen marching under their own banners (Lu, 1991). The example of 'Solidarity' in Poland was a possible inspiration of the BWAF's emergence. Wang Dan, a prominent student activist (repeatedly imprisoned since) had written an article in the illicit publication *New May Fourth* in March earlier, extolling its virtues (Schell, 1994, p. 66).

Dissident staff of the ACFTU were said to have given the labour dissidents support by handing out leaflets in the Square in May 1989 calling for greater union autonomy and asking that 'trade unions should work and speak for the workers and masses' (Fathers and Higgins, 1989, p. 66). In addition, the headquarters of the ACFTU donated 100 000 RMB (27 000 US dollars) to the Red Cross for the student hunger strikers (*SWB*, 2 June 1989). There had even been rumours of an unofficial one-day general strike in Beijing. Activities of the 'free' trade union organizations were also reported in Chengdu, Guangzhou, Hangzhou, Hefei and Shanghai, amongst other places (*Echoes from Tiananmen*, nos 1 and 2, June and August 1989). As late as 9 June, at least a thousand workers were reported marching behind the Shanghai Workers' Autonomous Federation banner in the demonstrations there. The autonomous trade unions were accused of usurping the name of the working class, fabricating rumours and attempting to overthrow the people's government in the official press. Such illegal organizations, it was predicted by offical spokespersons would 'certainly become the rubbish abandoned by history' (*Gongren Ribao/Worker's Daily*, 18 June 1989, p. 1).

By 25 July, the official Chinese news agency reasserted that:

China's trade unions must work under the leadership of the CCP and no trade unions opposed to the CCP are allowed to be established (according to the then) Ni Zhifu, President of the All-China Federation of Trade Unions (ACFTU). (*Xinhua News Agency* report in *SWB*, 28 July 1989)

Addressing the third meeting of the Eleventh ACFTU presidium which opened there on that day, Ni stressed that any attempt to work outside the CCP leadership and put the trade unions into an opposition role must be resisted. 'Otherwise, we will miss the correct political orientation of trade union reform and construction leading to great errors' (ibid.). Ni then stressed the trade unions' role in representing and safeguarding workers' rights and interests. He then went on to argue that:

The trade unions must avoid simply acting as agents of the government and work independently so as to increase the attraction to workers and enjoy more confidence from the workers, leaving no opportunity to those who attempt to organize 'independent trade unions'. Otherwise we will also make great errors. (Ibid.)

By early 1992, an underground labour network, the 'Free Labour Unions of China' (FLUC) was reported as distributing pamphlets in many factories in Beijing (*Reuters News Agency* report, 5 February 1992; Schell, 1994, p. 269). Its bold manifesto read:

The right of workers to organize free trade unions is internationally recognized ... Didn't Poland's 'Solidarity' get banned and suppressed ten years ago? And what were the results? 'Solidarity' won and its oppressors fell. (Schell, 1994, p. 269)

Two years later, in April 1994, an account of clandestine trade union activity described:

Serious outbreaks of industrial unrest [which] have flared in parts of China as a result of Dickensian factory conditions and widespread abuse of workers' rights. The problem, disclosed in the normally tame official press, suggests that many workers – deemed 'masters of the country' under communist rule – are in danger of becoming an underclass. The authorities now champion entrepreneurial flair to fuel China's economic boom. An official report says 250 000 labour disputes have broken out since 1988, including 1 100 during the past two years in the prosperous economic zone of Shenzhen, near Hong Kong. They include strikes and incidents of shop-floor violence (*Daily Telegraph*, 1 April 1994, p. 6).

By 1994 a 'League for the Protection of the Rights of Working People' led by Liu Nianchan and the 'Chinese Workers' Autonomous Federation' led by Shen Yin Lan had been set up (see Wilson, 1995, p. 8). As many as 800 underground unions, it was claimed, had been formed in Guangdong province. Many of these allegedly had the characteristics of secret societies, they were based on personal loyalties and lacked formal rules, but 'were feared by employers and government' (see *Daily Telegraph*, 1 April 1994, p. 6). A group of activists used the 'Shenzen Volunteers Association' – an officially recognized body – to organize classes on labour laws for workers, but many were arrested in May 1994 (ibid., p. 8).[8]

A later account – in mid-1995 – of an unofficial labour organization apparently operating with official acquiescence if not actual tolerance in the North-East was reported by a Japanese-based source as follows:

> The 'self-help organization' was set up at the beginning of the year by workers of small and midsize state-run corporations in Harbin and other cities in Heilongjiang Province. The organization's unofficial character is to improve the working and living conditions of state-company employees and help the growing ranks of unemployed. It has 10 full-time staffers. Despite its technical illegality, there are no clandestine meetings for this group. 'The local authorities are willing to cooperate with us in finding new jobs for the workers', said an official of the association. In fact, the organization is already making demands. It has called on the provincial government to force companies to pay overdue wages and ensure the payment of unemployment pensions. (*Nikkei Weekly*, 10 July 1995, cited in *SWB*, 10 July 1995)

The credibility of this report may however be qualified by the overwhelming weight of contrary evidence based on other cases. Even so, one of the present writers had seen 'sit-down' demonstrations openly held and sustained outside the main local government administrative building in the same city in the Summer of 1993 and had been told that such peaceful protests were not infrequent, particularly related to the expression of grievances against urban rehousing programmes. Reports of openly-held labour demonstrations against late payment of wages and redundancies have been extensively reported (see recent issues of the *China Labour Bulletin*; *The Economist*, 26 July 1997, p. 67).[9]

Clandestine labour organizations appear to have the following character-istics: first, they clearly state their identity in their name, for example, the 'autonomous' this or that (denoting that they are not part of ACFTU-related organizations); second, they are mostly limited in scale and numbers of workers involved – typically 3–4 people in membership-cells according to Han Dongfang (see Wilson, 1995, p. 7), but had involved a critical mass of labour activities in major cities in 1989; third, they have sometimes appeared 'simultaneously' in more than one location, or belonged to a very loose network of similar organizations – particularly in Guangdong Province or in the Shenzen Special Economic Zone (SEZ); fourth, they have been largely linked to specific grievances, such as fatalities due to health and safety negligence, usually in the foreign-funded enterprise sector in coastal regions or redundancies and unpaid wages in the older industrial areas.

From official and unofficial press sources or scholarly accounts avail-able the unofficial labour movement probably involves key groups of activists and organizers numbering nationally many hundreds, but not many thousands (although those involved in incidents they have organized may sometimes have run into more), with a maximum size of single inci-dents or demonstrations of a thousand, at the most. The number of 'sleeper' activists or 'passive' potential supporters or sympathizers is difficult to estimate but could run into hundreds of thousand, albeit in a a total urban industrial workforce of over 150 million people. According to the International Confederation of Free Trade Unions (ICFTU) annual report on workers' rights, 'China has one of the worst records of trade union repression' (*Financial Times*, 13 June 1997, p. 6), it was alleged.

The regime had assiduously tried to 'ring-fence' student demonstrations in summer 1989 and kept sympathetic workers away from these crowds. Fearing a Polish-style, *Solidarity*-style movement, they dealt with worker activists more harshly than with student dissidents, although it is hard to document precisely executions and fatalities arising from suppression of both groups (see Schell, 1994, pp. 171–2, 191, 217–18).

An official step after the events of summer 1989 – through a CCP circu-lar of December later that year – was to cement an even-closer union-Party alliance (*Renmin Ribao/People's Daily* 1 February 1990, p. 1). As White (1996) points out:

the post-Tiananmen CCP leadership also moved to stop the institutional reforms already underway and strengthen Party control of the unions.

At the same time, however, they realised that they needed the unions to help prevent an even more threatening recurrence of the 1989 unrest, this time involving greater participation from urban workers. This mixture of dependence on the unions with the desire to control them was the basis for a post-Tiananmen pact between the Party and the unions. This was a *de facto* political arrangement whereby Party leaders were to grant the trade unions greater access to policy-making and more influence in the enterprise in return for their continued support for the Party leadership. (White, 1996, pp. 456–7)

3.5   CONCLUDING REMARKS

Rather than any novel organizational response to such dissidence, the authorities may have responded by recently re-emphasising and augmenting party discipline at enterprise level but it is often difficult to disentangle the roles of Factory Director and Party secretary when both posts may be held by the same person.[10] Increasingly often, a senior manager may be asked to become the Party secretary, or even trade union chairperson in some cases.

To sum up, we have outlined the strategy and structure of Chinese trade unions in this chapter, as well as looking at the nature of the grass-roots membership and their unionization-level *vis-à-vis* that of other countries. We have also analyzed the ACFTU's representative rationale and challenges to this through the rise of autonomous trade unions in recent years. We now turn to the legal context of Chinese trade unions and management in the next chapter.

Part II
Reforming

'There must be less empty talk and more hard work.'
(Deng Xiaoping, Closing Address at the Eleventh National Congress of
the CCP, in Chi, 1978, p. 150)

4 Trade Unions and Management in China and Their Legal Context

4.1 INTRODUCTION

Many of the crucial reforms of Chinese labour legislation relevant to the role of trade unions and management prior to the 1994 Law were introduced in the 1980s (see for, example, Josephs, 1988; 1990; 1995; 1996, Zheng, 1989).[1] About one-third (over 600 laws) were implemented in between 1978–88 (Xia, 1991, p. 36). Often, laws were tentative and inadequate (for the Chinese legal background see Dicks, 1989; Potter, 1994; Tanner, 1994). The legislation has been described as 'an aggregation of all existing labour regulations' (Korzec, 1992, p. 6). Discussion among Chinese legal experts reveals a growing dissatisfaction with 'semi-law': the absence of proper codification of administrative law and administrative procedure law in the People's Republic of China (Xia, 1991, p. 7). Labour legislation in the PRC was in the past paradoxically weak, given the repeated claim that the workers were 'masters of the country', with the system mainly protecting workers in SOEs, as noted in Chapter 1 (see Xia, 1991; Korzec, 1992; Leung, 1993; Warner, 1996a).

New issues, such as redundancies, individual and collective labour-contracts, and efficiency-based payment systems, have come to the fore in recent years. Social and unemployment insurance have now to be dealt with as well as how to react to joint-ventures where foreign multinational companies are involved, or to other sources of overseas investment (see Friedman, 1996). Not all of these problems could be dealt with at national level, so provincial- and municipal-level labour organizations had to be instructed how to respond (interviews at ACFTU Headquarters, July 1993). Even so, Chinese trade unions were at best *re-active vis-à-vis* the momentum of rapid economic change (see Howell, 1995). Parallel to the workers' side, there is now an embryonic businessmen's body, the All-China Federation of Industry and Commerce (ACFIC) which had existed in the 1950s and, which was revived in the mid-1980s. However, tripartite consultation on formulating the 1994 Labour Law was carried out with another organization, the Chinese Enterprise Directors' Association (CEDA) together with the ACFTU and the State Ministry of Labour. This triumvirate represents the PRC externally on international labour matters, as we shall see later.

4.2   LABOUR LAW OF THE PEOPLE'S REPUBLIC OF CHINA

The National People's Congress passed the new Labour Law on 5 July 1994 (implemented on 1 January 1995). The text was then published in the *Renmin Ribao (People's Daily)* in 13 parts. The main goals of the new legal framework may be summed up as follows:

- workers have the right to choose jobs, to be paid, to have rest and holidays, to have protection in the workplace and to receive training to improve their *skills*;
- no employment permitted of children below the age of 16;
- no discrimination on the basis of race nationality, sex or religion;
- women to enjoy same rights as men;
- minimum wage-levels to be set by local governments and reported to the State Council;
- contracts must be customary between employers and workers, setting out pay, conditions, tasks to be performed and terms when contracts can be terminated;
- enterprises on the brink of bankruptcy or in grave difficulties may reduce working staff; provided that the decision is agreed upon by the trade union organization in the enterprise or after consultation with all staff members;
- average working week not to exceed 44 hours, with one day off per week;
- working day to be limited to eight hours;
- women not to work in mines, in conditions of extreme temperatures and after seventh month of pregnancy. After birth, at least 90 days of leave should be given;
- dispute committees to be set up in work places and to include both employers and workers.

Li Boyong, the Minister of Labour at the time, presented a draft on 2 March 1994 to the legislators at the sixth session of the Standing Committee of the Eighth National People's Congress (NPC) stating that: 'The rights of enterprises to dismiss workers for reasons other than workers' faults will guarantee the legal rights of employers to run business independently and will give enterprises a certain edge in market competition.' However, he continued, the limits set for job reductions are 'necessary for China's social stability.' Because China has far more workers than required and such a disparity could not be changed in a short time, massive job reductions would lead to social chaos, he argued. The draft also included the introduction of a new form of 'collective contract' between the trade union and the enterprise on matters of rewards, working conditions and welfare (*Xinhua News Agency/SWB*, 2 March 1994).

The new Labour Law clearly had not had an easy path through the political decision-making process, with successive drafts revised more than 30 times over the past ten years. Legislation in the PRC points out 'can no longer be considered as a unified top-down policy-making system'. Instead, it is better thought of as 'a multi-stage, multi-area system' (ibid., 1994, p. 39). Several interested actors, whether Party, ministries, trade unions, and others, worked out a legislative compromise in the end. The ACFTU claim that they gained the 'five-day week' as the *quid pro quo* for the concessions they had to make (interviews at ACFTU headquarters, November 1995). The degree to which the Labour Law is fully enforceable and the degree to which it *will* be strictly applied is, of course, decidedly moot. The initiative is probably aimed partly to meet the needs of a modernizing economy and partly to answer international criticism of China's labour practices. Unlike much previous legislation in this field, it sets out its general principles and then ways of implementing them (see *Xinhua News Agency/SWB*, 2 March 1994; *SWB*, 5 March 1994 *Gongren Ribao/Workers Daily*, 6 July 1994, p. 1; *Renmin Ribao/People's Daily*, 7 July 1994, p. 2; *Reuters News Agency* report, 6 July 1994; *Financial Times*, 7 July 1994, p. 4).

An evaluation of selected parts of the Labour Law is presented in this chapter, particularly looking at clauses whose practical consequences may affect the management of human resources whether in state-owned enterprises, joint-ventures or foreign-funded firms, although we recognize that those we do not have space to cover in detail may be in some cases just as relevant.[2] It is based on a translations into English of the original Labour Law document (see PRC, 1994; also Warner 1995, Appendix 2 for a full text). The interpretation of the new Labour Law should also be closely related to the 1992 Trade Union Law, parts of which we have referred to in Chapters 2 and 3 (see PRC, 1992; also Warner, 1995, Appendix 1, for the complete document).

4.3   KEY FEATURES OF THE 1994 LABOUR LAW

The 1994 Labour Law is divided into component chapters each dealing with a specific subfield (see Table 4.1). We first set out the statement of principles elaborated in the first of these, concerning its broad remit.

Table 4.1   Main headings of 1994 Labour Law: contents

---

  1. Principles
  2. Employment promotion
  3. Labour contracts and collective contracts
  4. Working hours and holidays
  5. Wages
  6. Labour safety and hygiene
  7. Protection of women and young workers
  8. Vocational training
  9. Social security and welfare
 10. Labour disputes
 11. Monitoring and inspection
 12. Legal obligations
 13. Supplementary

Source: 1994 Labour Law, p. 1.

General

We now go on to deal with the introductory clauses of the 1994 Labour Law, in order to highlight significant features of the 13 chapters, which are in turn divided into 107 subsections.

Chapter 1: No. 1

> *This Law is formulated ... in order ... [to] regulate labour relations, establish and maintain a labour system compatible with a socialist market economy.*

The full statement of principles (see Figure 4.2) sets out the main motives underlying the Law. Broadly speaking, the Law is mainly intended to clarify and to codify the relations of the three actors: the *State* (representing the People, as a whole) the *Employers* (an ambiguously defined grouping) and the *Trade Unions* (on behalf of workers in enterprises – see below) that have been affected and challenged by the reforms. The role and function of the state is now made more explicit; that of the trade unions is formally (at least) enhanced, with more autonomy ostensibly aimed for; while that of the employers (employing units) is possibly rendered more complex, whether in SOEs, JVs, TVEs, FFEs or private firms.

More narrowly, the law clarifies relations between those working in enterprises, referred in the Marxist terms as 'labourers' (*laodongzhe*) literally those who labour, but whom we will address as 'workers', and

Table 4.2   Principles of the 1994 Labour Law

Chapter 1: Principles

1. This Law is formulated in line with the Constitution in order to protect the legal interests of labour, regulate labour relations, establish and maintain a labour system compatible with a social market economy, and promote economic development and social progress.

2. This labour law is applicable to all enterprises, individual economic organizations (named employing units hereafter) and workers involved in labour relations. State organizations, institutions, social organizations and workers in labour-contract relations, are all covered by this law.

3. Workers shall have rights of equal employment and choice of job, remuneration for work, rest and holidays, labour safety and hygiene protection, vocational training, social security and welfare and also the rights to seek labour arbitration and other legally regulated labour rights. Workers shall complete their given tasks, enhance vocational skills, abide by labour health and safety regulations, as well as labour discipline and professional responsibilities.

4. Employing units shall establish and perfect regulations in systems according to the law, to ensure workers can enjoy their labour rights and also carry out their work duties.

5. The State shall, by all possible means, promote employment opportunities, develop vocational education, establish labour standards, regulate income levels in society, perfect social security, co-ordinate labour relations, and incrementally enhance living standards of workers.

6. The State shall encourage workers to take part in voluntary work for social ends, promote labour competition and offer constructive suggestions regarding work-improvements, encourage and protect workers in carrying out scientific research and technical innovation, as well as praise and reward workers and professionals.

7. Workers have the right to take part in and organize trade unions according to the law. Union representatives shall protect the legal rights and interests of workers independently and autonomously and develop their activities according to the law.

8. Workers shall take part in democratic management, and equal consultation with employment units on the protection of legal interests and interests of workers through worker conferences, worker representative congresses and other similar forms within the framework of legal regulation.

9. The Labour Administrative Department of the State Council shall be in charge of labour affairs for the whole country. Labour Administrative Departments of local People's Governments at and above county level shall be in charge of labour affairs within their administrative districts.

Source: 1994 Labour Law (see Appendix 2, in Warner, 1995, p. 179).

those referred to as 'employers' – whether the state or the various types of employing unit, based on the newly-introduced contractual relations. The law essentially applies to industrial workers in a wide range of enterprises, from SOEs to foreign-funded firms; it does *not* apply to those with civil servant status or to the vast majority of Chinese workshops in the agricultural sector, for example. At first sight at least, workers' rights appear to be central to the new law (see Figure 4.2) but as we shall argue in this chapter, many basic protections are not guaranteed in the new formulation, several previous 'rights' have been dropped and a new status quo is set out which, in effect, erodes the 'iron rice bowl' policy enjoyed by Chinese workers since the early 1950s (see Walder, 1986). However, Josephs (1995, p. 564, n. 21) argues that once assigned to jobs, SOE employees were never, strictly speaking, guaranteed a 'right' to permanent employment in law.[3] Other social reforms, embodied more or less in the 1994 Labour Law, such as those dealing with child labour, gender equality and so on, also leave many concerns as to how effective implementation will be.

Trade Union Autonomy

Chapter 1: No. 7

Trade Unions shall represent and protect the legal rights and interests of workers independently and autonomously and develop their activities according to the law.

Past and contemporary empirical evidence hardly supports the notion of trade union autonomy in the PRC, whether we are looking at the position of the unions in the large state-owned enterprises or in other types of enterprises, whether private or foreign-owned (see Warner, 1995). What the workers confront in the latter may not be the state-employer, but a new 'class' of 'bosses', unrelated to the state and unconstrained in many cases by any trade unions at all; or, if working in the state-owned enterprises, they may face unions which may still act as the 'arm' of the state-employer (see Chan, 1993). In the latter case, the unions lately have been in potential danger of being challenged by independent ones, such as the Beijing Workers' Autonomous Federation as happened for a short while in the Spring of 1989 (see Chapter 3 for further details). In 1992, the Free Labour Union of China (FLUC), for example, was set up but soon prosecuted and suppressed (*China Labour Bulletin*, October 1994, pp. 1–4).

Since then, as we have already noted, several other unofficial reformist labour organizations have sprung up as we noted earlier, including the League for the Protection of the Rights of Working People, the Workers' Forum and the Chinese Workers' Autonomous Federation, which faced similar harassment (see Howell, 1995, p. 24).

Labour Contracts

Chapter 3: Item 17

Labour contracts shall be legally binding when signed according to the law.

The new 'contract-relation' – formerly referred to as an 'exploitation-relation' and thereby contrary to 'socialist' theory and practice – is now explicitly institutionalized in the 1994 Labour Law, following its earlier introduction in the 1986 regulations, amended in 1992.[4] It does, on the other hand, remain within the Chinese cultural tradition of *bao* or reciprocity, with rights balanced by obligations. The necessity arises mainly because of new types of enterprises where the employer is no longer the state but private or foreign. The 1994 law makes labour contracts applicable to such firms. This step is especially relevant to the various SEZ in the coastal areas, where foreign investment is not only dependent on the cooperation of the workers, but where industrial conflict may potentially deter further investors. By demanding a contract, the state attempts to regulate the situation and, in the long run, may gradually isolate itself from direct confrontations and act as an *arbitrator* as well as a *regulator*, as is often the case in many countries in East and South-East Asia (see Deery and Mitchell, 1993). Interest by Chinese IR specialists in such countries' models has been common since the early 1990s, particularly regarding those of Singapore as well as 'Greater China' (see Interviews at the ACFTU Headquarters, July 1993, and November 1996). We will return to this theme later in Chapter 7.

Chapter 3: Item 20

When a worker has worked in the same employment unit for over 10 years and both the worker and the unit agree to renew the contract, indefinite contracts shall be made if demanded by the worker.

At first sight, this clause looks like a perpetuation of the 'iron rice bowl' system. The offer of an indefinite contract can however still be vetoed by management. 'Firing' is a very sensitive issue at present in Industrial Relations (IR) disputes, as life-long employment is no longer in effect guaranteed (see Warner, 1995), although some legal observers believe there is still a 'strong commitment to job security' (Josephs, 1995, p. 570).[5] With this law, the large state-owned enterprises 'facing bankruptcy' can confront the redundancy problem by not agreeing to renew workers' contracts, even after they have worked for ten years in the firm. Workers' Congresses can debate management's proposals, but ultimately with limited *de facto* decision-making powers, except possibly *vis-à-vis* employee welfare schemes, housing and so on (Interviews with Ministry of Labour officials, May 1995).

Chapter 4: Item 26

> *Now the employing unit can terminate the contract with 30 days notice in written form directly to the worker.*

This enhanced power of termination of contract is almost unprecedented but has been defended in the face of chronic over-manning in SOEs.[6] 'Workers' will not only no longer enjoy 'socialist' privileges, but will also be made vulnerable to market forces without the back-up of a quasi-capitalist social security system (see Hussein, 1993). Labour insurance to date had been mostly limited to industrial workers in SOEs. Unemployment insurance was introduced in the mid-1980s, mainly for this category of employees, and was financed by a payroll tax. The new Labour Law in fact uses the term 'unemployment' rather than the older euphemism 'awaiting employment' (see Feinerman, 1996, p. 124). China however, has yet, to fully overhaul its social safety-net and introduce a nation-wide system (see *Financial Times*, 15 November 1994, p. 3; Friedman, 1996, p. 153 ff).[7]

Redundancy

Chapter 4: Item 27

> *When reducing the amount of personnel ... the Trade Union or the whole staff shall be notified 30 days in advance.*

Previously, redundancy (which was rare) was dealt with by the Labour Administration Department. Now, the most important parties are the employing unit (the Director within the Director-Responsibility system) with the trade union next. The latter now has a key role in determining *who* will be made redundant, while the Department will merely receive a report and carry out the paper work.

Consultation

Chapter 4: Item 30 – Trade Union Rights

> *The Trade Union has the right to give its opinions when the termination of a contract is improper.*

This item further clarifies the role of the trade union and calls for the strengthening of the tie with its members. It proposes that their opinions have to be dealt with, and must not be neglected or ignored. The unions are now in a difficult position, as they are rather 'thin on the ground' in private, joint-venture and foreign-funded enterprises (as we shall see later in Chapter 6). In such instances, the establishment of unions and protection of worker rights is now seen as a priority, as opposed to the state-owned enterprise sector where the unions' role has long been institutionalized (Interviews with Ministry of Labour officials, December 1995). Even in the latter, the unions' voice has been somewhat undermined by the 'three systems' enterprise reforms of the early 1990s, subsequently extended to the whole of industry, as the factory directors' power have been substantially enhanced, according to empirical research (see Ji, 1992; Child, 1994; Warner, 1994; 1995).[8]

Collective Contracts

Chapter 4: Item 35

> *The collective contract signed according to the law is legally binding on both the enterprise and the workers of the enterprise.*

At the closing ceremony of the Twelfth ACFTU Executive Committee, Wei Jianzing (the Chairman at the time) said:

> For trade unions, the important link and crucial issue is the signing of collective contracts with enterprises by trade unions on behalf of

workers and staff members. To keep a firm hold on collective contracts is the crux of implementing the Labour Law, with the result that 'a slight move in one part will affect the situation as a whole'; and the various endeavours carried out by trade unions in implementing the Labour Law will be promoted. (*SWB*, 17 December 1994)

Whilst the 'collective contract' appears to be more adaptable to the larger state-owned enterprises – as we shall see in Chapter 5 – any attempt at enforcing it where trade unions are weak seems doubtful.

Chapter 4: Item 41

> *Employing units may extend working hours ... due to the demands of production ... after consulting the Trade Unions and the workers.*

When regarded as involving the whole workforce, formal 'consultation' on such matters between management and trade union is now clarified – although it was long carried out informally – a question arises as to how it should act if the staff do *not* agree to extend hours. There was no legal formulation of its scope until 1992 and it was reformulated in 1994 (Interviews with Ministry of Labour officials, May 1995).[9]

Wage Determination

Chapter 5: Item 47

> *Employing units can autonomously decide their own wage distribution and wage level according to the law, production level, management characteristics and economic efficiency of the unit.*

This clause mostly (and formally) endorses the earlier wage-reforms and the shift to efficiency-based rewards (see Child, 1990; Tung, 1991; Howe, 1992; Takahara, 1992).[10] The State's policy of 'eating out of one big pot' (*daguo fan*) is to be phased out, replacing the egalitarian ideal and the planning-mechanism in the wage-system, as discussed elsewhere (see Warner, 1995). Such a development perhaps recognizes *de jure* what was beginning to happen *de facto*.

Health and Safety

Chapter 6: Item 52

The employing units must establish and perfect their health and safety systems.

Health and safety problems are relatively less problematic in SOEs, with the exception of construction and mining (for further details, see Wilson, 1995, pp. 21–3). This part of the 1994 law is particularly aimed at the increasing problems in new and small-scale employing-units, especially the township and village enterprises (TVEs) and foreign-funded enterprises (FFEs). As discussed above, its effective application must remain moot as the number of labour inspectors (and their training) in China may be a major constraint (Interviews with Ministry of Labour officials, May 1995 and at ACFTU Headquarters, March 1997.).

Conciliation and Arbitration

Chapter 10: Item 77

Labour disputes between employing units and workers shall be resolved through conciliation, arbitration and litigation according to the law or through consultation.

By 1994, there were 2800 Labour Arbitration Committees which handled for example 1482 collective dispute cases, involving 52 637 persons (see Table 4.3) and the numbers are still growing. The trade union appears to enjoy a seemingly more active role in such conciliation and arbitration processes than previously (see Zhang, 1997: 143ff); it is still, however, expected to perform as an arm of the state which organizes workers, and if grievances surface, it is thought that they are better expressed through such an organized official body. Such a practice is possibly suggestive of Japanese enterprise unionism, where the trade union is not expected to be principally an external party, but an internal channel leading to the expression of worker opinions to management, hopefully promoting common interests in the unit concerned – see later in Chapter 7 (Interview with Ministry of Personnel official, July 1994). Until the 1980s, there were no formal legally prescribed mechanisms to which workers could go to try to resolve work-related grievances (Josephs, 1995, p. 562).[11]

Table 4.3   Settlements of labour disputes accepted and handled by Labour
Arbitration Committees in the PRC, (1993–4)

Item	1993	1994
Disposition of accepted cases		
Number of cases	12 368	19 098
Collective disputes	684	1 482
Number of persons	35 683	77 794
Collective disputes	19 468	52 637
Cases accepted for disputes of contractual employees	5 131	8 367
Due to contract performance	2 327	4 159
Due to termination of contracts	486	812
Due to change of contracts	209	263
Due to cancellation of contracts	1 552	2 078
Due to extension of contracts	140	208
Other	417	847
Persons accepted for disputes of contractual employees	12 276	41 532
List of cases handled	11 403	179 629
Number of closed cases		
Cases by mediation	6 004	362
Cases by arbitration	1 709	3 465
Cases solved by other methods	3 690	5 135
Results of settlements		
Lawsuit won for enterprises	2 676	3 592
Lawsuit won for staff and workers	4 426	8 585
Lawsuits partially won by both parties	4 301	5 785
Number of persons	31 800	67 766
Disposition of accepted cases for disputes of contractual employees		
Number of closed cases	4 768	7 687
Cases by mediation	2 683	3 942
Cases by adjudication	709	1 395
Cases solved by other methods	1 376	2 350
Results of settlements		
Lawsuit won for enterprises	1 184	1 770
Lawsuit won for staff and workers	1 878	3 687
Lawsuits partially won by both parties	1 706	2 230
Prosecuted due to disobedience of arbitration	105	259
The same result with settlement adjudication	53	137

Source: Adapted from State Statistical Bureau, 1995.

Monitoring of Compliance

Chapter 11: Item 88

The Trade Unions [are] to monitor that the employing units abide by labour disciplines and regulations.

This now newly-regulated monitoring-role seems to be encouraging trade unions to function more actively than before, especially where the enforcement of 'interests and rights of workers' may have been weakened. Viewed in relation to the above, this clause is intended to achieve a rebalancing of the power-distribution in enterprises in line with newer and more competitive market conditions (Interview with Ministry of Personnel official, July 1994). How far it is a realistic proposition, given past and contemporary empirical evidence on the role of trade unions in the Chinese enterprise, is moot (see Warner, 1995; Warner, 1996a).

The code lays down that employers found in breach of state standards for industrial safety rules will be fined 50 000 yuan (one yuan RMB currently stands at 8.3 to the US dollar at the time of writing). It covers articles on the rights and interests of female employees, notwithstanding pregnant women and new mothers (cf Jacka, 1992). Employers found in violation of these articles will be fined 3000 RMB; those trying to block the supervision of labour officials or retaliate against informants will pay 10 000 RMB as a penalty (*Beijing Review*, 16 January 1995, p. 4). Enforcement of such penalities, given the limited staff available in Labour Bureaux, on safety and other issues like child labour, is another matter (Interviews with Ministry of Labour officials, May 1995). An official survey in late 1996 noted 'working conditions in many foreign funded firms were appalling' (*Xinhua News Agency*, 21 November 1996).

Compensation

Chapter 12: Item 89

Labour rules and regulations formulated by the employing units which violate the laws and regulations can be challenged and correction by the Labour Administration demanded; those workers harmed shall be compensated.

Under the new Labour Law, employers who fire workers will be required to pay compensation to those losing their jobs. In December 1994, The

Ministry of Labour issued regulations guaranteeing workers fixed compensation according to length of service. One year's service now merits compensation equal to one month's salary. Employees injured while off-duty or ill will get medical assistance equal to six months wages. There will be an increasing number of people seeking assistance here because the government will allow the loss-making ones engaged in restructuring to make many employees redundant.[12] The 1994 law is also being used as the basis for additional laws on social insurance (Interviews with Ministry of Labour officials, November 1995).

4.4 COMPARISONS WITH INTERNATIONAL LABOUR ORGANIZATION BENCHMARKS

The 1994 Labour Law sets out to codify a number of workers' basic rights, notwithstanding choice of job, rest and holidays, social insurance and so on. What is left out may be as important as what is included, such as the omission of the right to strike (this featured in the 1975 Constitution but was removed by constitutional amendment in 1982, as noted earlier) although this is also constrained in varying degrees in other East and South-East Asian countries (see Deery and Mitchell, 1993). Other issues related to forced labour (see Wilson, 1995, p. 14 ff) are absent, as are those relating to rehabilitation through labour (*laojiao*) – (see Wu, 1992, pp. 81–107). Critics have pointed to China's limited ratification of International Labour Organization (ILO) conventions (see Table 4.4). There are up to present a total of such 174 Conventions and Recommendations largely dealing with hours of work, days off and holidays, health and safety, child labour, and so on.

China was represented in various political guises since the ILO was founded in 1919. In 1939, it had a seat on the Governing Body. In 1971, the PRC rejoined the ILO replacing Taiwan, and in 1983 set up a tripartite delegation on the lines noted earlier in Section II. More recently, its record on human rights (and allegations regarding the use of child and forced labour) may have weakened its position:

> China has always been active since re-entering the ILO. In April 1989, China held an international labour conference in Beijing to discuss labour protection, the working environment, and the role of unions. However, as a result of the Beijing massacre on 4 June, 1989, China was voted out of the Governing Body in 1990. (*China Labour Bulletin*, July 1994, p. 2)

The 1994 Labour Law is possibly aimed at rehabilitating its status in international labour circles. Yet, as Feinerman points out, 'At times of

Table 4.4   Chronology of ratification of international labour conventions
(ILCs) by China

China has ratified a total of 16 International Labour Conventions concerning
minimum working age, rest days, industrial accidents, compensation, minimum
wage, protection of female labour, employment of the disabled, and the right to
organize for agricultural workers

ILO no.	Subject	Year ratified
7	Minimum age (sea)	1920
11	Right of association (agriculture)	1921
14	Weekly rest (industry)	1921
15	Minimum age (trimmers and stokers)	1921
16	Medical examination of young persons (sea)	1921
19	Equality of treatment (accident compensation)	1921
22	Seamen's articles of agreement	1926
23	Repatriation of seamen	1926
26	Minimum wage-fixing machinery	1928
27	Marking of weight (packages transported by vessels)	1929
32	Protection against accidents (dockers, revised)	1932
45	Underground work (women)	1935
59	Minimum age (industry, revised)	1937
100	Equal remuneration	1951
144	Tripartite consultation (International Labour Standards)	1976
159	Vocational rehabilitation and employment (disabled persons)	1983

Source: *ILO in Asia and the Pacific – A Review of Activities in 1991* (Bangkok:
International Labour Organization, 1991).

stress in international relations, ideological formulations thought to
have been long discarded come to the fore remarkably quickly' (1995,
p. 186).

China has up to now failed to ratify a number of key ILCs, these include
numbers 87 and 98, explicitly guaranteeing the right of workers to have
collective bargaining and their right to enjoy freedom of association,
respectively. To date, 16 ILO conventions have been ratified by successive
Chinese governments since 1920, but only *three* in recent times (number
100 on equal remuneration in 1951, number 144 on tripartite consultation
in 1976 and number 159 on vocational rehabilitation and employment of
disabled persons in 1983 – see Figure 4.3). Such conventions however,
are not legally binding and depend on whether national governments
adhere to recognised labour standards. Josephs (1995, p. 577) cogently
points out that the US Government has signed even fewer ILO conventions than China. As a recent report pointed out:

Though there are over 150 ILCs, although most member countries have signed only a few. The average number signed by European countries is about 47 and about 20 for Asian countries. The reasons usually given by governments for not signing the conventions are that they do not suit the conditions in their own countries or that the clauses are to complicated and the countries have to take time amending their own national legislation accordingly. The ILCs, however, remain a useful means of setting up an international standard for the member countries concerning labour protection and working conditions. (*China Labour Bulletin*, July 1994, p. 3)

The degree to which the PRC will conform to international benchmarks *vis-à-vis* labour standards in the coming years is uncertain, although a greater degree of *formal* compliance than previously may be conceded for diplomatic reasons, especially to counter human rights criticisms, if nothing else.

4.5 COMPARISONS WITH FORMERLY 'SOCIALIST' COUNTRIES'

Whereas the PRC has remained, at least nominally, a 'Socialist', even 'Marxist' economy, the former Soviet Union and other members of its bloc have mostly carried out 'free elections', adopted pluralist political institutions, in varying degrees privatized many of their basic industries, and institutionalized their market-economies to a degree unimaginable even a decade ago. Many of them now have a form of 'free collective bargaining' and multiple trade union bases, as in the Russian Republic (see Borisov *et al.*, 1994; Ashwin, 1997). Industrial relations and human resource management have, for example, also been reformed in Eastern Europe (see Borisov *et al.*, 1994; Thirkell *et al.*, 1995; Tung and Havlovic, 1996).

Until recently, the Soviet Union and Eastern Europe provided the model for Chinese industrial relations; (see Granick, 1987; 1991) for example, as we have seen earlier in Chapter 1, the trade union movement in China – the All-China Federation of Trade Unions (ACFTU) – was based on the Leninist 'transmission-belt' (see Warner, 1995, p. 21 ff). This model remains relatively intact in the PRC in spite of the substantial changes in the economy and labour market. As Chan (1993, p. 5) puts it: 'Terms like "socialism", "Marxism", the "Communist Party", etc, have to be preserved, if only to provide a last line of defence against inroads made by the languages of other ideologies.' 'Socialist Corporatism', she argues, is a possibility, but the main precedent only lasted a short period at the end of the 1980s when the Jaruzelski government in Poland legally recognized '*Solidarity*' as a trade union (ibid., p. 59).

On the other hand, like the former Soviet Union and its bloc, China appears to be seeking convergence with Western and Asian practice in many aspects of its labour-management relations and human resource management (HRM) although as usual 'with Chinese characteristics'. The 1994 Labour Law is conceivably an exercise in damage-limitation in some ways in that China's leaders understand that such a Labour Code may be a step forward in terms of the 'Open Door' policy and more closely integrating itself with the international economy, but also, as far as internal matters are concerned, balancing 'social stability' with 'enterprise efficiency'.

4.6   CONCLUDING REMARKS

In the final analysis, the 1994 Labour Law (as well as the revised 1992 Trade Union Act) may be usefully interpreted in part by outside HRM experts and practitioners as a *reflection* of ongoing developments in the economy and labour-force in China (see Warner, 1995; 1996a). The move to a 'socialist market economy' has led to an emergent labour-market (involving contracts, redundancies and so on) and this in turn we would argue has called for an appropriate legislative framework. The new law codified many existing practices introduced in the mid-1980s dealing with the demand for and the supply of labour. Even so, it is, one might say, clearly a gesture in the direction of Weber, rather than that of Marx!

Yet to make such an observation on the theoretical inspiration for the new framework may be misleading. Dissident criticism (published in Hong Kong) argues that

> a law which is unfair can be no better and sometimes worse than having no law at all ... The first labour law was formulated without a fair and just principle and philosophy. Therefore it can only lay the basis of an unfair industrial relationship and may even strip workers of their basic rights ... As the labour law does not provide workers with adequate job security, there is much room for improvement. (*China Labour Bulletin*, September 1994, pp. 1–4)

Law has long been an instrument of social control for most of the history of the PRC. The calls for a 'strong legal system' to maintain 'political stability' and 'good social order' continue (see Lubman, 1995, p. 10). On the other hand, the economic reforms have induced legal reforms such that 'a market economy is an economy governed by law' (Ibid 1995, p. 12).

Enforcement of any existing legislation is, however, a major obstacle in China (see Feinerman, 1996, p. 130); this is a particular problem *vis-à-vis* certain categories of firms, such as loss-making SOEs, or firms run by the military, or small workshops in remote places. Corruption or favouritism may also raise difficulties in this domain.

Given that the 1994 Labour Law is only a preliminary form of regulation of human resources in a vast country with various local interests to be considered, its impact should not be overestimated by actual or potential joint-venture participants whether they be foreign investors or HRM managers; in the long term, local protectionism and the difficulties in setting up unions autonomous of employers (or of the state) will be amongst many major problems in carrying it out. To a large degree, the effective implementation of the 1994 Law relies on adequate inspection[13] as well as the introduction of a well-functioning social security system, which, owing to severe financial problems, does not seem likely to appear overnight. While the goals of the 1994 Labour Law aspire to maintain and develop harmonious IR between workers and employers (thus cementing social stability) industrial conflict cannot be legislated away that easily and is likely to remain a key issue for the foreseeable future.

Over-tight, rigorous labour legislation may potentially increase costs and frighten foreign joint-venture investors away; on the other hand, ineffective over-elastic laws may stoke the fires of workplace discontent in the late 1990s. If labour standards are strictly enforced in a country, then its economic competitiveness may be undermined. Such consequences of the literal enforcement of the 1994 Labour Law might deter new investors in China and lead them to set up business in say Vietnam or another mini-Dragon economy. Since labour inspection in the PRC is somewhat sporadic and underfunded to say the least, this is unlikely to occur in the short- or even the medium-run.

Conversely, the lack of a robust labour code may carry with it several disadvantages. One drawback may be that, as in the case of economic laws generally in China, too many decisions by government agencies or Chinese joint-venture partners may be arbitrary. The lack of *predictability* in economic relations and of legally enforceable rights, whether by domestic or foreign litigants, may hinder business dealings. Another disadvantage of the Chinese system has been the 'indeterminacy' of the whole regulatory framework for foreign investment (see Lubman, 1995, p. 13).

To sum up, the 1994 Labour Law may represent a move to relatively greater 'convergence' between the internal and external systems in theory at least and may go further in practice than the *status quo ex-ante* in terms of 'regulation' of the workplace, but many problems remain none the less regarding the integration between this comprehensive national labour code and local regulations (see Feinerman, 1996, p. 130). It does however codify important areas of labour legislation relating to such areas as labour contracts, redundancy, consultation, collective agreements, wage determination, health and safety, conciliation and arbitration, compliance and compensation, as has been seen above. In the next chapter, we turn to the role of Chinese trade unions *vis-à-vis* management in the state-owned sector.

5 Trade Unions and Management in the State-Owned Enterprise Sector

5.1 INTRODUCTION

As has been made clear earlier, Chinese trade unions largely represent workers in the state-owned sector (and related urban collective enterprises) as opposed to the other parts of the economy. Given the nature of the relatively recent industrialization of the economy, this description is not surprising. There has been a significant institutional time lag, thus causing the official representational bodies to be currently out of 'synch' with the most recent structural changes in the economy and labour force. Given the latest phase of the economic reforms since the early 1990s (see Table 5.1), we shall argue that even in the state-sector there is a management–union 'crisis' in the making.

The primacy of the state-sector cannot be underplayed in the context of union power in the PRC. State-owned enterprises ('owned by the whole People', in the official jargon) have long been the main pillars of Chinese industry. They are mainly located in large industrial cities like Beijing, Shanghai, Shenyang, Wuhan and so on. Large and medium-sized SOEs in this sector formerly produced the bulk of total gross value of industrial output, nearly 80 per cent in 1980; now they produce well below half of this total (Nolan, 1995). Employing over 110 million workers in all by the 1990s, SOEs were heavily subsidized, overmanned and often loss-making (Byrd and Tidrick, 1987; Tidrick and Chen, 1987; Nolan, 1994a; 1994b). Most such firms had the full stereotypical apparatus of Chinese management–union relations under the 'Director Responsibility System' and distinct organizational culture (Barnowe, 1990; Ji, 1992; Bu, 1994). They claim to have almost complete unionization with Workers' Congresses as well as branch union committees, as we have set out in Chapter 3. Currently, their formal presence is still considerable with most industrial workers formally belonging to the ACFTU-affiliated unions at plant level.

The 'iron rice bowl' (*tie fan wan*) employment policy for many years characterized the state-owned sector. It originally had its roots in the early 1950s and was inspired by first Japanese and then later by Soviet

Table 5.1   Reform of the Chinese employment system

System characteristic	Old	New
1 Strategy	Maoist	Dengist
2 Employment	Iron rice-bowl	Labour market
3 Conditions	Job security	Labour contracts
4 Mobility	Job assignment	Job choice
5 Rewards	Egalitarian	Meritocratic
6 Wage system	Grade-based	Performance-based
7 Promotion	Seniority/political fidelity	Qualifications-based
8 Union role	Consultative	Co-ordinative
9 Management	Economic cadres	Professional managers
10 Factory/party role	Central	Ancillary
11 Work organization	Taylorist	Flexible
12 Efficiency criteria	Technical	Allocative

Source: Based on Warner 1995, p. 50.

practices, as we have seen earlier in Chapter 1. The system was originally intended to protect skilled workers after the Liberation in 1949, but eventually spread to cover a large number of urban industrial workers (for further details, see Warner, 1995, ch. 2). After leaving school, young Chinese workers were allocated jobs by local labour bureaux. They were then assigned to work-units (or *danwei*) which registered their citizenship status (or *hukou*). Citizenship registration confined the worker to their original *danwei*. Urban dwellers without their *hukou* were non-persons. The influence of the former Soviet Union was thus, as we have seen earlier, considerable not only in terms of industrial and enterprise organization (see Kaple, 1994), but also in the very model of trade unions adopted, suggesting a form of Leninism 'with Chinese characteristics'.[1]

5.2   TRADE UNIONS AND WORKERS' CONGRESSES

The Cultural Revolution that beset China during the 1960s and early 1970s – as we have seen earlier in Chapter 2 – seriously disrupted the functioning of the economy in general and production in the enterprise in particular. The twin machinery of the Factory Management Committee and Workers' Congress was suspended throughout the country, and enterprise management fell under the control of the Revolutionary Committee at the workplace (Andors, 1977, pp. 214–16). In the aftermath, the official search for economic vitality under the 'Four Modernizations' drive encouraged the state to foster enterprise autonomy and to do so by restoring a unitary system of workplace democracy (Ng, 1984, p. 59). Consequently, in place of the 'dual structure' preceding the Cultural Revolution, the Workers' Congress was revived but not the Factory Management Committee. In 1978, Deng Xiaoping declared before a national conference of trade unions that 'democratic management should be put into effect and the system of workers' congresses should be established and perfected in all enterprises' (see Morris, 1986; 1987). Three years later, the Central Committee of the Chinese Communist Party and the State Council promulgated the '*Provisional Regulations Concerning Congresses of Workers and Staff Members in State-owned Industrial Enterprises*'. Later, in the early 1980s, because of Yugoslav and later Polish experience with *Solidarity*, the leadership blew 'hot and cold' with the notion of workplace workers' organizations (see Wilson, 1990a). In a discussion of the early reforms, Wilson (1990a, p. 265) notes that even when the establishment of Workers' Congresses was on the agenda in 1980, their role *vis-à-vis* trade unions was not debated. She suggests that they might have been seen as a 'less threatening avenue for democratization' than more powerful unions (ibid , p. 265).[2]

Just as Soviet trade unions were integrated into the Soviet system, so are their counterparts inside China ideologically conceived as mass organizations led by the Party? As 'transmission belts' between the Party and the workers, they were distinct from, but in effect organizationally under the leadership of the Party, as we have already made clear earlier.

The history of the organized labour, the All-China Federation of Trade Unions (ACFTU), therefore, has essentially, been one of passive alignment to harmonize with the Chinese Communist Party's (CCP) changing political needs. In the aftermath of the 1949 Liberation, when economic recovery was a central concern of Party leadership, Chinese trade unions were observed to be 'conciliatory ... towards managements, often siding with them against striking workers and approving reductions in wages and welfare benefits' (Hearn, 1977, pp. 161–2). During the 1950s, they were 'reduced to little more than agencies responsible for ensuring enterprise control by the State's representatives', enforcing labour discipline, regulations and organizing contest or emulation campaigns (*laodong jingsai*) to increase productivity (ibid., pp. 162–3). 'At the 1957 Eighth Congress of the ACFTU, the unions were reorganized on a regional basis with industrial branches, to facilitate the decentralization required by the Great Leap Forward' (Turner *et al.*, 1980, p. 148). During the Cultural

Revolution, the position of the unions had become increasingly untenable and later suspended in 1967–8. But during the late 1970s, reconstruction of the union movement began, and with the reconvened Ninth ACFTU Congress in 1978, they were once again to be regionally-based organizations with industrial or trade branches. The restored ACFTU subsequently took on the form of a complex hierarchy – as suggested in Chapter 2 – constituted at the upper tier of regional federations 'to link with the Party structure organized on a geographical basis', below which further division is based upon 'vertically organized industrial unions to parallel government ministries responsible for particular industries', that is, industrial bureaux in the district at the time (Henley and Chen, 1981; Lansbury *et al.*, 1984; Warner, 1993).

Despite the institutional docility of the Chinese labour movement, the Party's fears that the trade unions were establishing their own bureaucratic power-base have often strained the relationship between the political and the union movements. Such apprehension prevailed, even before professional expertise appeared to be taking precedence over political purity. Virtually, the party's distrust of the labour movement was rooted historically in its early experience of political struggles:

> The reliance on the peasantry after 1927 ... was an adaptation to a rural environment forced upon the communists by the annihilation of their numbers in the industrial centres by the Kuomintang nationalists; ... isolation for urban environments and from the working class did, however, leave an undeniable stamp of primary reliance on revolutionary peasant consciousness and a consequent implicit denigration of the urban proletariat. (Hearn, 1977, pp. 160–1)

The friction erupted into an open repudiation of unionism during the Cultural Revolution. The purge of Liu Shao-ch'i (whose power-base originated in the labour organization of the urban proletariat) coincided with the suspension of the unions in 1967–8. Liu was condemned for promoting 'counter-revolutionary economism' in the trade union movement. Even when the ACFTU was redeemed in 1973, the suspicion of the Party bureaucracy towards unionism as a rival political force persisted. The resurrection of the Workers' Congress system and the trade union structure could, therefore, be interpreted as a purposive strategy to decentralize the organization of workers' power, otherwise feared by the Party if the labour movement were allowed to enhance its centralized bureaucratic strength (Ng, 1984, p. 65). With Deng's reforms, the Party's policy has thus been to devolve the union structure to the grass-roots level and make its functional presence more conspicuous at the workplace in the individual enterprise. In 1981, the ACFTU made the first of its five tasks to 'mobilize' and 'organize' the workers and staff to carry out reforms. Not only its grass-roots affiliation but also its 'independent' image was emphasized.

The union's workplace functioning was to be sharpened by merging the union branch with the Congress in the same plant into a 'twin machinery' of worker representation, as noted earlier in Chapter 2. Like the Workers' Congress, each enterprise was to set up its trade union under the relevant industrial union of the district, with its chairman, vice-chairman and the trade union committee members 'democratically elected by the workers'(Xian, 1980, p. 22). Thus, the production unit itself was said to be further highlighted as the focus of work for the unions. In the context of China's self-seeking drive to reform the economic management system, such development was said to be a logical corollary to the ACFTU's newly assigned mission: 'to educate their members to understand the meaning of the "Four Modernizations"' (Henley and Chen, 1981, p. 90). Most of this chapter will be concerned with the functioning of this 'twin machinery' referred to above.

The reconstruction of the augmented Workers' Congress system may be possibly interpreted as a 'quasi-liberal' strategy to reinforce the 'grass-roots' organization and influence of the (formerly) centrally-administered union bureaucracy in the enterprise, where its presence used to be feeble. The union would become more visible in the workplace, in that it would deputize for the Workers' Congress during its recess. Such processes, it may be argued, would enable the union to enjoy an 'agency' role. Structurally speaking, this 'hybrid' arrangement appeared to entail a more practical approach to 'orthodox' socialist unionism, for both the planning process of the enterprise and for encouraging its members 'to participate in production conferences for the fulfilment of the workers' plan' (Ng, 1984, p. 66). The relative success of harmonizing such a 'Workers' Congress-cum-union' merger would depend upon the degree to which their respective functions were seen to be mutually concordant or identical. As previous experience shows, however, there is a limit, even in the Communist states, to the extent to which the union can substitute or usurp fully a workers' representative body and *vice versa*.

To the extent that the union and the Workers' Congress were to be consolidated into one at the workplace level, the reconstituted union structure in China confronted role-conflicts of an intense nature. Moreover, it was imperative for the union to monitor the Congress in the shop. Given the volatile record of unionism in China since 1949, however, one might argue whether the ACFTU was an institution of sufficient credibility and competence to be entrusted by the Party leadership with such a strategic role.

Indeed, a related but perhaps more fundamental question to raise is whether this type of combined machinery would be more conducive to the *bona fide* articulation of workers' occupational rights and interests than in its absence. Evidently, a socialist country cannot free itself entirely from the problem of labour protests and their authentic representation as it evolves towards industrial pluralism (see Kerr *et al.*, 1973). The Webbs had earlier noted that the Soviet workplace was equally prone to 'sectional' industrial conflict and 'economistic' haggling, as in Western capitalist societies (see Webb and Webb, 1935). Nor has China been immune from the spontaneous and sporadic eruption of industrial upheavals. Indeed, for a brief period during the 1950s, unions were described as 'instrumental' in exposing sweat-shop conditions and other forms of worker exploitation resulting from the drive for increased productivity. During the Cultural Revolution, workers' opposition was voiced through spontaneous protests and through unions which elicited fresh charges of 'economism' by the Party leadership (Ng, 1984, p. 67).

By the late 1980s, there were over 360 000 Workers' Congresses (Zhang, 1988, p. 35; Gong, 1989, p. 3) but this total had fallen to just under 300 000 by 1995 (see Table 5.2). Liu (1989) enumerates their formal responsibilities as follows:

> According to the provisions of the Law of the People's Republic of China on Industrial Enterprises Owned by the Whole People, the Workers' Congress is the basic from of democratic management in enterprises and the organ for workers to exert such powers. It has the right to deliberate such major issues as the policy of operations, annual and long-term plans and programmes, contract and leasing responsibility systems of management; it may approve or reject plans on wage reforms and bonus distribution as well as on important rules and regulations; it may decide on major issues concerning workers' conditions and welfare; it may appraise and supervise the leading administrative cadres at various levels and put forward suggestions for awards and punishments and their appointment and approval and it democratically elects the director. (pp. 5–6)

A demand for direct elections of union officials surfaced again in the late 1980s (it had previously been a demand of the Democracy Movement of 1979) with a third of incumbent officials said to have been voted out of office in over one hundred enterprises sampled (Zhang, 1988, p. 23). While this may have been a 'straw in the wind', further evidence of such displacements are relatively scarce.

Union representation in the workplace – to make the workers 'masters of the country' in the above representational model – was, it was said, formally built into the system. Workplace institutional control may have in fact evolved over four decades, although the changes in form may have changed with shifts in function. The role of the Party secretary in the enterprise according to some observers (for example, Walder, 1989) had long been relatively central whatever the changing institutional arrangements, whether managerial or representative.[3] The Party controlled the union's work and appointments in the trade union with the latter's chairperson often holding the same rank as Deputy-Director. Such officials sometimes swapped roles with managers and sometimes held both offices. The Party committee was responsible to 'guarantee and supervise' policy implementation (Child and Xu, 1989, p. 10). In this context, full-time union cadres supported policy-making bodies in the enterprise on sensitive workforce issues, however. Granick, for example, points out that:

> Although the issue of dismissing workers for personal fault was mentioned in several of the sample enterprises, none of the informants suggested that the enterprise trade union was any obstacle to such dismissals. Instead, objections came solely from the local authorities of the area where the worker had his official residence. This is in sharp contrast to the situation in the (former) Soviet Union, where no dismissal is legal unless it wins the prior explicit approval of the enterprise trade union committee. (Granick, 1990, p. 238)

It is therefore doubtful if trade unions have played much of an *independent* role in Chinese enterprises – according to the sceptics. Their argument goes as follows: union officials do traditionally support the Party line; the Workers' Congress has not been functionally that distinct from the union; its sessions are often said to be just a formality; workers elected to the Congress are drawn from the Party faithful; the traditional 'hard-liners' in the Party are usually the 'pro-worker' faction; the 'reformers' support the 'managerial' line. In the Special Economic Zones and joint ventures, there was often neither a union nor a Workers' Congress – see Chapter 7 later for further details.

5.3 THE CHANGING ROLE OF WORKERS' REPRESENTATIVE BODIES

Trade unions in China have tended in the past, as several authorities have argued, to stress mainly production questions, but have also had to look after the everyday welfare of their members and their leisure activities (see Lee, 1986; Chan, 1993; Kaple, 1994). They have not bargained freely, or fixed wage levels as in Western countries, but have been concerned with 'mobilization and socialization' (Lee, 1986, p. 160). Unions in China have thus been traditionally required to discipline and to ensure the production commitment of the labour force at all costs (ibid.). They pass over 12 times as many motions on production matters as they do on welfare ones (see Table 5.2).

Indeed, in a recent report to a seminar of senior ACFTU leaders, one commentator pointed to the Chinese labour movement's current dilemmas:

> The reconstruction of labour relations has had a dual effect upon trade unions, at one and the same time giving rise to both challenges and opportunities. Opportunities arise from the new conflicts and contradictions. In the newly emerged market, the distinction between labour and management is being clarified. The roles and functions of workers and managers are becoming increasingly differentiated in production. This brings us the hope of solving a fundamental problem which unions have long felt uneasy about but unable to handle under the old system. As we know, Chinese unions have long been claimed to be the 'workers' own organization'. In reality, however, whenever unions took any initiative in fighting for workers' interests, they would immediately meet strong resistance. Under the old system, enterprise managers always emphasize their role in working for the worker's material interests; indeed, the Party secretaries explain their position in representing the Communist Party at the enterprise level in terms of the Party, as the vanguard of the working class, naturally representing the highest interests of the workers. Enterprise unions then inevitably find themselves in a thankless position. Although defined in principle as a representative body for the workers, in reality unions found their position extremely ambiguous. The reconstructed labour relations differentiate management from labour, as this in turn helps clarify their respective roles and functions in management and production. Consequently, the prospect of a closer relationship between unions and workers is in the offing. This is an inevitable consequence of the introduction of the market economy. (Feng, 1996, p. 9)

Thus, plant-level industrial relations in China have further devolved to the trade unions and Workers' Congresses working together, the latter

Table 5.2   Role of Workers' Congresses in Chinese enterprises (end of 1995)

Number of enterprises with Workers' Congresses	297 033
Number of worker's representatives on Workers' Congresses	12 411 762
Number of women workers representatives on Workers' Congresses	4 139 765
Number of enterprises convening Workers' Congresses at regular internals	259 585
Number of motions proposed	
(a) on production and management	26 443 367
(b) on workers' welfare	1 958 771
Number of units with 'Democratic Appraisal' of managerial cadres	188 199

Source: ACFTU statistics, 1996.

revived with the economic reforms to balance the new powers of factory managers (Lee, 1986, p. 166; Henley and Nyaw, 1986). The former have provided the day-to-day continuity, with the latter meeting periodically to effect 'rubber-stamp' policy.

The remit of the trade union committee itself was set out in the 1992 Trade Union Law as follows:

Article 30   In an enterprise owned by the whole People, the Congress of Workers and Staff members shall, as the basic form of democratic management of the enterprise and the organ by which the Workers and Staff members exercise their right to democratic management, discharge its functions and powers in accordance with the stipulations of the Law of the People's Republic of China on Industrial Enterprises Owned by the Whole People.

The trade union committee of an enterprise owned by the whole People shall, as the working body of the Congress of Workers and Staff members, take care of its day-to-day work and check and supervise the implementation of its decisions. (*Trade Union Law*, 1992; see Appendix 1 in Warner, 1995, p. 173)

Trade unions are thus expected to implement the details of resolutions passed by the Workers' Congress. In the everyday work of the enterprise, union officials are, for example, expected to defuse conflicts between the workers and management. If the latter act out of order, for example by reducing bonuses, or when there is a stoppage by the workers involved, the union is asked to intervene. Congresses were also encouraged to involve themselves in 'democratic appraisal' of cadres, as Table 5.2 shows (Interviews at ACFTU Headquarters, March 1997).

Table 5.3 Collective negotiations and contracts in Chinese enterprises (end of 1995)

	No. of units setting up collective negotiations	No. of representatives involved in collective negotiations	No. of units setting up collective contracts	No. of units signing collective contracts	No. of units implementing collective contracts
National total	52 493	912 108	49 928	48 431	43 152
Categorized according to scale of unit (person):					
1–10	478	1 796	454	28 521	25 209
11–50	11 166	84 031	9 945	17 382	15 681
51–100	11 870	130 945	10 475	150	148
101–200	11 437	190 170	10 632	9	1
201–300	4 920	94 879	5 414	64	60
301–500	5 305	132 307	4 982	843	762
501–800	3 247	86 314	3 446	1 220	1 097
801–2 999	3 417	139 940	3 818	225	179
3 000 and over	653	51 726	762	17	15
Categorized according to economic type:					
State-owned	32 015	609 902	29 237	444	400
Collective	17 759	269 236	17 992	9 582	8 557
Privately operated	231	1 624	172	10 275	9 067
Individual	30	1 712	20	10 186	8 952

90

Table 5.3 (continued)

	No. of units setting up collective negotiations	No. of representatives involved in collective negotiations	No. of units setting up collective contracts	No. of units signing collective contracts	No. of units implementing collective contracts
Joint Venture	105	871	71	5 216	4 720
Stock-holding	915	16 646	925	4 942	4 467
Foreign invested	1 168	10 085	1 287	3 422	3 035
Hong Kong, Macau and Taiwan invested	242	1 704	207	3 657	3 306
Others	28	328	17	707	648

Source: ACFTU statistics, 1996.

In the recent years, trade unions have promoted a system of so-called 'collective agreements', now a formal requirement of the Labour Law of 1994 (see also Ministry of Labour Circular, No. 485, 5 December 1994). By the end of 1995, around 50 000 work-units (mostly SOEs) signed 'collective contracts' in their new version (see Table 5.3). These accords are based on individual enterprises and define the respective roles of managers and unions, but must be distinguished from Western-style 'free collective bargaining'. The old pre-1994 'collective agreements' gave the unions a formal say in managerial decision-making, but the new ones sanctioned by the 1994 Labour Law are mostly 'framework agreements' which deal with wages and working conditions for a given enterprise.[4] According to informal sources, new-style 'collective agreements' were only just being introduced 'so it was too early to say what their impact was' (Interviews with Ministry of Labour officials, November 1995). On key issues such as dismissals, management usually does meet with the union officials representing the Workers' Congress, but it is difficult to disentangle their role from that of the union's. In recent years, health and safety matters have become increasingly a Congress responsibility (Interview with ACFTU officials March 1997). The ACFTU has also asked them to 'appraise' the performance of top enterprise managers (see *China Daily,* 22 March 1997, p. 1. In any case, the links between the Party and the trade unions are also close because of overlapping membership. In addition, the union chair-person is normally a member of the enterprise Party committee. There are now further dilemmas because of the increasing phenomenon of the 'twin-leadership' (*yijian tiao*) where the role of Factory Director and Party secretary are fused. Previously, the Party secretary could arbitrate between the union and management. At present, the future role of trade unions at both macro- and micro-levels is in a state of flux.

As Feng points out:

In reality, the Workers' Congress finds it difficult to assert its right to participate in enterprise management despite the fact that such a right has been legalized by the Enterprise Law. The State Council issued 'Regulations on the Transformation of the Management Operational System in State Industrial Enterprises' in August 1992 to accommodate the implementation of Enterprise Law. The Regulation elaborates itself into dozens of clauses. But none of these clauses mention democratic management – the workers' right to participate in enterprise manage-ment has been totally ignored...

The Corporation Law, passed by the NPC at the end of 1993, came into effect in July 1994. Heated debates had been going on between the government and the ACFTU regarding whether the Law should include clauses detailing the rights and role of trade unions and the Workers' Congress. The controversy amply illustrates the unions' sensitivity to new challenges posed by the increasingly complex legal context (Feng, 1996, p. 21).

As we have seen earlier in Chapter 4, the role of the trade union is further clarified in the 1994 Labour Law but the Workers' Congress is given no great prominence there.[5]

In the first chapter of the Labour Law where its principles are enunciated, Articles 7 and 8 set out the role of the workers' representative institutions:

7.   Workers have the right to take part in and organize trade unions according to the law. Union representatives shall protect the legal rights and interests of workers independently and autonomously and develop their activities according to the law.
8.   Workers shall take part in democratic management, and equal consultation with employment units on the protection of legal interests and interests of workers through Worker Conferences, Worker (Representative) Congresses and other similar forms within the framework of legal regulation. (1994 Labour Law, ch. 1)

There are many further references to trade unions but Workers' Congresses do not figure much further in the text.

As a result, the roles of the trade unions and Workers' Congresses have remained ambivalent *vis-à-vis* management policy with no new signs of independence emerging. In an empirical investigation carried out in 1993 (see Warner, 1995; 1996b) several case studies undertaken did not indicate much change in their activities, whether for unions or Congresses – some examples follow.

In one-case study investigated in Capital Iron and Steel (*Shougang*) in Beijing, the Workers' Congress met only once a year to review the previous year's performance and to discuss the coming year's plans. In between, every section had to report to the General Manager, who was said to be formally elected by the Workers' Congress. The trade unions were described as 'active' in supervising the work of the different departments. The grievance-channel was first, to the trade union; second, to the 'Supervisory Committee' – set up 'like a court to hear workers' complaints' including those regarding contracts, with the same membership as the Examinations Committee; third, directly to the General Manager (see Warner, 1995, p. 108).

The activities of the trade union and Workers' Congress in another case study in the Dalian Shipyard, were assumed to be more or less a formality in the implementation of the latest reforms. They had been involved in the

Figure 5.1   Key authority relationships in Chinese enterprises

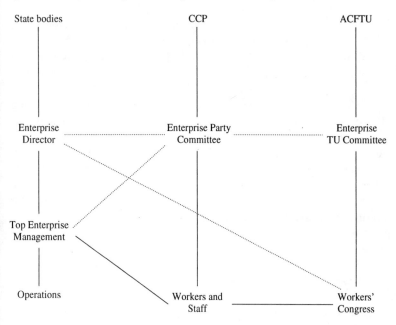

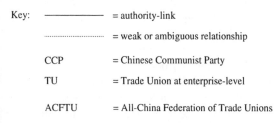

Key: ——————   = authority-link

....   = weak or ambiguous relationship

CCP   = Chinese Communist Party

TU   = Trade Union at enterprise-level

ACFTU   = All-China Federation of Trade Unions

Source   Adapted from Child, 1994, p. 67.

approval of 'three systems' reforms', as well as in their traditional concerns such as welfare and leisure, as well as labour protection. They also helped in discussions of production levels and promotions. There were two meetings of the Workers' Congress, one to review the previous year's progress and the plan for the coming year, with the second one to monitor the half-yearly achievements of the enterprise (see ibid., pp. 109–10).

The role of the trade unions and Workers' Congress in another case, in Harbin Power Equipment, for example, was emphasized relatively more sharply than elsewhere. There were frequent 'model worker' and 'emulation' schemes organized by the trade union which was active also in soliciting ideas for productivity improvements. The Workers' Congress met regularly four times a year to discuss important decisions such as the system reforms, income distribution and dismissals. The Party Secretary was also the Factory Director, a process described as 'combining the Party and leadership as one' (see ibid., p. 111).

In a later set of case studies carried out in the Winter 1995 in Beijing, all the firms studied there had functioning Workers' Congresses (see Warner, 1996b). In one example, in Peony TV, it met only once a year; in Beijing Transformers, it met similarly rarely. However, in Beijing Pharmaceuticals, it was convened twice a year. *Ad hoc* sessions could be called, if necessary, in all cases. The Congress members normally did not take a direct part in managerial decision making in these SOEs, but met as a formality to discuss policy matters such as the previous year's company performance and the plan for the next one, as in the earlier case mentioned.

5.4 CONCLUDING REMARKS

To sum up, the role of the ACFTU unions grew *pari passu* with the emergence of the state-owned sector of the economy. The typical SOE enshrined the 'iron rice bowl' system for its almost totally unionized permanent workforce. At grass-roots level, the ACFTU's top-down role was mediated by plant-level Workers' Congresses which met infrequently and which worked in tandem with the factory trade union committee who implemented policy on a day-to-day basis (see Figure 5.1). Since the latest phase of the economic reforms were introduced in the early 1990s, the roles of both trade union and Workers' Congress (see Rosen, 1989; Wang and Heller, 1993; White, 1996) have been diluted as managerial autonomy has grown stronger than it was under the enterprise legislation of the 1980s. Even here, Lu (1996) reported that in five out of the six state enterprises he studied in the mid-1980s, neither the Congress nor the union was encouraged to get involved in major decision-making on organizational charge directly affecting workers' interests. Whether the unions can take on a more differentiated role as the reforms deepen, given the growing degree of worker alienation referred to earlier in Chapter 3, remains to be seen. In the non-state sector, the role of unions *vis-à-vis* management remains problematic. In the JVs and foreign-funded enterprises, the ACFTU has yet to catch up with the rapid growth of this burgeoning part of the economy. It is to this largely unorganized sector that we now turn in the next chapter.

6 Trade Unions and Management in the Joint Venture and Foreign-Funded Enterprise Sectors

6.1 INTRODUCTION

Foreign capital has re-entered China for almost 20 years now, since it was admitted in the late 1970s when Deng Xiaoping launched the ambitious 'Four Modernizations' and opened up the economy through the 'Open Door' policy to investment by sources from outside the country. In retrospect, the foreign-funded enterprises, including the joint ventures (JVs), have been a pioneering force not only on the frontier of productivity and technological innovations (see Vogel, 1991) but also in managerial and labour reforms for a China now in search of a new realm of 'market socialism'. After these years of experiments to advance 'socialism with Chinese characteristics', the question worth investigating is whether the once 'enclaved' practices adopted in these foreign-owned enterprises will be increasingly emulated by their 'native' counterparts in the state-owned sector, now in a vigorous process of restructuring and rationalization, as suggested by the thesis of 'institutional convergence' brought about by the unifying imperative of 'industrialism' (Kerr *et al.*, 1973).

In this context, we refer to 'internal' convergence as between the state and non-state sectors. Otherwise, inasmuch as a 'divide' is still ascertainable between the state-owned enterprises (SOEs) and the foreign-funded enterprises (FFEs) (as well as privately-owned firms) on these dimensions like workplace industrial relations and human resources practices, we can further ask if it is legitimate to interpret the diversities in terms of a new state of 'dualism' – which can appear to coalesce with the integrative notion which Deng Xiaoping has canvassed in the 'one country, two systems' formula as the blueprint to integrate and unify China across the Mainland, Taiwan and Hong Kong (see Deng, 1985, p. 31).[1] It is around the theme of these two alternative perspectives that this chapter intends to review the latest terrain of workplace industrial relations in the joint-ventures and other foreign-funded enterprises in China.

6.2   JOINT VENTURES AND FOREIGN-FUNDED ENTERPRISES

The general impression has been that, since their re-entry into China, JVs and FFEs have enjoyed a substantial degree of autonomy in personnel decision-making. The JV enterprises are heralded as the pace-setters, pioneering nationwide managerial reforms. Those in Guangdong Province, for instance, have been distinctive in their ability to '(attract) personnel of senior secondary graduates and above' by paying attractively high wages (Sit and Wong, 1990, pp. 224–5; see also pp. 222–3 and 158). The autonomy hitherto extended by the state to these foreign enterprises, enabling them to organize their own wage and personnel activities almost independently, is an approximation in practice of a nascent labour market, although some doubt its extent (see Knight and Song, 1995). Since the beginning of the present decade, the manpower utilization of these enterprises has been made even more 'market responsive' because of newly-sanctioned personnel practices, such as contract-worker hiring, which were later emulated in the SOEs and urban collectives. Apparently, these enhanced flexibilities experienced (and experimented) in the labour market practices of these foreign enterprises have displaced and helped emasculate the formerly Soviet-style system of central state manpower allocation, now rejected for having bred widespread rigidities and stifled incentives (see Davis, 1993; 1995). These reforms have far-reaching implications not only for human resource management in both the foreign-funded and Chinese enterprises, but also for the work agenda of the Chinese trade unions, as we noted earlier in Chapter 1.

The paradoxical mix of the nation's hospitality with its apprehension about the revisit of foreign guest capital (the presence of which dated back to the imperial Manchu reign, the 1911 Revolution and the Nationalist-led Republic in the earlier decades of this century), epitomized in such anachronistic institutions as the 'unequal treaties' and 'foreign settlements', and instigating large-scale industrial upheavals like the Canton – Hong Kong Strike-Boycott of 1925–6[2] has created a mood of national ambivalence which was represented in the elaborate legislative code which the state first evolved in the 1980s for governing the activities of foreign capital in China. These legal prescriptions were intended to enshrine the special privileges extended to the foreign businesses as incentives, but at the same time were induced by a historic anxiety to hold the 'aliens' under rein. They sanctioned the strategic role of the Chinese trade unions, to act as both 'ambassadors' in bridging links with the foreign employers as well as protectors of the Chinese workers hired in these JVs and other FFEs – a dualistic set of 'agency' roles which are not always necessarily compatible.

6.3   REGULATION IN THE JOINT VENTURES AND FOREIGN-FUNDED ENTERPRISES

The principal legal instrument governing labour–management relations in the foreign business sector has been for a decade or more the *Regulations for the Implementation of the Law of the People's Republic of China on Joint Ventures Using Chinese and Foreign Investment*, promulgated by the State Council in September, 1983. It was preceded by the *Regulations of the People's Republic of China for Labour-Management in Chinese Foreign Joint Ventures* which the State Council decreed earlier, in July 1980. By virtue of these provisions, the foreign employer is legally obliged to recognize a workplace union organization, which is part of the national labour movement under the ACFTU. Specifically, chapter 13 of the *Regulations for the Implementation of the Law in Joint Ventures* is devoted to the subject of the recognition and functions of grass-roots unions inside these enterprises. Its Article 95 guarantees to the workforce of a joint venture enterprise the basic right to 'set up grass-roots trade unions and carry out trade union activities' in the same fashion as governed by China's Trade Union Law and the *Articles of Association of Chinese Trade Unions*, a brief recently revised in 1992, regarding the unions' legal status. Yet, symmetrically, the same set of Regulations, in its Article 39, explicitly acknowledges and buttresses the prerogative of the foreign enterprise management by confirming the latter's autonomy. It is hence reminiscent of the legal status of the employment contract (and relationship) in Western capitalist society that the Regulations of 1983 declare that 'the general manager shall (be) empowered ... by the board, have the right to appoint and dismiss his subordinates, and exercise other responsibilities and rights as authorized by the board within the joint venture' (Article 39).

The union, however, enjoyed a legal right under the Regulations to help conclude labour contracts on behalf of the individual workers and staff members and was responsible for their enforcement (Article 99 of the Regulations). The union was also the competent organ to regulate, jointly with management, the 'welfare and bonus funds' held by the enterprise (Article 97) – the provision of which was sanctioned by Article 10 of the ancillary *Regulations for Labour – Management in Chinese – Foreign Joint Ventures*. Where the foreign-funded enterprise can be exempted from an obligation to establish the workplace participative organ of the Workers' Congress, the union was to act, almost *ipso facto*, as the 'sole' agent to deputize for the entire workplace in the plant. All these measures seem to suggest an official anxiety to prescribe an obligation incumbent upon the foreign businesses to recognize and to deal with the Chinese trade unions, at the enterprise level, as the representative organ acting on behalf the Chinese workers in their employment.

The 1983 Regulations also made the provision of specified employer's facilities to the workplace union organization obligatory for the foreign enterprises. Thus, these legal norms required the foreign employer to furnish the union with such concessions as space to house the union's office and its meetings, as well as back-ups for it to organize welfare, cultural and sports activities. Analogous to the case of the SOE, a fund amounting to a standard 2 per cent equivalent of the enterprise's payroll has to be subscribed by the foreign employer as his legal duty to support the 'house' union and its activities.[3]

However, in spite of these legally-backed arrangements of state sponsorship for the All-China Federation of Trade Unions (ACFTU) to organize the JVs and other enterprises in the foreign-funded sector, the national trade union centre has always reckoned as problematic the regulation of industrial relations and labouring standards in these workplaces owned and managed by visiting overseas capital. The explanation of these problems is highly intricate and complex; but in many instances, it reflects the lingering psychology of the Chinese ambivalence, deeply rooted in history, towards the foreigners and the 'hegemony' of their 'capitalist' penetration into the country. The 'dualistic' dictum of having to welcome as well as tame the 'alien investors' probably helps shape and sustain the ACFTU's 'neurosis' about the JVs and related enterprises of foreign capital. In addition, it has resulted in a new terrain of workplace industrial relations which, although still distinctive because of the variety of officially-sanctioned concessions extended to the foreign-funded sector as an 'enclave' industry, is likely to be replicated, at least in part, in the other important domain of the state-owned enterprises currently going through a vigorous process of renewal. However, is it legitimate to look upon the JVs and FFEs in China as the standard-bearers of advances and innovations in labour market reforms and labour-management restructuring in order to achieve the enshrined realm of 'market socialism'? To answer this question, a review of the development of the JV practices in the area of 'human resource management' since the early 1980s among the foreign-backed businesses in China may provide a glimpse of the shifting industrial relations terrain in this sector.

6.4   HUMAN RESOURCES AND LABOUR MARKET REFORMS

It appears that labour market reforms in China began ostensibly with the JVs and the foreign-owned sector as the standard-bearer for piloting innovations which were to be later emulated by the SOEs. In the Shenzhen Special Economic Zone, for example, all FFEs have, since 1983, ceased to recruit workers by the centrally allocated system and substituted with contract labour arrangements. Literally, all foreign enterprises since the early 1980s have been able to enjoy a latitude of freedom in their wage and personnel activities that approximates to a labour market of sorts. Joint ventures in Guangdong province, for instance, have 'demonstrated a high degree of flexibility in the most critical aspects of operation' – notably in paying high wages to 'provide sufficient incentive' to the workforce and 'attracting personnel of senior secondary graduates and above' (Sit and Wong, 1990, p. 158). Later, this flexibility has been increased by the practice of hiring contract workers. Such an innovative system of labour-hiring was ratified by the Chinese government in 1986 (but piloted in Shenzen in the early 1980s) by virtue of a body of State regulations reforming the nationwide system of permanent lifelong employment which was the 'mainstream' practice prior to the 'labour market reforms', at least for new employees.

However, it was apparent that in spite of the advances which the JVs represented in their potential 'labour market' freedom and flexibilities, these FFEs were still the captives of considerable restrictive constraints due to pre-reform practices and institutional controls. One major source of such normative and institutional limits practised in the JV enterprises, at least before the resumption and enhancement of the reform policies heralded by Deng Xiaoping's 'Southern Tour' to the coastal provinces in 1992, was the almost unwritten 'rule' that personnel administration in the enterprise be placed under the jurisdiction of the Chinese partner, which conserved an implicit 'home vs alien' divide in spite of their business collaboration. Such a division of labour or in cruder terms, the internal demarcation of spheres of influence, was vividly narrated in Pearson's (1991) observation that:

> The personnel manager uniformly came from the Chinese side. Chinese personnel managers and Chinese deputy general managers in most cases had final authority over disciplinary actions taken against workers … Indeed, many foreign managers reported strong and successful resistance from the Chinese partner or from local labour authorities to their efforts to fire workers … Moreover, in labour decisions that required negotiations between partners (such as increasing or decreasing wages), the Chinese deputy general manager sometimes claimed to represent the workers against management. (p. 173)

Such an 'enclave' was probably useful, inasmuch as the Chinese partner or manager became a *de facto* agency or labour service subcontractor deputising for the foreigner partner – especially in the earlier periods when foreign business began to make its reappearance in the early and mid-1980s. This role was reminiscent of the 'compradore' role performed by the Hong Kong staff in British trading houses dealing with China almost a century ago, because of a mutuality of alienness between the visitors' and the hosts' culture and interests.[4] However, the negative implications of such jurisdictional demarcations were also obvious in upholding an overtly bureaucratic and parochial 'divide' of conserving a 'we–they' identity which not only separated the foreign from the Chinese side in the managerial echelon but also insulated foreign capital from any direct dialogue, haggling or control *vis-à-vis* the workers. What emanated in some joint ventures could therefore be a 'fictitious' terrain of labour – management relations which gave the foreign managing partner an illusion that the JV was tantamount to a labour (service) subcontracting shop – where workplace industrial relations were either irrelevant or could be conveniently assumed away because of the Chinese intermediary 'buffer'. Given such a delegated jurisdiction which suggested almost a *laissez-faire* detachment of the foreign partner from any 'in-house' human resource issues, it was logical to suspect that the latitude granted to the foreign-funded business as a privileged concession could have been more apparent then real in the joint ventures. Practices existed in some JV enterprises whereby wages paid to Chinese workers did not go directly to the individual worker 'but, rather, were distributed through the local labour bureau, to the Chinese partner's *danwei*, or to the labour organization' (Pearson, 1991, p. 173).

However, within this generic class of JV and FFEs, a heterogeneous rather than a uniform pattern of human resources pervaded the diversity of overseas businesses belonging to different industries and ethnic ownership. Child (1994) in his study, has added to this spectrum of diversified practice by making explicit the role of such variables as the centralization of control on strategic decisions desired by the foreign partner, as well as whether the rationale of the overseas participation was to search for a production base or to secure an inroad into and consolidate a share in the Mainland's lucrative market. In the former case, the management of human resources tended to remain more indigenous, with the Chinese partner or deputy manager acting like a labour subcontractor or agent, subject to loose, or even a *laissez-faire* type of nominal intervention or control from the foreign partner. Personnel management practices in this type of joint venture situation hardly betrayed the 'novel' property which accorded with the stereotyped image of the foreign-funded sector as the 'primary' pattern-setting employers in China's nascent labour market, but instead could be potential grounds for poor labour conditions, which have perturbed the ACFTU. Child summarized its characteristic profile:

> These are low technology products requiring relatively simple production processes. Both the level of investment and time-scale of the foreign partner tended to be limited. The foreign partner has therefore generally not felt the need to intervene a great deal in the Chinese management process, except to ensure productivity and quality standards. The Chinese operation is primarily a sub-contracting one, with wider commercial, financial and product development matters being retained by the foreign company. (Ibid., p. 253)

Unwittingly, this type of JV business was and is still vulnerable to the notorious 'sweat shop' hiring of Chinese labour by overseas capital, conceivably drawn 'by the attraction of low cost labour as a manufacturing base and export platform for products' (ibid., p. 253). At this lower reach of the overseas investment sector, which comprised a sizeable contingent of cross-border capital transfer and migration from Hong Kong, Macau and Taiwan, the 'wage' factor was and is still the principal incentive in pulling the Chinese workers (which has in turn helped sustain the rush of mobile rural labour to the cities). However, it is suspected that the vicissitudes of industrial capital are also most conspicuous among this type of workplaces – confirmed by press reports of overcrowding, substandard provisions of dormitories and insanitary shopfloors, as well as a sequence of factory fires and occurrence of other industrial hazards and accidents.

These propensities towards industrial impoverishments (in work and working conditions) suggest a 'secondary' lower tier in the labour market of the JV sector which has been segmented and 'balkanized', precipitating in turn a basic issue of work humanization and labour protection under the squeeze of the less scrupulous 'outside' investors. That the 'labour-aristocratic' image of employment in the foreign capital sector can be highly illusory has been demonstrated graphically in the following piece of criticism:

> Since the late 1970s, foreign capital has been introduced into China in a greater and greater scale ... Chinese workers' 'fifteen years' of experience in this sector has shattered many of their illusions about foreign capital. These workers' own experience furnishes a stark contrast to the frequently made claim that foreign firms or joint ventures scrupulously abide by international laws and conventions. The behaviour of many such firms is in reality a fairly dramatic departure from the image of

themselves they like to project. In Guangdong, for instance, firms with foreign capital always elaborate on the responsibilities and liabilities of the workers in the labour contract ... Many of the firms set extraordinarily high task quotas of workers, in some cases 50–60 per cent higher than that set for workers in the country providing the capital. Overtime is always adopted as an effective way to extract extra profit from the workers. Some firms force their workers to work as much as 134 hours overtime per month, severely violating the limit of 48 hours per week set by the Chinese government. Many workers become so exhausted by overtime that they faint in the shopfloor during protection. Compulsory overtime is also used by many foreign firms or joint ventures in other parts of the country. (Feng, 1996, pp. 26–7)

In addition, a host of such complaints represented to the ACFTU have been reported also in other industrial centres like Beijing, Shanghai and Shenzhen (ibid., p. 27). Apprehensive about these reported workplace abuses while being aware also of the 'marketplace' *impasse* now that both the state and the Chinese workers attach a high premium to the lucrative employment opportunities that these enterprises afford, the All-China Federation of Trade Unions (ACFTU), has responded to the problems of the JVs and foreign employers by enhancing its organization work in this type of workplace, placing its apparent faith upon the presence of the 'grass-roots' unions in the plant as the most efficacious safeguard in protecting 'the legitimate rights and interests of the Chinese employees'. Part of the trade union centre's national agenda laid down at its Twelfth National Congress in October 1993 propagated, accordingly, the importance of strengthening the work of the Chinese trade unions in the FFEs (ACFTU, 1994, p. 35).

6.5   THE ACFTU AGENDA

The Twelfth ACFTU National Congress has indeed detailed an elaborated body of guidelines for the Chinese labour movement and its union organs in dealing with the enterprises of the guest capital. Such prescriptions for governing labour-management activities in the JV and foreign-funded sector were articulated, in summary, by the instructions that:

(i)   trade unions be established at 'earliest possible' time in enterprises already in operation while preparatory work of organizing unions be started simultaneously with the preparation of any new enterprise;

  (ii) the political status and legitimate rights of the workforce in foreign-funded and private enterprises are 'naturally' protected by the nation's Constitution and laws, as 'masters of the country';

 (iii) trade unions are to safeguard the legitimate rights and interests of workers and staff members in these enterprises; and to co-operate and work together with investors in order to strive jointly for the development of the enterprise 'to serve the masses of workers and staff members' and to contribute to promoting reforms and opening to the outside and the economic construction ...'; moreover, 'trade unions should support the legitimate operations of enterprises';

 (iv) trade unions should sign collective contracts with enterprises on workers' behalf with enterprises and help workers and staff members to sign individual labour contracts with enterprises and supervise the implementation of these contracts;

  (v) trade unions should check and supervise the implementation of state laws and regulations on wage, working hours, social insurance, labour protection, safety in production, special protection of female workers and worker training;

 (vi) trade unions should attend the full or non-voting members board meetings and working meetings of management in these enterprises to voice the opinions and demands of their workers and staff members;

 (vii) a system of consultation or bargaining be established 'in exclusive foreign-funded enterprises and private enterprises' and the participation of the unions in the management of these enterprises be constantly explored;

(viii) the Workers' Congress system be conserved and improved in those Sino-foreign equity and contractual JVs where such a system has been established and in existence already; and

 (ix) the work of organizing the grass-roots unions be enhanced in those foreign participating enterprises because problems such as serious law-breaking, holding back workers and staff members from organizing unions, violating the human rights of workers and staff members and arbitrarily extending working hours, deducting wages and firing workers and staff members as well as lacking in labour protection measures, etc. were more serious and abhorrent in enterprises where trade unions are not yet organized; and

  (x) the Chinese trade unions in the foreign-funded enterprises should seek to cultivate stable labour relations in and promote the healthy development of these enterprises, while the overall role of the ACFTU in participating in labour policy and law formulation be strengthened for safeguarding the interests and rights of the workers and staff members in these enterprises.

6.6   THE UNION'S DILEMMAS

Behind such an overt posture of a clear official concern which the ACFTU canvassed in holding the personnel and industrial relations terrain purportedly 'under rein' among these foreign-funded businesses in China, is an apparent yet subtle paradox of a dualistic 'agency' role which the Chinese trade unions are expected to perform. The context is historical, rooted in China' century-long 'chiliastic' encounter with the 'alien' West.[5] The union's role is now additionally double-edged – ushered upon it by the imperatives both to modernize the nation industrially as well as to conserve the state under the sacrosanct ideology of 'socialism with Chinese characteristics'. The first role is hence to serve the state in dealing with and receiving foreign capital – a role which has become enhanced and now imperative because of the nation's steady withdrawal from a past tradition, inspired by the Soviet model of containing foreigners' interests and investment. Instead, in its place is now the state's design of deputizing the Chinese trade union with a 'quasi-ambassadorial' role in the workplace, in order to act with hospitality towards the foreign investors and partners (as noted earlier in Chapter 2), as well as a 'chaperone' role to educate the Chinese workers to accommodate with an alien employer, whilst at the same time keeping them immune from the vice of Western 'spiritual contamination'. Such a 'diplomatic-cum-guardian' task of the Chinese unions is especially conspicuous where the FFEs are exempted from the representation by such organs as the Party as well as the Workers' Congress. This strategic workplace duty of the Chinese trade union in a JV/FFE has been interpreted with such a significance:

> Where the Party abstains from the workplace of the FFE, it is likely that the grass-roots union organization will fill the gap by acting as its proxy. One of these tasks, consistent with the state's policy of working with foreign capital, is for trade unions to educate workers and staff in supporting the enterprise administration. Even though 'some of them do not understand the policy of opening to the outside world and feel that they are selling their labour in those enterprises', the trade unions endeavour to 'help workers and staff members realize that they are equally masters of the country and that running well those enterprises is beneficial to China's modernization drive and therefore conforms with the fundamental interests of the working class'. (Gong, 1990, p. 4, cited in Ng, 1994, p. 20)

The second role, liable to contradict the first one where the foreign capital is a 'secondary sector' employer in the lower reach of the labour market, is basically self-vindicating, now incumbent upon the ACFTU's newly revitalized agenda – which is its 'native' mission to act on behalf of the Chinese workers in order to shield these protected beneficiaries from the excesses of unscrupulous employers from overseas.

However, in this connection, what could have been a more thorny challenge of increasing urgency for the ACFTU has been the problem of workplace tensions and vulnerabilities uncovered in the hybrid sector of JVs and FEEs. The increasingly visible syndrome of poor working conditions, workers' grievances or even open agitations, coinciding with the widely publicized episodes of industrial accidents (noticeably, fires and explosions) has created such an irony of capitalist-fashioned 'sweat shop' exploitation inside socialist China that the ACFTU could no longer stay lukewarm and dismiss such a phenomenon as just the 'teething troubles' of 'Third World' industrialization. Heavy pressure upon the foreign employers by the ACFTU was unequivocal, at least in nominal language when the state was about to reconstitute and develop a more rationalized and humanized industrial system of institutional safety-valves to address workplace grievances particularly after mid-1989 – in part to stabilize the administration and in part to pre-empt any undesirable drift towards an alternative underground labour movement, as described in Chapter 3. In a public statement published in 1994, the ACFTU leadership articulated 'its greatest concern' over the recent frequent violations of the legitimate rights and interests of the workers in some overseas-funded enterprises. When interviewed, Zhang Dinghua, the vice-chairman and first secretary of the ACFTU, lamented that in these enterprises that there existed:

– Serious violation of China's labour legislation and neglect of safety in production, putting in jeopardy workers' personal safety and health;
– Abuse of workers. Some have violated the workers' human dignity, imposed corporal punishment on them, and even encroached their civil rights;
– Forced overtime work. Some overseas-funded enterprises have forced workers to work 10 to 12 hours a day, in defiance of the 44-hour work week system as defined in China's law;
– Failure to implement the minimum wage standard as set by the local governments. Some overseas-funded enterprises have arbitrarily cut down or pocketed workers' wages; and

– Refusal to sign labour contracts with the workers in an attempt to show
   legal responsibilities.
   (*Chinese Trade Unions*, 1994, vol. 7, no. 5, p. 2)

What has compounded the HRM and industrial relations pattern featuring
the JVs, however, is the relatively better employment opportunities which
the modern corporate employers in this foreign-funded sector are more
likely to offer in China's vast employment market. Offering important contrasts to the employment types in these foreign enterprises as documented
in the preceding profile are the comparatively advanced managerial practices in human resources and associated activities located in the upper-
echelon of the Chinese labour market, often attributed to what have been
commonly labelled as the 'model' overseas enterprises. Other than the rep-
utation enjoyed by the visiting multinational corporations for their greater
abilities to pay (wages), these foreign businesses have been typically rated
superior as the more preferred employers in the domain of employment and
personnel practices, notwithstanding those dire working conditions
identified at the other end of the spectrum, as mentioned earlier. According
to official statistics, JVs and FFEs paid over twice the wage levels of SOEs
by 1994 (see Table 6.1). The stereotyping is by now probably well crystal-
lized but it is still useful to make a brief reference to the Sino-foreign differentials in how human resources are managed, which are observable in
the context of investigating workplace industrial relations among the JVs
and FFEs *vis-à-vis* the SOEs inside China today. As Child notes:

the Chinese conception of the personnel management role is quite at
variance with that normally held by foreign managers today. The personnel management role in Chinese organizations is geared towards the
maintenance of control and conformity, supplemented by an ideological
appeal to the virtues of work. This clearly contrasts with the foreign
concept that the personnel function exists to provide a service to management through assisting the selection, training, assessment, motivation and organization of employees, doing this systematically with
reference to their contribution to organizational effectiveness.

Differences between foreign and Chinese personnel practices appear
in a number of areas within joint ventures. A combination of the control
over staff just mentioned with traditional attitudes means that Chinese
managers tend to emphasize negative discipline: punishment, restric-
tions and personal loss of face. By contrast, many foreign managers
today favour positive (or self-) discipline: motivation through praise and
reward, and encouragement of initiative. Foreign personnel manage-

ment tends to rely on standard practices for selection, appraisal, time-keeping, assessment of attitudes and discipline. (Child, 1994, p. 259)

In short, the profile of human and industrial relations configuration that can be construed from these reports is so heterogeneous that any generalizations about such terrain is necessarily a simplified imagery which has to consider, at least, the role of such corporate features as first, the ethnic character of the foreign investment as well as the style and cultural traits associated with it; second, the collaborative strength and linkage between the Chinese and foreign partners which depend not only upon such nominal instruments as the formal business contract but more importantly upon such hidden influences as norms of reciprocity, *guanxi* (networking) and *mianzi* ('face') relationships; and third, the cultural mix of the workforce management in joint ventures. Again, such diversities raise an interesting question as to the prospects of industrial relations development – not only between the home state-owned and the foreign-funded sectors but also internally among various clusters and sub-groups within the industry of overseas investment, including those coming from Hong Kong, Taiwan and Macau. Moreover, to the extent that the nation's labour market is segmented, with increasing evidence of a 'primary–secondary' divide between the more 'sophisticated' employers and the 'marginal' petty shops at either ends, it is also problematic to ascertain the relative location of the JV and other FFEs on this spectrum, *vis-à-vis* such home establishments as the SOEs, the JVEs, as well as the petty labour contract-shops.

Table 6.1   Average annual wages of staff and workers by sector (1985–94)*

Year	1985	1991	1992	1993	1994
State-owned	1 213	2 477	3 371	3 532	2 592
Urban collective	967	1 866	4 538	4 797	3 245
Jointly managed	1 269	1 789	3 336	3 741	4 982
Share holding	–	–	–	5 171	6 383
Foreign-funded	1 847	3 918	4 347	5 315	6 533
Overseas Chinese from Hong Kong, Macao & Taiwan funded	2 143	7 071	4 740	5 147	6 376
Others	1 000	2 622	3 371	3 279	4 954

* Annual average wages are given in yuan (RMB) but not at purchasing power parity
Source: State Statistical Bureau, 1995.

The myth once enshrining the JV and the wholly foreign-owned multi-national corporations as the pattern-setting 'model' employer is now increasingly diluted, and the nexus of workplace relations between the managed and the manager is now the 'marketplace' one between so-called mercenary capital and waged labour. Consequently, there is an emerging arena of industrial conflict and wage haggling, workplace grievance and discipline, organizational commitment and labour force stabilization. In the context of China's dualistic structure of the state-owned and the foreign-funded sectors, another basic issue is: how vulnerable are the JVs industrial relations *vis-à-vis* explicitly capitalist systems of production and social relations?

It may still be assumed that in spite of the compounding features that first, the JVs and FFEs are far more varied, internally differentiated and stratified as a source of employment than apparent; and second, empirical evidence suggesting the beginnings of at least partial convergence in human resources' practices, in part emanating from the unifying effects of common statutory labour standards which the state promulgated recently (noticeably, in the 1994 Labour Law and parallel *Regulations on Labour Management of Enterprises with Foreign Investment*), between the JVs and the SOEs (Warner, 1996b, p. 31), the imagery of the foreign business as the 'primary sector' employers in China's labour market probably still prevails today.[6] In spite of the growing fluidity and interorganizational mobility of key techno-cratic personnel, such as the managerial and professional staff, which is liable to characterize the guest MNCs, it is suspected that their managerial bureaucracies, mostly carriers of relatively advanced hardware technologies and managerial practices, are able to conserve themselves as elitist 'enclaves' – demarcating themselves with relatively distinctive boundaries of their consolidated (if not 'privileged') internal labour markets:

> Since these foreign-funded businesses ... are able to offer their workers and staff members better wages and conditions of employment than other employers, they may be described (in the language of Western theories on labour market segmentation) as 'primary sector' employers. Further, insofar as they are able to attract and retain the more highly trained personnel from China's manpower reservoir, these enterprises may be seen as potentially creating a quasi-layer of 'labour aristocracy' more advantaged than the average mass of the working proletariat inside China. (Ng, 1994, p. 24)

Nonetheless, it has to be reiterated that the JV and foreign business sector is not entirely a 'standard-bearing' sector of efficient and problem-free employers to be emulated by the Chinese home enterprises in human resources' practices and industrial relations. Several writers (see Child, 1994; Warner, 1996b) have identified problems which beset foreign managers in Sino-foreign JVs. Amongst these: employee appraisal was confounded by job demarcation; tightening up on time-keeping was spoilt by lax work practices; promotions were not easily accepted due to the residual egalitarian norms, and so on. Dismissing workers was still resisted in most JV's experiences according to such studies. It was thus easier (as Warner, 1996b notes) to transfer 'hard' technology than its 'soft' counterparts: this clearly delayed improvements in productivity and overall enterprise performance':

> Thus far:- we have seen how far China has opened up to Western (and East Asian) management ideas since the Open Door policy was introduced in 1978. It is also clear that management knowledge-transfer has been largely injected via foreign-funded firms especially joint ventures, with apparently only partial pay-offs in terms of organizational performance, at least in terms of the ones referred to ... It is also the case that foreign HRM practices have made some headway on a limited scale in Chinese JVs, if less so in SOEs. (Ibid., p. 26)

Earlier, Tsang (1994) has also documented extensively such contours of problematic wages, human and industrial relations in his review of Sino-foreign JVs. Other than the much reported legacies of official and other institutional constraints on the nominal abilities of these firms to hire, transfer and discharge freely according to the rules of the contract and the 'reign' of the market, it was the once highly-structured and now liberalized wage domain that was probably most vulnerable to disarray, inconsistencies and inequity, as well as poor cost-effectiveness and incentives. As this critical view argues:

> Although many investors are attracted to China by the low labour costs, the whole remuneration package is more expensive than expected when compared with other developing countries. The Chinese regulations stipulate that the wage level of a joint venture is to be set at 120 per cent to 150 per cent of that of state enterprises in the same line of business and same locality ... The complete wage package consists of the basic wage, bonuses, and subsidies take-home pay, which includes the basic wages plus bonuses, amounts to about three-quarters of the package. The subsidies – insurance, welfare, pension and housing funds – are paid to the Chinese partner or local authorities...

The introduction of the bonus system ... is meant to provide monetary incentives ... Owing to the ideological legacy of egalitarianism,
bonuses have been distributed rather evenly to all workers within a
work group or production floor. This practice of 'collective assessment'
has made bonuses less effective as a motivational tool ... Remuneration
of expatriates presents another problem. In Beijing Jeep, it is said that
the great difference in remuneration received by local versus foreign
staff has been the cause of resentment. Each Chinese worker 'is highly
aware that the compensation package for one foreign expatriate is
several hundred times the annual salary and benefits that he or she
receives. (Tsang, 1994, pp. 8–10)

6.7   WORKPLACE RELATIONS

Understandably, much of the problems as documented above are endemic
to the 'dualistic' characteristics of the managerial structure of the joint
ventures and the problems of their internal governance. Adding to and
compounding the 'dialectics' of labour – capital interests in these enterprises is also the divide separating the foreign and local identities – which
are still reputed to have generated a sizeable amount of managerial strain
and intraorganizational strife (Pearson, 1991, p. 174). In this context, the
JVs and other overseas-funded enterprises have been a 'conducive'
brewing ground, in spite of their image as a better-paying employer, for
workplace grievances, industrial strife and worker agitation which have
been found by the national labour movement in its criticisms of the labour
conditions in these business organizations. Such a 'contested terrain' has
been narrated in a graphic portrayal by the ACFTU of a work stoppage
affecting a overseas-funded company in their official review, *Chinese
Trade Unions*, as follows:

On June 21 this year, more than 300 workers of its paint-spraying workshop went on strike, demanding a better working condition. Soon after
receiving the workers' complaints, the Shenzhen Federation of Trade
Unions sent an investigation team to the company, heeded workers'
opinions and investigated their workshops and accommodation. They
discovered that more than 30 workers lived in a simple living quarters
of 30 square meters, with bad ventilation and lighting and without any
fireproof installations.

In the company with a workforce of more than 1000, there was no
dining hall so the workers had to eat in the open. The paint spraying
workshop was full of poisonous gas and there were not any protection

measures for workers' safety and health. The company never provided medical examinations to them. Workers were paid 80 yuan (10 US dollars) less than the minimum wage of 280 yuan (33 US dollars) as defined by the local government, and worked 100 extra hours every month without any extra pay. (Wei, 1994, p. 11)

These workers' grievances and the strike emanating subsequently in the overseas-funded enterprise investigated by the ACFTU led subsequently to the unionization of the workplace, when the Shenzhen Trade Unions Council convened a preparatory team for a 'grass-roots' trade union to be created 'upon the request of the workers', in order to institutionalize its agency role of representing their job interests and safeguards 'on a proper footing'. In this narrative, the leverage role of the Chinese trade union both as a protector of labour as well as in policing the workplace conduct of the overseas- and foreign-funded businesses is naturally emphasized, as follows:

the Shenzhen Federation of Trade Unions ... would, in co-operation with other relevant departments, continue to urge the Shenzhen Guangyue Industrial Co. Ltd. to enforce laws and regulations till it has corrected its wrong-doing and the first Trade Union Committee comes in being ... the company was urged to meet [the demands] within one month. Otherwise, it would demand, the municipal government to punish it according to law. (Ibid.)

Indeed, the shifting terrain and property of workplace industrial relations in these JV enterprises attest to a creeping yet noticeable redefinition inside China of the official view in interpreting and approaching strike behaviour, as its reformed economy is evolving towards the practice of 'market socialism'. Previously, 'managerial bureaucratism' was the only officially sanctioned reason for a strike – otherwise 'in socialist China, the workers and staff members are the 'masters of the country' and the enterprises (so that) under ordinary conditions there is no need for them to achieve their end through strikes' (Ng, 1994, p. 68). However, the admission into the country of foreign capital has since instituted a new and distinctive configuration of workplace relations by virtue of the 'dualistic character' of foreign business for being both 'alien' and 'capitalistic' in employing Chinese labour on a 'wage' basis. It was at the beginning of the present decade that the ACFTU began to acknowledge formally that in the JV sector and associated categories of foreign enterprises, the workers' identity and interests could be so intrinsically distinctive from the employers' that these workplaces featured a *bona fide* type of labour–capital relations analogous to what have been typical of Western capitalist societies (Lao, 1990, p. 7). Even in the relatively well managed, 'model' joint venture businesses such as the Fujian Hitachi TV Set Corporation Ltd., labour–management relations could not be seen apart from its intrinsic nature of a paradoxical 'antagonistic–cooperative' relationship – which vests the Chinese workers with a new legitimacy to strike in order to wrest a 'better deal' from the 'mercenary' capitalists. This perspective was introduced because of and consistent with the adjusted strategy which the ACFTU adopted, partly proactive but mainly responsive.

Even such an enhanced industrial role has remained constrained by the prudent concern of the state with attracting and retaining foreign and overseas investment – and in this connection, the strategic function of a 'workplace ambassador' to be played by the Chinese trade unions, which is conciliatory rather than adversarial, cooperative rather than conflictual or antagonistic. The main union goal in this context is 'mutual understanding' (Interviews with Shenzen ACFTU officials, September 1996). Trapped in such a 'dualistic' role and the dilemma it hence posed, it is still probably true that the ACFTU – in spite of its increasing vocal zeal in articulating the workers' interests and grievances encountered in this type of workplaces – will continue to treat industrial militancy stemming from labour–capital conflict as negative, and hence, in general to be decried. Inasmuch as the Chinese trade unions continue to opt for the consultative approach of dialogue-building and conflict-resolution as the preferred style of structuring the system of workplace industrial relations here, it may be suspected that in the event of an outbreak of industrial conflict, they are more inclined towards a stance of reasoned and restrained intervention to remove misunderstandings, accommodate differences and resolve shopfloor disputes. Indeed, such an imagery was propagated in the early 1990s, when the ACFTU's reports of amicable dispute settlement owed to its mediation were typical, as follows:

> On Spring Festival, the Japan Sanyo Corporation in Shenzhen decided that workers and staff members would have five days off. But some workers and staff members demanded to have 15 days off so that they could stay longer together with their families. Learning of the matter, the trade union of the corporation explained to those workers and staff members that the Sanyo Corporation had not violated the stipulations of three days of holiday during the Chinese Spring Festival, so that they should respect the decision of the corporation. The workers and staff members accepted the advice of the trade union and gave up their demand. (Gong, 1990, p. 4)

However, what appears to be a hiatus in more recent developments of workplace industrial relations in this non-state sector has been the more sceptical and probably less accommodating orientation of the national labour movement towards capital and its hiring defaults uncovered in glaring scale by the ACFTU. The reason could be quasi-political – in giving the trade union organ the *raison d'être* to enhance its agenda of organizing, with greater interventionist rigour, the industrial plants and business enterprises of foreign and overseas capital. However, the growing visibility of workplace issues heralded by the ACFTU in its recent disclosures could also be a disturbing signal. Indeed, the indictments brought up by the ACFTU in its recent reports against the vicissitudes of 'alien capital' were well corroborated by 'media' coverage in the press (both domestic as well as outside the nation, notably in Hong Kong). Thus, the lack of industrial safety has been lamented in such a commentary by the nation's trade union centre, as follows:

> The findings report reveals that some overseas-funded enterprises, small ones in particular, have neglected safety in production with noise, toxic gases and pollution well above the standards set by the State. In a toy factory solely funded by a Hong Kong businessman, a big fire broke out, burning 84 women workers to death. Investigation into the tragedy shows that it was because the workers were forced to work in a precarious condition. With almost all exits sealed off, the workers could not manage to escape with their lives quickly. (Wei, 1994, p. 3)

A series of surveys conducted by the ACFTU, at both the national as well as local levels of the provinces and municipalities, have indicated, in particular, the vulnerability of the Chinese women workers in these workshops in the non-state sector run by either JVs or solely FFEs. Glaring examples of their industrial deprivations were reported in such areas as discrimination, including risks of discharge for reasons of maternity and other defaults in protecting the working mothers, such as during pregnancy and post-natal childcare; in addition, denial of the protection of the regular 'work contract' instrument, for example in Guangdong, the survey revealed that '33–87 per cent of them had not concluded work contracts, and 23–46 per cent of the signed contracts had not been testified. A large number of overseas investors only recruit[ed] single women aged between 18 and 25 and sign[ed] with them only short-term contracts of three years or below' (*Chinese Trade Unions*, 1994, vol. 7, no. 5, p. 3). In addition, women experienced low and inferior pay compared with their male counterparts, nonpayment of overtime pay for work outside the scheduled daily hours, congregation in overcrowded, congested and fire-prone conditions on the shopfloor; and openness to abuses, insults, beatings and sexual harassment.

These reports and disclosures about alleged maltreatments and impoverishments of labouring women in such workplaces have elucidated an urgent case for the ACFTU to advance its organizational realm to cover those foreign-funded enterprises still not unionized, or still resistant to unionization. The logic follows that the presence of the Chinese trade unions was hence imperative in this context in order to protect and represent the otherwise inarticulate women workers when they were exploited by these employers. As pledged by the national trade union centre:

> The ACFTU report stresses that 'women workers in overseas-funded enterprises, like their counterparts in other enterprises, are the masters of the country, and their political status, economic interests, personal dignity, civil liberty and other lawful rights and interests allow of no infringement'. It urges trade unions at various levels to carry out careful inspection of the implementation of legislations on labour protection for women workers together with the labour and public health departments ... In accordance with China's Trade Union Law and other relevant legislation, the Chinese employees in overseas-funded enterprises are entitled to establish trade union organizations, and women workers' organizations should be set up in enterprises with 25 female workers or above. The report urges the setting up of trade unions and committees for women workers in overseas-funded enterprises at a faster pace in order to safeguard the workers' legitimate rights and interests organizationally and forge a link between the workers and the management so that labour relations can be stabilized. (Wu, 1994, p. 3)

Given such alertness which the national labour movement registers *vis-à-vis* the problematic nature of labouring conditions and industrial relations in the JV and foreign-funded enterprises, are these workplaces particularly prone to industrial conflict and disputes? Again, the brief published by the ACFTU on the nation's labour disputes profile for 1993 (cf Table 4.3) seems to suggest their vulnerability, as it concedes:

> What merits attention is that collective labour disputes are on the rise. Statistics complied by the ACFTU show that mediation committees across the country handled 14 313 collective labour disputes in 1993. The collective disputes in some provinces have multiplied several times, bringing about a considerable increase in stoppages, strikes and their participants. Xiao Zhenbang, member of the ACFTU Secretariat, attributes

the direct causes for labour disputes to the problems in labour remuneration, insurance, welfare and the punishment of workers. In 1993, 35 208 labour disputes were related to wages and insurance benefits, representing 41.5 per cent of the total ... Xiao said that 'most labour disputes have been caused by the workunits' infringement of the legitimate rights and interests of labourers. This is more striking in overseas-funded enterprises. (Wei, 1994, p. 8)

The ACFTU made no pretence in naming the non-state sector, essentially funded by overseas capital, as the primary source of the more troubled industrial relations terrain appearing now in the country, as it observed that these employers' defaults in their duties and responsibilities have 'resulted in tense labour relations, including many disputes and occasional strikes in some overseas-funded enterprises' (Wu, 1994, p. 3). Concluding on the basis of such evidence that this sector is vulnerable to labour abuses and exploitation which can in turn breed widespread shopfloor discontents and agitation, the ACFTU has apparently viewed it as a proper corrective and an urgent lever to intervene by organizing the inarticulate Chinese workers employed by these foreign business interests, and restraining them in their role as the representative mass organization of Chinese labour. Such accentuated intervention would be consistent with the state's directive issued a decade ago, ratifying the right of the ACFTU to unionize the workforce hired in every JV and FFE. Intervention has been deemed imperative now in light of the experiences accumulated over the years indicating glaring gaps of workplace deprivations and injustices which need addressing promptly in order to help stabilize industrial relations in these enterprises.

The recognition provides an explanation of the urgency with which a 'deadline for unionization in overseas-funded enterprises' was rushed onto the ACFTU's agenda in 1994. It prescribed that:

trade unions should be set up in all overseas-funded enterprises in the coastal provinces that had started business before June 1994. As to other cities, regions and provinces, trade union should be organized in over 60 per cent of the overseas-funded enterprises by that time. (Wei, 1995, p. 6)

The Vice-Chairman of the ACFTU, while issuing such a normative statement of its intended organizing work on this frontier, also made explicit his instructions that 'the setting up of trade unions in newly founded overseas-funded enterprises shall be written in agreements or contracts according to the Chinese relevant laws, the prescription for the setting up of enterprises and trade unions shall be done at the same time, and when the enterprises start business, trade unions shall be organized simultaneously or no later than one year' (ibid., p. 7).

6.8   UNIONIZATION IN FOREIGN-FUNDED ENTERPRISES

The rhetorical appeal by the ACFTU's Vice-Chairman to the Chinese trade unions to endeavour 'to work harder to make a breakthrough in organizing trade unions in overseas-funded enterprises' betrayed indirect symptoms that such unionizing efforts by the national trade union centre could have encountered, in the previous years, a salient amount of handicap and even resistance – which is probably recognisable, vicariously, from the sluggish pace with which the ACFTU has been advancing its ambits of organizing the non-state sector (see Table 6.2). That grass-roots union organizations are not universally found in all FFEs but have featured a relatively erratic spatial distribution among local districts was already noticeable at the beginning of the 1990s, as the ACFTU then reported:

> In Guangdong province, which has three economic zones, 41.9 per cent of foreign-funded enterprises that have opened for business had set up trade unions and 43 per cent of workers and staff members in those enterprises have joined the trade unions. In Shenzhen Special Economic Zone, 96 per cent of foreign-funded enterprises employing over 25 people have trade union organizations. (Gong, 1990, p. 2)

However, the scope of unionization in the foreign-funded enterprises has, by the mid-1990s, appeared to remain trapped in a more or less comparable level, in spite of the rigours with which the ACFTU has canvassed such a task on its agenda. By the end of 1995, just over two million employees worked in unionized enterprises which were in foreign invested or overseas compatriot categories (see Table 6.2). This relatively low level is symptomatic in the relatively equivocal profile of the Chinese trade unions' penetration of these workplaces which has been set out by the ACFTU, as follows:

> Recently, the ACFTU has conducted investigations on the unionization in such provinces and municipalities as Jiangsu, Shangdong, Guangdong and Shanghai, where overseas-funded enterprises are comparatively concentrated. The investigation showed that 52 340 overseas-funded enterprises had started business in these provinces and muncipalities by the end of June 1994. Among them, 17 477 trade

unions had been set up, accounting for 33 per cent of the number of the enterprises. Compared with December 1993, 4017 new trade unions were set up and unionization rate increased 4 percentage points. In Jiangsu Province, the number of trade unions in overseas-funded enterprises increased from 2800 at the end of 1993 to 4260 at the end of last June, and in Shangdong Province, the number increased from 1690 to 2632. (Wei, 1995, pp. 6–7)

Such figures, however, were inconsistent with those for FFEs and those nationally set out in Table 3.2, unless only referring to workshop union committees rather than basic ones.

In Shenzen SEZ, there was perhaps greater success. Over 70 per cent of all enterprises had basic trade unions and about the same percentage of employees had joined them. There were over 8000 basic unions with over half a million members. There were over 40 000 enterprises in the SEZ, of which over 11 000 were state-owned and these had both a trade union and a Workers' Congress; many FFEs had neither of these (Interviews with Shenzen ACFTU officials, September 1995).

Two factors have been perhaps crucial in helping explain such a dubious terrain of unionization in the JV and foreign-funded sector compared with large mostly SOE firms (see Table 6.2). In the first place is the probable scepticism of the multinationals, especially those of US origin, who are known for their apathy or even hostility towards unionism, seeing it as posing a challenge to managerial prerogative. Such an 'aversion' psychology could have been even more pervasive in China among foreign capital participating in joint ventures who 'are likely to feel apprehensive about a labour organization belonging to the central quasi-official bureaucracy of the ACFTU, especially since the JV law enables the union to participate in the enterprise's decision-making process by direct access to the board of directors' (Ng, 1994, p. 18).

A common strategy adopted by foreign management in coping with the Chinese workplace unions has hence been one of containment. As observed by Pearson in 1991, 'foreign managers ... were able to confine ... [labour organization] ... activity to after regular work hours', reducing it in some cases to just a nominal 'friendly society' which concentrates upon organizing sports activities (Pearson, 1991, p. 186). The suspicion of foreign capital as a partner in JVs towards the inroad of the Chinese trade unions is acknowledged openly by the ACFTU which laments that 'most foreign investors looked on trade unions with distrust. They believed that trade unions would organize strikes, and interfere with their work, thus giving a negative effect on production and performance' (Huang and Bao, 1991, p. 10).

Table 6.2   Number of employees in unionized enterprises (end of 1995)

	Number of employees	Female employees	Contract employees
National total (persons)	113 213 930	45 152 722	49 658 015
Categorized according to scale of unit (persons):			
1–10	111 263	38 094	21 736
11–50	6 402 950	2 359 741	1 636 147
51–100	10 322 194	4 125 417	3 065 574
101–200	15 347 106	6 343 007	5 371 368
201–300	9 863 835	4 182 923	4 046 077
301–500	12 841 399	5 435 769	5 870 840
501–800	12 277 946	5 139 118	6 145 830
801–2999	26 748 416	10 697 110	13 616 093
3000 (and over)	19 262 821	6 831 543	9 884 350
Categorized according to economic type:			
State-owned	90 709 616	34 781 191	38 126 176
Collective	17 299 815	7 967 526	8 186 439
Privately operated	193 942	83 614	82 238
Individual	116 657	43 615	49 932
Jointly managed	223 809	103 809	114 168
Stock-holding	2 237 697	955 946	1 605 212
Foreign invested	1 819 449	922 136	1 247 541
Hong Kong, Macau and Taiwan invested	426 506	230 398	219 979
Others	186 439	64 487	26 330

Source: ACFTU statistics, 1996.

In this ambivalent context, it has been conspicuous for the Chinese labour movement at the local levels of the provincial and municipal authorities to have adopted a nominally active yet intrinsically lukewarm stance towards the agenda of organizing the JV and FFEs, in order to avoid confronting and antagonizing these foreign businesses or participants in such enterprises. Such a prudent inactivity has worked in the past, presumably because of a quiescent Chinese labour force. However, industrial affluence now made possible by the nation's advances towards the market economic system has apparently inflated shopfloor expectations as well as accentuated its sensitivity to industrial hazards, inhospitable working conditions and other workplace abuses of the workers' rights and benefit entitlements.

That there is now a creeping increase in the amount of workplace unrest in the non-state sector that has caused alarm in the state leadership is attested by reports in the Chinese press that China officially registered around 260 strikes occurring in JVs and FFEs in 1993 (*Associated Press*, 22 June 1994).[7] Similarly, the statement by the CCP General Secretary, Jiang Zemin, also in mid-1994, that the strike-weapon was deplored by the state as the most harassing item among the 'eight hidden perils' now besetting the nation and its stability should be noted in this context (*SWB*, 24 May 1994).

The state responded to such an escalating 'industrial relations' syndrome – falling short of a quiescent HRM scenario – in the 'Sino-foreign equity joint ventures, Sino-foreign contractual joint ventures, foreign-funded enterprises and Sino-foreign joint-stock limited companies' in the PRC by promulgating, in August 1994, the *Regulations on Labour Management in Foreign-funded Enterprises* (noted earlier) under the joint jurisdiction of the Labour Ministry and the Ministry of Foreign Trade and Economic Cooperation. This code declares, that first, the Labour Ministry be responsible for supervising the enterprise's staffing, training, pay, insurance, worker safety and hygiene, as well as fringe benefits in this sector; second, the enterprise be allowed to recruit its workforce through the local employment agencies and labour service companies approved by the Labour Ministry; third, the hiring of child labour be proscribed; fourth, the enterprise be required to recruit only Chinese workers but be allowed to hire recruits from Taiwan, Hong Kong and Macao and from abroad, provided that this is with the approval of the local labour bureau and in conformity with the relevant state regulations; fifth, minimum wages be prescribed for the workforce in the enterprise on the basis of wage guidelines stipulated by the Ministry of Labour or the local labour bureau; sixth, such employment benefits as holidays, old-age insurance, maternity, sickness and workmen's compensation, as well as the rules governing overtime work and pay and those regulating the dissolution of labour contracts be rationalized and standardized in the enterprise; seventh, the publication of a 'labour handbook' ('employee handbook') and its circulation to the workforce be made mandatory within the enterprises; and eighth, an array of official sanctions be instituted to censure the enterprise for breaches of these regulations (cited in *SWB* 30 March 1995).

The growing qualms articulated by the national labour movement centre, the ACFTU, about the vulnerabilities of the Chinese workers hired in the foreign-funded business sector, as well as the JV enterprises, are probably not entirely surprising. Ideologically, at least, the defensive apprehension expressed by the Chinese trade unions about the exploitative potential inherent in the 'cash-nexus' epitomized by the system of waged employment relations in these enterprises seems consistent with the official emphasis on 'mainstream' Marxist socialism, still upheld by some as sacrosanct, in spite of the 'contract-relationship' now legitimized in the 1994 Labour Law (see Chapter 4 earlier). Indeed, the embattled experiences of the Chinese labour movement in the early days, especially during the decade of upheavals of the 1920s has always been a patent reminder to the ACFTU leadership, even of today, of the vicissitudes of Western business activities which were, and still are, 'alien' and 'capitalistic'. The historical background of the 'unequal treaties' and labour strife, such as the Seamen's Strike of 1922, the Hong Kong–Canton Strike-Boycott of 1925–6 and the Shanghai strikes of the same period, have always been alive in the background in alerting the state and its union organs to both the industrial benefits as well as the costs implied by the current 'Open Door'.

The situation is, however, paradoxical – and compounded by the specific character of trade unionism in the PRC. Chinese trade unions have hardly evolved through the analogous experiences that 'mature' Western trade unions have developed to their present status as adversarial industrial institutions but basically enshring the capitalist system of 'waged' production and economic relations. The history of the Chinese labour movement (first, during the prewar era of gestation and anti-foreign struggles and second, in their subsequent configuration as Soviet-prescribed socialist unions) after 1949 attests sparsely, if at all, to properties Anderson has defined as the notion of trade unionism in Western 'conventional wisdom':

> Trade unions are an essential part of a capitalist society because they incarnate the difference between capital and labour which defines the society … trade union are dialectically both an opposition to capitalism and a component of it … As institutions, trade unions do not challenge the existence of society based on a division of classes, they merely express it. (Anderson, 1967, p. 264)

However, the Chinese society basically lacks such a structural history and hence the Chinese unions, albeit emulative in organizational forms, have never been that type of spontaneous workers' combinations espousing a defensive 'working class' solidarity to challenge the ills of industrial capital. China's trade unions in their prewar heydays achieved their unusual strength of workers' solidarity and militancy not because of their commitment to a 'class' struggle against capital (virtually, they were political allies to the patriotic Chinese capitalists and merchants, who provided even more depressing workplace conditions than their Western counterparts trading in China), but more because they were the 'vanguard' in a nationalistic crusade against Western and foreign aggrandizement and imperialistic assaults on China, the nation and its interests, as noted in Chapter 2 earlier. As a sequel to the 1949 Liberation, 'socialism' may have replaced and substituted 'nationalism' as the main factor cementing the Chinese labour movement but this is still moot.

The implications of the above for the present terrain of workplace industrial relations in the foreign-funded sector are not necessarily negative. Ironically, such a union's 'Chinese' intrinsic and historical character can be argued to be a 'blessing in disguise'. The reason is, paradoxically, that the Chinese trade unions have always been allies to or agencies for the established order rather than as 'alien' institutions or alternative power centres that need to be incorporated, as hypothesized in such notions as those of 'union integration' and 'union incorporation'. Thus, in principle there is a potential here for the successful implementation of Western (or Japanese) HRM practices

Inasmuch as the Chinese trade unions are always located within the 'mainstream' of the establishment (in spite of their 'chiliastic' agitations against foreign capital in the 1920s), the authenticity and applicability of recently popularized arguments in Western IR literature that the Chinese trade unions are increasingly becoming 'corporatist' (Chan, 1993) should be qualified – because, unlike the situation in the capitalist 'Western world', the institutional integration of the union system has hardly been problematic in the Chinese milieu.

This probably means that a collaborative relationship of 'mutual partnership', is more readily attainable in workplaces where the tradition has not been conducive to the workers and their unions' antagonistic opposition to managerial authority, insofar as its exercise has been sanctioned by the state. Up to present, such an official strategy of accommodating and offering foreign capital and business a hospitable investment environment in the Mainland has seemingly been upheld. Some firms, especially US–Chinese JVs, have developed from personnel management to HRM, but only on a limited scale.[8] In spite of the unequivocal signalling now by the ACFTU that the labour movement could not be expected to stay acquiescent about attempts by foreign businesses to exploit unscrupulously cheap labour, the official policy has appeared intact: that the union organ shall continue to sustain 'an ambassadorial role towards the visiting capital, exemplifying the State's policy on mutual nonconflictual co-operation' (Ng, 1994, p. 25) – in order to 'help foreign investors acquaint themselves with the national conditions and relevant policies of China so that they can run enterprises without any worries within the scope provided by China's law and encouraged by China's policies' (Gong, 1990, p. 5).

6.9   CONCLUDING REMARKS

To sum up, all these observations, albeit tentative, suggest that the tendencies for many foreign multinationals to sometimes import into China their classic strategy of avoiding trade unions or aversion from dialogue with them could have been unwittingly transferred from their home societies, yet applied to a context where the Chinese trade unions have not been nurtured as adversarial bargaining agencies of the workforce against management. Where the structural conditions, as given by historical legacies, are not intrinsically associated with the adversarial model of 'Western' industrial relations, there exists a potential for China to evolve a distinctly 'Asian' non-conflictual model of labour-management collaboration, instead of confrontation. Such a development could be consonant with a 'hybrid' model or form of labour-management, but falling short of a general trend to full HRM 'with Chinese characteristics' (Warner, 1995, p. 161). That such an option may be attractive is made apparent by first, the current doldrums in which the adversarial Euro-American tradition of Western-style trade unionism is seemingly trapped; and second, the recognition made earlier by Thurley (1988) and other industrial relations' specialists about the prospect of an alternative, 'Asian' model of industrial relations and unionism. As he stated:

> Asians often reject the conflictual, adversarial basis of Western industrial relations argument. Asians ... are frequently horrified by strikes and attached to values of co-operation, mutual commitment and harmony. Collective bargaining, itself, is seen as overlapping with consultative discussions. If this is true, then, of course, the basis of trade unions in Asian countries is indeed very different from that current in the West, certainly in the United Kingdom. (Thurley, 1988, p. 26)

Evidently, there are clear constraints handicapping such a prospect of a new 'model' industrial relations style emanating from the joint-venture and foreign-funded enterprises in China. Of these, two factors are perhaps most strategic. The first is the level of suspicion which the state may espouse, at varying times, towards the aggrandizement of 'obscure interests and ambitions' of foreign business and capital in China. Such distrust is historical and has never disappeared totally.

The second condition is probably more specific to the shopfloor itself, suggested by the ACFTU's anxiety to enhance its activities in the workplace and its organization – otherwise it might invite disillusion at the grass-roots level with its authentic image as the spokesman of the latter's occupational interests and grievances. The pressure of such a challenge emanating from the shopfloor yearning for the ACFTU's 'delivery of the goods' has become increasingly evident, given 'its newly discovered role of assisting the State to absorb and cushion any emerging agitation which now appears imminent in the urban areas under the impact of accelerated industrial growth' (Ng, 1995, p. 72). Indeed, the credibility crisis for this giant union bureaucracy is liable to explode, if the ACFTU consistently betrays an incapacity of coping effectively with workers' disaffection related to issues such as 'the inflated expectations and the creation of diverse interests stimulated by economic affluence and its uneven distribution in the populace' (ibid.).

Where a wide spectrum of varying work and employment conditions exist among enterprises in the overseas and foreign-funded sector, it is arguably a prudent strategy for the national trade union to attach its priority of the present work agenda to the harmonized betterment of labour conditions in this sector, lest it might serve as the breeding ground for an alternative and 'undesirable' worker movement, especially if the competence of the ACFTU as the *bona fide* representative agency of the Chinese labour became seriously questioned. Clearly, the ills of deprivation and other economic vicissitudes arising from such advances of economic affluence need to be held in check by an effective labour movement. How far Chinese trade unions can learn from models elsewhere in this respect in East and South-East Asia, particularly those in 'Greater China' will be pursued in the next chapter, to which we now turn.

Part III
Comparing

'The diversity of Asian countries is based on historical precedence and should thus be fully respected.'

(Li Peng, Speech: 'The impact of China's development and the rise of Asia on the future of the world', 4 September 1996 in *Beijing Review*, 30 September 1996, p. 9)

7 Outside the Mainland: Trade Unions and Management in Three Overseas Chinese Societies

7.1 INTRODUCTION

This chapter sets out to sketch a profile of trade unionism as it has evolved in three predominantly overseas Chinese societies in East Asia, located on the fringe of the Mainland, in what has sometimes been called 'Greater China' and sharing basic Chinese values (see Bond, 1986; Bond and Hwang, 1986; Shenkar and Ronen, 1987; Lockett, 1988; Whitley, 1990). They are namely, Hong Kong, Singapore and Taiwan. Each of these three societies has captured the world's attention as a case of successful industrialization within the regional league of the East Asian newly industrialized economies (NIEs) (see Redding, 1990). Their industrial experiences of organized labour provide an interesting comparison to what has been documented in the preceding chapters about the labour movement in the PRC, as canvassed from either a historical or a contemporary perspective. Such a comparative glimpse on trade unionism in these four societies (including the Mainland) is hoped to reveal some preliminary evidence on first, the propensity of Chinese trade unionism towards a collaborative stance, *vis-à-vis* an adversarial one, in approaching management and employers in the workplace; and second, its aptitude, within the labour movement itself, for 'unitary' or alternatively 'pluralistic' unionism within a 'corporatist' contest. We propose to look at the situation of organized labour in Hong Kong and then in Singapore, before reviewing the contrasts in the profile of Chinese labour unions across the 'Straits', between Taiwan and the Mainland, in order to enable comparisons to be made.

7.2 TRADE UNION PLURALISM IN HONG KONG

The Hong Kong labour movement is probably distinctive for its internal diversity, which is perhaps reminiscent as well of the Mainland movement before 1949.[1] Before that, the combinations of 'Chinese labour under

British rule' in this territory were notoriously an extension or virtually, an overseas 'arm' or base of the Mainland workers' movement. (See earlier discussion of this historical phenomenon narrated in Chapter 2 of this volume.) However, continuities of such a linkage did and have persisted beyond 1949 – the polarization between the left-wing and the right-wing sectors of the Hong Kong labour movement, sponsored respectively by the PRC Government in Beijing and the Nationalist administration (having consolidated its withdrawal) in Taiwan, has become almost institutionalized since 1949 in this territory, with the inception of two formal and rival trade union centres, the pro-Communist Hong Kong Federation of Trade Unions (FTU) and the pro-Nationalist Hong Kong and Kowloon Trades Union Council (TUC).

During the 1950s and 1960s, this vanguard labour movement seemed to have withdrawn from a militant stance of organizing widespread labour protests and work stoppages in the agitational years of the late 1940s – which represented probably a recalcitrant workers' response to inflation and economic insecurity caused by both postwar reconstruction and political upheavals in the Mainland (before the 1949 Liberation). Increasingly purged of its 'chiliastic' character after the establishment of the People's Republic and, in Hong Kong, of the 'dualistic' structure of the two rival trade union centres, the territory's labour movement started to retreat to an industrially more docile posture as its trade unions behaved more like occupationally based 'friendly societies'.

When the labour market began to be glutted by the stampede of refugees and immigrants arriving from the Mainland, these unions delivered the much needed materialistic support of 'mutual aid' benefits and other supplementary provisions to their veteran members, who were constantly threatened by the insecurities of unemployment and low pay. Given the poverty of social wages (now in the form of public housing and inexpensive public medical and health services and so on) available from the government, whose welfare and social service administration was rudimentary at that time, the rationale for these unions' activities and provisions was probably understandable – inasmuch as many of the socially dislocated workers, including both the refugees as well as locals, had to look to their private fraternities such as the unions or clan associations, or even voluntary charities for such assistance as income supplements, dormitories, clinics, education classes and other welfare contingencies. To both the Communists based in the Mainland and the Nationalists operating from Taiwan, the trade union arms functioned as an important 'transmission-belt' (as noted in earlier chapters on the ACFTU) in helping the parties to foster the political organization of labour in Hong Kong. Such a phenomenon of 'peaceful' contest between competing union fraternities on mutual aid provision was probably a reflection of the ideologically split labour movement's strategic response to the macro-constraints of the territory's political economy at that time. Sheltered by the British administration in Hong Kong, there was a pragmatic accommodation of each other's existence between the left-wing and right-wing blocs of the labour movement in the territory, where multi-unionism (often coalescing with such a FTU versus TUC 'divide') began to thrive and consolidate – not only at the occupational and industrial levels but also in the workplace, where large-scale enterprises such as the public utilities were, and still are, liable to be confronted by the competing representation of both the left-wing and right-wing union branches purportedly organizing their workforce.

It was apparently difficult as well for organized labour to challenge the employers during this period of 'industrial take-off' (made possible, amongst other things, by an abundant supply of cheap labour) in the territory with industrial unrest and concerted worker militancy – at a time when its manual labour market was flooded with refugees who were preoccupied with searching for a job which promised a stable income, and were understandably suspicious of any overt expression of collective action hostile to capital. This period has been relatively free from any sizable eruption of industrial conflict, save a brief interval of open industrial antagonism organized by the FTU as the vanguard of the pro-China forces in Hong Kong during the 1967 Civil Disturbance – itself a historical benchmark in the contemporary development of this industrial society. These upheavals largely owed their politico-ideological inspirations to the spillover of the Cultural Revolution afflicting China in the late 1960s. By the turn of the decade into the 1970s, their effects had by and large subsided, giving way to a new epoch which witnessed China's opening to the West, its pragmatic external relations and concomitantly, as a sequel, the 'de-politicization' of the trade union movement in Hong Kong.

As Hong Kong advanced industrially into an affluent city economy from the 1970s into the 1980s, its trade union institutions have also became increasingly modernized and less trapped in its hitherto image as a cluster of conservative fraternities serving little more than the role as the political standard-bearers of the archaic Communist versus Nationalist 'divide' which dated back to the 1940s.[2] As labour's representative bodies and spontaneous combinations, these predominantly blue-collar trade unions in the 'mainstream' of the labour movement were beset more and more by the internal problem of their organizational stagnation – as their initial cohorts of membership began to age and retire – as well as the challenge of having update their conservative union platforms in order to harmonize better with the shifting expectations of a younger, more inquisitive and better educated labour force for whom the refugee-bound labouring psychology of their earlier generation had become increasingly irrelevant. Moreover, the impending need for the trade unions' renewal was accentuated and compounded by other developments in the labour and employment sector: first, the employment of an essentially 'white-collar' constituted and salaried 'middle-class' and its organization into a 'white-collar' union movement catering to, and conspicuous for its 'presence' within, the civil service and the public employment sector; second, the rise of an articulate fringe of non-union, labour pressure groups (noticeably, the Christian Industrial Committee, CIC); and third, the substituting effects that emanated from a reformist labour administration, whose declared programme of labour legislation (which has been formalized since the early 1970s in the aftermath of the 1967 civil upheavals) visibly upgraded workers' standards and strengthened the latters' safeguards.

In the background, the modernization of China and the 'Open Door' policy *vis-à-vis* the outside world also induced the veteran 'mainstream' unions to respond to these pressures by gradually rescinding their former obsession with ideological rhetoric. Instead, they had to respond to a rapidly shifting environment by looking ahead to a renewal strategy to pragmatize and 'depoliticize' their union programmes. These initiatives began to crystallize in the early and mid-1980s – coinciding with the inception of government-sponsored political reforms in the territory as well as Sino-British negotiations on the arrangements beyond 1997 (see Yahuda, 1996).[3]

The first measure has been to modernize the unions' provisions of membership's benefits and services. There was an evident move away from their early-day concern with philanthropic supply of wage supplements to those in need or in distress – whose number has drastically shrunk as the territory improved in affluence during the 1970s and 1980s. Instead, these unions now increasingly sought to appeal better to the average wage-earner both as a consumer patronizing the services and goods they deliver, as well as a yearning for after-work education and associational activities. In this connection, many of the large unions, and the major union centres, have stepped-up their cooperative enterprises by providing their members with retail outlets for various popular merchandise items at concessionary prices, and often extending these arrangements to include catering and travel agency services, or even discount and credit card facilities. Other popular fixtures can include, among others, sponsoring recreational and sports activities, or organizing extra-mural programmes on a variety of adult education and training courses for developing either leisure interests or vocational skills.

The second measure widely adopted by the unions for consolidating and attracting their membership has been their assumption of a more vocal spokesman's role in representing the occupational interests of the workers whom they organize. At the micro-level of private industry or enterprise, there were attempts by different unions to regularize their dialogue with individual corporate-employers, especially with a view to establishing or re-establishing the basis of union recognition for collective bargaining. This step was paralleled by an ascending readiness of unions to intervene in employees' trade disputes and work stoppages – partly as a resource support to the workers in dispute and partly to help reconcile their differences with the employers against whom these industrial actions were levied.

In addition, the trade unions and labour organizations have sought to enshrine themselves as the workers' representative bodies and spokesmen of their occupational interests at the workplace, and to do so by lobbying the government at the central level of public policy- making. Where pluralistic sectional interests now proliferate in society, the trade unions have ascended in societal status as one among the more vociferous and resourceful pressure groups characterizing a 'permissive' political economy in the territory since the 1970s (see Lethbridge and Ng, 1995). Directed at a politically sensitive civil-service-controlled administration, which is purportedly technocratic and now anxious to decolonize and democratize its hitherto image of 'alien' British rule, these pressure groups' lobby and activities were initially organized as essentially 'street-corner' social actions outside the 'corridor of power' within the establishment. However, as the government-sponsored democratic reforms became settled in their pace, there has been a noticeable tendency for the labour movement to be incorporated and integrated into the establishment and the mainstream arena of Hong Kong's newly evolved activities of electoral politics. This process of the trade unions' repoliticization, now as 'actors' in the home domain of domestic affairs, instead of serving as 'agencies' respectively acting on behalf of the Beijing and Taipei governments across the 'Strait', will be discussed again in a later section of this chapter. However, it is worth noting that by way of petitioning, public assembly, demonstration, or staging industrial actions, these unions have consistently been capable of presenting formidable pressure upon the government over topical labour issues and vigorously lobbied it for favourable legislative motions in order to protect and advance their members' cause.

A paradox is hence noticeable in Hong Kong's contemporary history of labour and organized labour. While Hong Kong's unions have visibly depoliticized their heavily ideology-laden image in recent years by indulging themselves less and less in doctrinal policies over the Mainland

– Taiwan issue, they have concurrently become more enmeshed in the internal administration and domestic politics of the territory. Such a reorientation in the nature and strategy of the local unions was given a crucial impetus by the democratic reforms sponsored by the government since the beginning of the 1980s (see Ng, 1996). These political reforms were initiated partly with a view to erecting an institutional or representative government in Hong Kong and partly to position the territory for the latter's transition towards 1997.

The political strength of Hong Kong's trade unions was stimulated as a by-product of these electoral reforms. Unions in the territory became enshrined in the 'estate of the realm', when designated as members of one of the earliest functional constituencies having two elected seats in the Legislative Council. This step was a benchmark measure heralding the labour movement's new inroad to political power and influence. In the 1985 inaugural election for part of the Legislative Council, a representative each from the FTU and the TUC entered the Council in the two seats designated for unions making up labour's functional constituency, while a veteran union leader was also elected to the Council in the teacher's constituency. Labour's presence in the legislative was again enlarged in the 1991 election, when in addition to the twin seats held over their own 'functional' demarcation, trade unions were able to furnish from among their leadership two successful candidates for the directly elected franchise, as well as retain and secure control of the teachers' and nurses' seats. At the same time, Hong Kong's leading political party, the Democratic Party, is known for having maintained a close, ally-like relationship with the new and third trade union centre, the Confederation of Trade Unions (CTU).

A consistent feature of the territory's labour movement and its membership since the Second World War has been a tradition of its internal division and associated diversity. Such a fragmented labour movement, justified on the one hand by the official explanation that Hong Kong's trade union laws and institutional heritage have always been able to give a liberal latitude to the freedom of association, and yet deplored on the other hand, by the movement itself because of the detriments to its solidarity due to the drift in small and loosely integrated unions within the labour movement, has been caused in the past by the perennial syndrome of 'union proliferation along ideological, political, ethnic, and other parochial lines, and leading to multi-unionism at all levels of the enterprise, industry and economy' (Lethbridge and Ng, 1995, p. 79). In 1995, for example, there were altogether 522 employee trade unions registered in Hong Kong organizing a declared membership strength of 591 181, yielding a union participation rate of 21 per cent (see Table 7.1 for background statistical data).

Table 7.1   Selected background statistical data on Hong Kong (1995, except where indicated)

Population (millions)	6.20
Labour force (millions)	3.09
% Real GDP growth	4.80
GNP per capita (US$)	> 27 500[*]
% Inflation	8.70
% Unemployment	3.50
No. of union members (millions)	> 0.60
% Unionized	> 21.00

[*] 1995 estimate at current market prices.
Sources: Various (Hong Kong Government Statistics, World Bank, World Factbook, etc.).

This patent feature of a pluralistic labour movement has epitomized, up to the 1980s, the impasse of deep ideological splits and rivalry between the polarized left-wing union centres. Such a dichotomization between the two opposing factional blocs has stifled the labour movement's strength, emasculating its solidarity and explaining its lukewarm aptitude in organizing concerted industrial actions and collective labour protests such as strikes and work stoppages.

As noted above, the half-century old legacy of the Communist versus Nationalist schism in Hong Kong's history of organized labour began to gradually wither from the mid-1980s onwards. There was glimpse of a new horizon of a better unified workers' movement in the earlier half of this decade (1980s), as suggested by growing signs of mutual accommodation, dialogue or even ad hoc collaboration between the old adversaries of the pro-China FTU, now with around 5 per cent of those unionized, and pro-Taiwan TUC, with around 33 per cent.

However, such a vision of a more solidaristic movement was (and is) illusionary when the 'mainstream' union organizations became afflicted by the 'imperative' challenge of the new unions catering to the sectional combinations of the white-collar as well as grey-collar workers (technicians alike) and the younger blue-collar ones. Initially sponsored by the Church-backed Christian Industrial Committee, these new unions coalesced by forming a third trade union centre in 1990. Partly inspired by the euphoria stemming from the officially sponsored electoral reforms, and partly as a strategic response to the territory's political transition, the CTU seemed to spearhead the labour movement as its new 'vanguard', instilling into it a renewed vitality of industrial activism and political popularity among the grass-roots populace in the domain of 'electoral' participation.

Quickly forging a close 'ally-like' partnership with the Democratic Party (the biggest and most influential political party in Hong Kong as the progressive standard-bearer of 'Western-style' freedoms) with cross-membership, the CTU has swiftly gained in popularity, dislodging and substituting the TUC, at least in terms of membership strength, as the second leading trade union centre and poising as the 'antagonistic' alternative to the pro-China FTU. As to be suggested in the ensuing discussion, the CTU's ascendancy to a new 'realm of estate' in political influence and power has compounded and to a considerable degree, strained industrial relations in Hong Kong by ushering to the scene its high flavour of 'politicking' and 'politicization' at the expense of almost disrupting labour-management dialogue (see Ng, 1996). Moreover, the theme of fragmented multi-unionism has become perpetuated, inasmuch as the emergent tripartite 'configuration' of unionism's 'trichorization' has now made the Hong Kong labour movement even more fragmented than before, in spite of nominal and sporadic demonstrations of inter-union solidarity on a territory-wide scale over such 'core' issues as imported labour and retirement security.

7.3   HONG KONG TRADE UNIONS AT THE CROSS-ROADS

In retrospect, it can be argued that since China's changing economic and political strategy with the 'Four Modernizations' reforms and its implications (see Warner, 1995, pp. 3–12), the Hong Kong labour movement has evolved through a cyclical experience of first, 'depoliticization' which implied pragmatic organizational rationalization – and, second, additional impetus by the gestation of the civil service based, white-collar movement which has contributed to a pluralistic fragmentation of the labour movement. This younger public sector unionism has been noticeable for having espoused an image of an 'organic', in Selig Perlman's (1949) terms, and sectarian 'labour aristocracy' consciousness in defence of their traditional advantages of pay relativities both within the civil service (intergrade differentials and comparabilities) as well as externally *vis-à-vis* the private sector wage markets. Wage negotiation and pay adjustment disputes which clustered in close succession in the government and public sector, pervaded this brief internal of ten years between the late 1970s and late 1980s.

Instigated by the officially sponsored political-cum-electoral reforms and boosted by the June 1989 events in Beijing, which touched off a strong local reaction and yearning for the protection of democracy and human rights, the newly constituted third trade union centre, the Hong Kong Confederation of Trade Unions (CTU) with around 15 per cent of those unionized, quickly grew in popularity. It acted in close solidarity with the leading Democratic Party and soon eclipsed the right-wing TUC to forcefully challenge the leadership of the FTU in the mainstream labour movement. The 'China factor' now recovered its pre-eminence as the pivotal 'divide' splitting the labour movement, just after a short spell of coexistence between the pro-China and pro-Taiwan factional groups among the territory's organized labour. Never able to insulate itself as an 'enclave' free from the Mainland influence (almost endemic to Hong Kong's labour history since its prewar urbanization), the local labour movement drifted visibly back to a politico-ideologically split movement in which confrontation, this time centred upon the polarized stance between the veteran pro-China vanguard organization, the Hong Kong Federation of Trade Unions (FTU) and the newly constituted, yet popular, third trade union centre allied to the Democratic Party, the Hong Kong Confederation of Trade Unions (CTU).

The trade unions in Hong Kong were then conditioned by the political impasse in which the territory was trapped in the 1997 transition, induced unwittingly by the Hong Kong Government in an assiduous (and, perhaps, paternalistic) endeavour to democratize the administrative-cum-legislative institutions in there (in a hasty agenda which has, unwittingly, antagonized China as it retorted by announcing instead a Mainland-fashioned system of gradualistic institutional advances from indirect to direct electoral arrangements). The Hong Kong unions have inadvertently waived their role as the sectional representative body of workers' industrial interest to drift into another internal power-struggle and embattled contest between the FTU and CTU as two adversarial vanguard union centres.

In spite of the appearance of its quick advance in political power by acting as a quasi-political organ, the labour movement has been eclipsed as a *bona fide* industrial organization. An offshoot of the rapid escalation of the vanguard unions into the rank of Hong Kong's new class of political 'nouveau riche' has been the polarization between the FTU and the CTU camps, fringed by other lesser union federal bodies like the pro-Taiwan Hong Kong and Kowloon Trade Union Council and the (purportedly) neutral Federation of Hong Kong and Kowloon Labour Unions. Their leaderships have successfully enshrined themselves as political activists, with a sizable number of their ranks co-opted now into the establishment as elected members of the legislature, the law-making Legislative Council. However, this 'new estate of the realm' is not achieved by the labour movement without paying a costly price, as some of the negative implications of excessive political bidding by the unions are now being slowly unfolded.

To begin with, as novice entrants into the territory's ruling elite, many of these trade unionists nominated as politicians are increasingly withdrawn or even detached from their former concern with trade union affairs, as vividly suggested by such classic notions of 'union integration' or 'union incorporation'. For many of the politically active unions, their sponsorship of sympathetic political candidates in elections are steadily purging themselves of their initial and authentic 'industrial' character. Instead, it has to be reckoned that, because of the expensive game of 'politicking', the role of the trade unions has been steadily weakened as the representative agencies of their members in catering to sectional occupational interests. Or, otherwise, at least, the labour movement is afflicted, on a number of occasions, by the competing priorities of whether to advance the protection of the strikers in industrial actions, or to legalize the mandatory disclosure of information on enterprise restructuring and down-sizing, or to weed out the pocket of 25 000 migrant guest workers on the peripheral economy admitted under the Government's hastily assembled Labour Importation Scheme of General Skills in 1990–91.

Next, both the FTU and the CTU, as the 'core' mutual contestants for organized labour's leadership and anxious to wield power in the exercise, campaigned against each other to elicit popular votes in political elections. The implications are two-fold: first, these two key union centres have never collaborated closely with each other on any coordinated or harmonized programme of organized labour's activities but, instead, contested vigorously with each other in 'cut-throat' rivalries on parochial issues which would appear to appeal best to the voters' nominal industrial interests and preferences. The most patent illustration here is probably the separate adoption of an almost identical yet overtly protectionist stance against the Mainland guest workers by both the CTU and FTU. Understandably, given its close association with the PRC, the FTU was locked in a dilemma which was embarrassing: the strategic imperative of having to deny the admission of its Mainland compatriots to work temporarily in Hong Kong is clearly paradoxical and helps explain its apparent reluctant militancy and lukewarm opposition to imported PRC labour at the beginning. On this issue, the FTU was seemingly incapable of formulating and offering an alternative platform which could have otherwise been instrumental in addressing the unemployment which beset the local workforce. The second implication is even more detrimental to industry and labour-management in Hong Kong as the two sides have been drifting into open and total hostilities between the unions and the employers and their associations on the all pervasive controversy of whether to continue or rescind the large-scale importation of guest workers from the Mainland or, elsewhere from overseas. The 'divide' between organized labour and management on this issue has become so sharp that the strong and unyielding mutual antagonism between the two sides is now impeding the time-honoured efficacy of the tripartite Labour Advisory Board.

Eclipsed in this orthodox role, the Labour Advisory Board has been substantially weakened further by the recent usurping acts of a number of vanguard politicians elected to the legislature under the trade union's sponsorship. Having now ascended to the echelon of political representatives in the Legislative Council, these trade union leaders-cum-Legislative counsellors jealously guarded their newly acquired legislative prerogative against the hitherto low-key, yet workable mechanism, of tripartite labour policy formulation and consultation at the lower level of the Labour Advisory Board. As a sequel, the tradition of a steady labour legislation programme for bettering workers' protection and employment standards, established since the early 1970s under the governorship of Lord Maclehose has been reduced into disarray because of aggrandizing acts of the more ambitious newly elected union representatives in the Legislative Council. Anxious to push forward a well-intentioned yet poorly coordinated programme of 'progressive' labour legislation, they coerced a weak Government to usher in a series of pro-labour private members' bills in anticipation of the '1997' changeover. Which were later suspended in mid-July. Such a policy of instigating labour enactments on the legislative agenda has alienated a number of small and medium-sized enterprises in Hong Kong and induced them towards cross-border relocation. The proliferation of fragmented items of new labour law has unwittingly added to the territory's unemployment by inflating production costs and helping to weaken Hong Kong by pricing itself out of the international/internal markets because of these escalating (labour and land) cost outlays.

After almost four years of protracted and socially divisive debate, ever since the idea of legislating on a territory-wide arrangement on retirement protection was officially conceived, the Government decided in mid-1995 to adopt a low-key system of forced saving-cum-deferred payment, now labelled officially as the mandatory provident fund (MPF) scheme. The newly sanctioned MPF scheme is itself virtually a reinstatement of an old idea, canvassed originally fours years ago but subsequently rescinded because of its highly unsatisfactory nature. The labour movement, in spite of its reluctant and recalcitrant orientation towards the revived blueprint, was visibly unable to articulate a concerted and well reasoned alternative. There was, indeed, an alternative to instituting such a territory-wide arrangement but this was itself also split between the option of a central provident fund and that of an old age pension which the Government at one time seemed to have advocated

Mirroring an ill-conceived union strategy has been an inexplicable default of Hong Kong's trade unions in having not advanced and improved institutionally their presence and representative status in the workplace, which has remained sparsely organized for a stable dialogue with management. The reason has been blamed by the labour movement upon the Government's doctrinal inertia and refusal to introduce legal norms conferring collective bargaining to unions by entitling them to mandatory employers' recognition by way of balloting procedures. However, the key trade unions, by indulging themselves in the newly instituted game of electoral politics, deserve indictment for having been lukewarm about uplifting their workplace status and negotiating for an equitable relationship of mutual recognition and dialogue with the employers.

Instead, unions remain feeble in the workplace as in the past. They are unable to make any significant inroads into either voluntary union recognition extended by the private corporate employers for collective bargaining to consolidate any collaborative relationship of consultation, cooperation in areas of mutuality (like productivity enhancement and work rationalization), or joint jurisdiction in processing workplace grievances, discipline and conflict. Over the past half-decade, sporadic incidents of union militancy have appeared but invariably collapsed, as illustrated by the industrial episode that led to the disintegration of the air-stewardesses strike waged against the Cathay Pacific Airways in 1993. Union feebleness in industrial actions was also echoed by other examples of the organized labour's collective acquiescence, as witnessed in the mass lay-off by Hong Kong Telecom in the early 1990s and its subsequent substantial staff-cuts. These 'down-sizing' exercises were emulated in other leading cases of corporate reorganization in the public utility and banking industries. However, crises over job security have touched off few militant acts of union protest and labour agitation.

The obsession of the trade unions with politicizing their programmes and activities as a 'short-cut' to power, encouraged and made possible by the Government-sponsored electoral reforms, has resulted in a lop-sided situation in which the Hong Kong labour unions, on the eve of their transition into a post-1997 industrial epoch, have remained no less immature in negotiating with employers in the industrial areas of workplace consultation, collective bargaining, conflict resolution and grievance settlement. Ironically, their new influence gained in the political arena has been of limited or little instrumentality in helping enhance their industrial strength *vis-à-vis* the employers at the workplace.

The future of the Hong Kong labour movement is hence an apparent paradox which betrays grounds of both optimism as well as pessimism (Ng, 1996). On the surface, the officially sponsored programme of democratic electoral reforms has uplifted the trade unions from their former doldrums of the 1960s and 1970s (at a time when the veteran FTU and TUC union groups were slowly withering away in their traditional vanguard roles as the quasi-agencies of the Mainland and Taiwan Governments). Their participation in popular electoral activities instilled these labour organizations with a new ministerial role as the workers' representative organizations in a reformed and gradually decolonized administrative establishment. However, instead of emulating the Singaporean 'corporatist' model (see later in this chapter) to forge and consolidate an industrial partnership with the state and the employers at both the macro- as well as the workplace-levels, the 'core' labour movement, led by the new standard-bearing 'CTU' group and its reluctant 'mainstream' rival centre, the FTU, has perhaps unwittingly adopted the Western-style adversarial approach which, in spite of its short-term 'progressive' appeal to the grass-roots voters in the electoral 'marketplace', has a negative effect on workplace labour–management collaboration, mutual dialogue and recognition. However, it is precisely the enshrining of these qualities and properties which has distinguished the Japanese-style enterprise unionism in cementing the workplace status of the trade unions as a (partner) institution to the management hierarchy in the enterprise, as noted earlier in Chapter 4. The labour unions can now be vested with a non-workforce's cooperation in organizational and technological re-engineering, especially where disclosure of crucial business information is involved and this may be a distinct and viable alternative to Western unionism. Such a non-Western, non-adversarial theme of trade unionism is not only specific to Japan but is also steadily taking root in other places in Asian societies like Singapore, Taiwan and now even Mainland China in its experiment with 'market socialism' (see Warner, 1995, p. 148).

A similar strategy of the future trade unions in Hong Kong as outlined above is hardly novel and is, in principle, quite conceivable. In fact, a move of the territory's union movement to dilute its highly, and yet deceptive, 'politicized' profile and to restore, instead, a more low-key presence in its industrial activities on the shopfloor at the workplace level can be a far more prudent, politically safer and institutionally more tenacious strategy for organized labour to adopt in Hong Kong. This step can be an attractive option for the leadership in the local labour movement, given the imminent uncertainty of a relatively fluid and uncrystallized political terrain to feature Hong Kong for at least a few years during the transition interlude before and beyond 1997. Such a move would point to a relative degree of 'convergence' with Mainland industrial relations.

Looking ahead, among the diverse (factional) sectors within the present labour movement of Hong Kong, it is most likely that the FTU will be, unsurprisingly, the most resourceful and adaptable one to excel both as a quasi-industrial as well as a quasi-political representative agency. It is likely to continue and advance its dualistic role of organizing the labour force in promoting the local people's cross-class unity and the prosperity of the Hong Kong Special Administrative Region (SAR), as well as in securing an effective dialogue with enterprise management in defense of labour's interests and rights. Its agenda is probably unequivocal in the context of the SAR's integration with the Mainland: assuming and resuming, as Turner *et al.* noted in the early 1990s, 'a doubly ambassadorial position: in relation to Hong Kong's economy and administration' (1991, p. 59). The prospect of such an institutional image and platform will become clearer as the contested political terrain in a closing era of British administration is waning away into the historical background after 1997.

The future position of the pro-Taiwan Nationalist trade union centre, the Hong Kong and Kowloon Trades Union Council (TUC), is actually less controversial than it appears to be for many of the less optimistic observers. For one thing, it has been restructured gradually along the line of a prudent strategy in order to maximize its resilience and versatility to survive. For another, in this context, it has been noticeable in having pulled itself, pragmatically, out of the 'mainstream' arena of interunion rivalry for leadership and staying content instead, with playing a minority role in partnership or collaboration with, for example, the apparently neutral Federation of Hong Kong and Kowloon Labour Unions.

Otherwise, the gaps in the labour movement, destined to remain pluralistic, and for that reason internally segmented rather than evolving towards a monistic or unitary organ, are likely to be filled by a number of established and relatively 'aristocratic' union bodies organizing the technical grey-collar workers as well as the white-collar workers in the civil service, public sector and new service industries. The more notable examples in this class of union organizations are first, the Chinese Civil Servants' Association, which is a federal-like association of grade-specific civil service combinations registered officially as a holistic 'general' union and having the biggest membership among all individual Hong Kong unions; and second, the Federation of Hong Kong and Kowloon Labour Unions. Of special strategic importance in holding the swing of balance in the future sustenance of this delicately split labour movement is the latter which, as portrayed in a classic critique of Hong Kong unionism, 'is hardly political in the sense of the older general federations, and has avoided any suggestion of hostility to them ...', let alone its prudent sensitivity in 'promoting the formation of new unions' (Turner *et al.*, 1991, p. 59).

Of course, what remains as the unfathomable abyss of the future of organized labour in Hong Kong is still the highly articulate combination of the CTU, which has in a sense been partially incorporated into the establishment of 'British-style' democracy. Masked by a spiralling mutual distrust between the Mainland authorities and these recalcitrant 'progressive' groupings, the CTU and its associates have adopted a 'polarized' strategy, by alienating itself from the future SAR administration in boycotting, amongst other things, the preparatory election of the China prescribed provisional legislature. These paradoxical acts of challenging the future establishment while staying a participant in the present British mandated establishment are perceived as uncooperative by the Mainland authority. The stereotyping of the CTU as a 'non-patriotic' mass organization is likely to impede or even preclude its potential role of contributing to a constructive and trustworthy labour–management–government partnership in the future SAR system of governance, whether political or industrial.

7.4 NON-ADVERSARIAL COLLABORATION: CONVERGENCE WITH THE ASIAN 'MAINSTREAM' APPROACH?

Given the propensity of the Hong Kong workplace towards spontaneous shopfloor agitation and an increasingly stratified labour market, it may be a pragmatic strategy for the Hong Kong trade unions during the transitional period to hold back from a less overtly politicized stance to a modest industrial role of organizing the average workplace, with a view to erecting a more consultative or even collaborative relationship with Hong Kong employers. Anyway, a non-adversarial approach towards the regulation of the relations between the managers and the managed is not at all new, as we have noted, in East or South-East Asia – as amply illustrated by the Japanese, Singaporean or possibly even (post-Modernization) Chinese models of enterprise unionism or 'work unit' basic labour organizations (see Wilkinson, 1994; Chen, 1995). Indeed, industrial relations in the future Hong Kong SAR may be converging with the workplace patterns in these Asian societies. This is a distinct possibility envisaged by such leading scholars as the late Keith Thurley in his vision of an emerging 'Asian alternative' to the class-based Western adversarial approach to trade unionism and workplace industrial relations (Thurley, 1988, p. 26).

In the currency of withering trade unionism throughout the Western world, beset by chronic crises of stagflation and the high costs of sustaining adversarial industrial relations institutions like antagonistic collective bargaining, the emerging Asian 'league' of practising a non 'zero-sum' institutional alternative of workplace industrial relations arrangements has offered an attractive option of 'strategic choice' for both the nation at large as well as the individual enterprises (see Moore and Jennings, 1995). Whether inspired by the Japanese, the Singaporeans, the Koreans or even the Chinese on their road towards 'market socialism', it is hardly incommensurate with the pragmatic dictates of both political, economic and cultural imperatives that the future Hong Kong SAR may aspire to join this Asian 'league' of evolving mutually emulative social and industrial institutions with in the region. However, the impending course of erecting a new Asian-style 'social-contract' in industry may be a thorny one. While confrontational electoral politics which had afflicted a faction-ridden Hong Kong society on the eve of its 1997 transition, will take time to subside, Hong Kong employers should also learn, as instructed by the Japanese and Singaporian models, to develop gradually a normative commitment of waiving their historical inhospitality and defensive suspicion towards unions, should they make and advance their presence in the workplace. Indeed, the binding nexus of Hong Kong industry is likely to be focused upon the shopfloor, where a 'normative consensus' of mutual respect and cooperation has to be nurtured by both parties, with patience, tact and tolerance. This may be achieved by employers in both the private and public sectors extending recognition to the unions, supported by stable consultative dialogue and institutionalized reconciliation of divergent industrial interest between labour and capital. If backed at the macro-policy level by a strongly state-sponsored and revitalized Labour Advisory Board of the ILO style which exalts tripartite participation and policy consultation, the evolving 'new' system of Hong Kong industrial relations may espouse a likely corrective to the present time-consuming process of fabricating cosmetic labour legislation Moreover, the present obsession of the labour movement with partisan legislative processes is pushing the economy along a costly path, drifting towards a drain of its competitive power in the global and Asian markets and a divisive gulf between labour and capital.

The dialectics of the 1997 political transition seem to have precipitated a dilemma for labour and management in Hong Kong, which can be 'alienating' for both parties and prove 'foreign' to the Chinese tradition of sanctifying industrial harmony between the employer and the employed, the manager and the managed. However, it is possible that such an 'alien' character in industry is just transient and it may subside to give way to greater labour–management cooperation and stability after 1997.

7.5   THE STATE AND ORGANIZED LABOUR: INDUSTRIAL PARTNERSHIP IN SINGAPORE?

In contrast to the Hong Kong system of institutional permissiveness which now accommodates a diversified state union pluralism (liable to be sustained beyond 1997), a 'monistic' labour movement characterized the organization of workers' combinations in Singapore shortly after its independence – featuring a classic case of 'industrial partnership' or 'social contract' between the ruling political party, the People's Action Party (PAP), and its ally of organized labour, a highly unified national labour movement led by the 'mainstream' trade union centre, the National Trade Union Congress (NTUC) with 72 trade unions and three associations affiliated to it, covering 240 000 members. Singapore has earned its worldwide image as a highly affluent and successful Asian industrial society, yet organized on a 'corporatist' model – due to a strategic collaborative pact of joint-regulation, binding together the state, employers and labour and the latter's representative organizations. Such an approach, non-adversarial but actually solidaristic in transcending the otherwise 'class' divide between the ruler and the ruled, the manager and the managed, is purportedly rooted in Asian's cultural heritage and temperament: it has not only been workable in stabilizing the nation's industrial relations but has also uplifted the economy because of a mutual, high-trust commitment of all parties to advancing their 'commonwealth'. It has been heralded as betraying an Asian spirit of 'altruism' mixed ingenuously with a Western inspired middle-class ideology of pragmatic accommodation. The ministerial role performed by the NTUC as the standard-bearer of the national labour movement perhaps epitomizes best such a notion in practice – helping to inspire labour movements elsewhere, even in Mainland China (see Warner, 1995) as well as other developing economies (see Maeda and Ng, 1996, p. 186) to emulate, at least partly such a theme in the latters' search for ways of reforming their trade union institutions.

Just as it has been the case in Mainland China or elsewhere in other contemporary societies, the specificities of Singapore's labour movement can hardly be understood as a pure workers' combination *per se*. Given its historical context, an appreciation of its character in industry and society cannot be made in isolation and divorced from the nation's specific historical experience after having attained independence from British rule and subsequently, announcing its detachment from the Malaysian Federation.

The early-day drama of the gestation of the Singaporean labour movement was probably no less politicized than what has been portrayed of organized labour and its quasi-revolutionary radicalism in the China–Hong Kong circuit. Ideology-cum-partisan division, paralleled by a nexus of Communist inspirations and a counter-Communist drift, was a pervasive theme that penetrated the country's pluralist union movement in its early days. Given its nature, its unionism helped instigate a sequel of labour-cum-social upheavals contributing to the young nation's instability. The subsequent consolidation of unionism and the withering away of its initial turbulent character – and the state's concomitant strategy to fashion such a reconfiguration of the unions' movement under the reign of the ruling People's Action Party – was a historical step. As such, the continuities and discontinuities experienced by the Singaporean unions on their path from an embattled state to a ministerial and unified status (today) attest to a process of institutionalization which has contributed importantly to nation-building. Leggett (1992) has documented this inaugural history of how a politically inspired labour movement has matured through the nation's historical metamorphosis (of domestic political contest, conflict and eventually, settlement into a consolidated ruling elite headed by the PAP) into a quasi-official partner institution allied to the Government. As he notes:

> A General Labour Union pre-dates World War II but the trade union leaders who had gone underground during the Japanese occupation confronted the returning British with a politicized labour movement ... The Singapore Trade Unions Council (STUC) established in 1951 supported a short-lived Labour Front government which deregistered the militant SFSWU (Singapore Factory and Shop Workers' Union). Subsequently the PAP, which had been formed in 1954, went on to win 43 out of 51 seats in the Legislative Assembly in 1959. However, it was not until the mid-1960s, when the PAP's protégé, the NTUC, formed in 1962, had established its ascendancy over the 'leftist' Singapore Association of Trade Unions that labour became 'depoliticized'. (Ibid., p. 59)

The partnership between the state reigned by the ruling party, PAP, and the unitary national labour movement, the NTUC, harmonized with the national employers' centre, the Singapore National Employers Federation (SNEF) has consolidated a system of centralized 'tripartitism' which emphasises, consensus among the parties, in spite of the diversity of sectarian (and, sometimes, antagonistic) interests inherent in labour – management relations. As reported by Cheng and Chang (1996) the Singaporean government, together with NTUC and the SNEF, has sustained at the national level a regular policy forum in the form of a high powered 'tripartite body that meets regularly to consult on national industrial relations issues such as annual wage increases and training' (ibid., p. 206). This highly institutionalized system of tripartite centralism epitomizes a non-conflictual model of unionism which has been instrumental, amongst other things, in helping the economy's industrial harmony and in turn, the nation's economic advance. Indeed:

> 'Incorporation' of the national labour movement in a social and industrial partnership with the State and business in the past three decades has led to the sustenance of a virtually strike-free industrial relations history in Singapore. (Ibid.)

The lesson of tripartite collaboration which Singapore purportedly personifies (an ILO-style tripartitism, apart from that the Singaporean version is more authoritarian, conciliatory and less partisan and dominated by the employer–employee 'divide' than the ILO 'blueprint') has been an important potential model for newly industrialized states, especially in East Asia or even in older ones like the PRC, to fashion their industrial relations and union policies in order to nurture a business environment conductive to foreign investment.

The gestation of this well-enshrined system of 'centralized tripartitism' governing the labour arena in Singapore owes much of its efficacy today to the dictates of the nation's history before and after its independence. However, it has also been argued that Singapore and its evolution of 'tripartitism' as a core politico-industrial institution attest convincingly to an Oriental 'cultural' trait of exalting 'altruism' and deploring sectarian conflicts in industry, which is reminiscent of the Japanese practice and is liable to be increasingly emulated inside, or even outside Asia, in place of the 'classic' adversarial model of Western-style unionism and industrial relations.[4] Such an alternative perspective of fashioning (or restructuring) the logic of union combination in the modern/postmodern context of organizing work and business was seen as distinctly prospective by one Euro-Asian scholar almost a decade ago:

> Asians often reject the conflicting adversary basis of Western industrial relations arguments. Asians ... are frequently horrified by strikes and attached to the values of co-operation, mutual commitment and harmony. Collective bargaining, itself, is seen as overlapping with consultative discussions. (Thurley, 1988, p. 26)

Inasmuch as such industrial assumptions are normative in or at least, vicariously embodied in the Asians' minds – it appears that the Singaporean system, which emphasizes a tripartite approach to labour relations at the national, industry or enterprise level, has 'best' articulated the strategic recognition of Confucian values in Asia today (see Tung, 1996). It has also helped to consolidate labour–management relations, and legitimize the State's steering role in the labour arena to make it less confrontational and more commensurate with new nations' concern with economic development. To a large extent, it is likely that the imagery of the Singaporean 'experiment' has offered a possible source of imaginative instruction to the architects of institutional and organizational reforms inside Mainland China as to how its national labour movement, the All-China Federation of Trade Unions (ACFTU), can be restructured in order to streamline its structure and rationalize and upgrade its activity platform (Interviews at ACFTU Headquarters, November, 1995). However, the 'optimistic' thesis of a future convergence in unionism between the Mainland China and the Singaporean cases is more problematic than it appears, for two reasons. One is the issue of comparability by virtue of the variation between the two nations in size and diversity, thereby making such an analogy fictional rather then tenable.

Another cause of reservation is endemic of the constraints bred by a highly structured system of 'union centralism' which has afflicted Singapore, seemingly impeding its economy's readjustments in the late 1980s and early 1990s. A highly centralized system of industrial tripartitism, consolidated in the early 1980s, has ironically undermined the industrial role of the Singaporean trade unions as the workers' spontaneous combinations for the *bona fide* articulation of their workplace collective interests. Instead, this power of organized labour became concentrated at the centre of the movement, which was ministerial as part of a corporatist governing elite. Such a heavily centre-led institutional arrangement of tripartite partnership, in spite of its collaborative nature in securing a trilateral dialogue among the otherwise adversarial parties of labour and capital, was conspicuously 'top-down', and hardly distinguishable from the orthodox 'transmission-belt' model. Such a state-sponsored system of voluntary now-adversarial/consultative unions was formally enshrined by legal enactments introduced in 1982. As noted in the following documentation on the restructuring of the workplace unions' role aimed at enhancing their institutional activity under the 1982 amendments to the Trade Unions Act:

the union's role was redefined primarily as a social and welfare organization and only secondarily for organizing and representing workers, thus supporting the national and corporate goal of increasing productivity. Workers and their representatives were encouraged to look to their companies' internal consultative channels such as the Work Excellence Committee and the Quality Control Circle for the resolution of workplace conflicts and productivity problems. (Ng and Cheng, 1994, p. 224)

The structural and institutional ramifications for the national labour movement and its internal character of union formation were evident: the shift towards building direct workplace representation and labour–management dialogue, while by-passing industry-wide negotiation, has made 'less relevant the representational role of the unions, in particular those still organized along occupational and industrial lines, which formed a vast majority' (ibid.). While Hong Kong trade unions have always been feeble as defensive industrial combinations and consolidated their historical image as instrumental collectivities catering to members' off-work association, extra-moral education and serving as mutual insurance cooperatives/friendly societies, the Singaporean trade unions have paradoxically advanced in popularity by also acting as a 'clubhouse' equivalent – a form of fraternity association. Their grass-roots appeal was symptomatic of an upsurge in the nation's union density (see Table 7.2 for background statistical data) which rose steadily to about 28 per cent by the end of the 1980s, after having been trapped at a much lower level of about 20 per cent in the early 1980s, and is now somewhat higher again. However, as noted by Leggett (1992), the nation's union density has been cyclically staggering as well, before the doldrums of the early 1980s. He reports that the labour history of Singapore reached a turning point in 1962 with the inception of the NTUC as the labour ally sponsored by the ruling PAP. It soon established its ascendency over the leftist Singapore Association of Trade Unions (SATU) thereby consolidating the labour movement into a monistic one and 'depoliticising' it. The NTUC subsequently began to promote cooperative business ventures and services, thereby improving its credibility and arresting its membership slide experienced in the early 1970s. With the sizable expansion of its organizational ambit in the manufacturing sector in the 1970s, the NTUC advanced its unionization level to a peak of 250 000 in strength, or 29 per cent of the workforce in 1979 (ibid., pp. 59–60). There is an implicit yet interesting analogy shared by Singaporean unions with 'welfare' unionism in Hong Kong: where the labour unions deliver their 'industrial' goods not by deputizing their memberships in collective bargaining but by working as 'service' organizations in merchandise sales and providing materialistic benefits to the 'worker' beneficiaries. Inasmuch as the workers in Singapore also perceive that their pecuniary benefits could be enhanced through joining the union, the reason appears that such a union has been able 'to provide its members with benefits', as distinct from and outside the jurisdiction of adversarial Western-style collective bargaining (Ng and Cheng, 1994, p. 224).

Such an official design of the national labour movement in the 1980s of detaching its industrial and other lower-level unions from an otherwise active involvement in labour-management wage-haggling apparently attests to the thesis of 'union incorporation (or integration)', which upholds and conserves the labour movement in an emasculated capacity to partner institutionally with the governing elite (the ruling political party and the employers, the capital) in a 'corporatist' state. The strategic rationale of such a model of 'tripartite centralism' – such as to enhance the status of organized labour in a 'ministerial' capacity, neutralize its recalcitrant tendencies and reduce the risk of its drift into an alternative power-centre which could have been disruptive to social stability by indulging in acts of industrial militancy and to, most importantly, marshal labour–management collaboration in the concerted enterprise of nation-building and advancing its economic development to a higher industrial realm – has made Singapore today, just like the Japanese case, widely cited as another classic example of resourcefully managing human resources giving Asian approval to trade unionism, inspired by the celebrated ILO model of industrial relations 'tripartitism'.

Table 7.2   Selected background statistical data on Singapore (1995, except where indicated)

Population (millions)	2.89
Labour force (millions)	1.65
% Real GDP growth	8.80
GNP per capita (US$)	> 22,900[*]
% Inflation	2.10
% Unemployment	1.40
No. of union members (millions)	> 0.25
% Unionized	> 25.00[**]

[*]   1995 estimate at current market prices
[**] based on the 'bargainable workforce', according to the NTUC in 1995
Sources: Various (Singapore Government statistics, World Bank, World Factbook, etc.).

At its zenith of development, the 'tripartite' National Wage Council (NWC), created since 1972, probably best eptomized the 'core' influence of this form of state-sponsored institution of 'tripartitism' in intervening in and actually regulating the private wage-market. Its primary prerogative in its inaugural days in the 1970s was to promulgate annual pay rise recommendations which were subsequently incorporated, almost as a rule, in the awards made or collective arguments approved by the Industrial Arbitration Courts. Through a series of assiduous steps to prescribe both the procedural and substantive wage norms announced to private enterprises to help govern their pay and annual pay adjustments, the National Wage Council, together with other parallel tripartite agencies like the National Productivity Board, the vocational-oriented Basic Education Skills Training and the Skills Development Fund, have coalesced and consolidated in the last three decades of government-orchestrated national construction a 'ministerial' system of tripartite consultative, advisory and even policy-making bodies which help ensure the government, or its ruling party, of its legitimacy and governing mandate.

In its capacity as the popular representative movement of organized labour, the NTUC has become and remains today a key pillar in sustaining this infrastructure of national consensus as the industrial ally to the PAP and a participant in its government, often at ministerial level appointments (Leggett, 1992, pp. 59–60). However, such a highly institutionalized design of state-led tripartite centralism, in spite of its appearance as a well-coordinated and harmonized system of integrated and consensual governance on national policies of social and economic development, can breed its own structural rigidities and inflexibilities due to over-regulation. These detriments to business flexibilities have become so stifling upon the economy and its resilience in coping with a rapidly shifting global order of trade and international division of labour that the nation began to embark upon a more prudent strategy of decentralizing and deregulating its economy – after experiencing the vicissitudes of the recession of the mid 1980s. Again, the union movement has been assigned a crucial contingent role of assisting the state to restructure the nation's labour-cum-wage markets and to rationalize its human resource infrastructure in order to uplift the economy.

The strains endemic in an over-regulated economy, dictated by the central prerogative masked by an apparently jointly negotiated and voluntary consensus, pledged by the trilateral partners of the state, the SNEF and the NTUC bureaucracy, have conspicuously betrayed themselves in the crisis of the 1985 recession, when these national endeavours to usher Singapore hastily into an advanced realm of 'post-industrialism' did not materialize but were beset and halted by various problems of institutional maladjustments and rigidities. The celebrated tradition of a technocratic-based and state-sponsored governance under 'tripartite centralism' has become increasingly problematic, in spite of its doctrinal (if not ideological) appeal of nation-building, when challenged by a rapidly shifting business terrain. It also faces uncertainty due to first, globalization and market competitiveness at both the regional and international levels; and second, technological advances, innovations and a consistent logic of changes in the marketplace and workplace. These bred have the paradoxical demands for both flexibility and commitment These contradictions are more taxing for such quasi-planned economies as Singapore (see Maeda and Ng, 1996, p. 183) compared to the 'laissez-faire' type of institutional permissiveness which has hitherto featured the Hong Kong case.

Readjusting its role, capacity and strategy, the NTUC has, as a sequel, embarked upon a new agenda of steering its member unions towards a novel design of 'organized pluralism', whereby the prerogative of industrial regulation over such issues as wages, bonuses and incentives is systematically devolved to the workplace level – to be negotiated jointly and directly between the enterprise and its 'house' union within a broad framework of wage norms or guidelines on pay adjustment criteria promulgated centrally by the National Wage Council, with the tacit blessing of the state and the NTUC. These latest developments, therefore, imply literally 'a devolution of joint decision-making to the individual workplace, now that growing emphasis is to be placed on voluntary collective bargaining and wage negotiations, industrial competition, private market adjustments and the inculcation of enterprise-level initiatives' (Maeda and Ng, 1996, p. 183).

7.6 TRIPARTITISM, PLURALISM AND UNITARISM IN SINGAPORE

There is the appearance of a more liberalized and decentralized structure of 'industrial government' in the nation, now that the 'nexus' of decision-making on wages and associated employment issues has shifted downwards from the national centre of the competent authorities and agencies to the workplace units – hedged with improved flexibilities to harmonize better with industry's parameters and organizational performance, productivity and profitability, and so on. Such a newly evolved measure of marketplace-oriented autonomy in wages and labour matters is probably efficacious in restoring the Singaporean labour union back to a more authentic role as the bargaining agent of the workplace labour force which

it organizes. However, as bargaining partners with the enterprise management, these basic workplace 'house' unions continue to betray the long-
cherished theme of conserving labour–management collaboration – along
a locus of 'consultative' negotiation in search for mutual consent, rather
than pursuing a 'zero-sum' type of 'we–they' divide in emulation of the
classic Western-style 'conflictual' adversarial bargaining. The official
rationale propagated has been, by such a devolution strategy, a nationwide vision to transform and reactivate the house unions 'as vehicles to
promote workers' identification with the company, so that house unions –
if supported by enlightened management, responsible union leaders
and expert advice from the NTUC – can become feasible workplace
mechanisms for the regulation of labour management relations as well as
for improving productivity' (Ng and Cheng, 1994, p. 225).

These initiatives of restructuring the trade union system with the
national labour management to align its role and activity better with the
state's economic development strategy has led an enhanced 'Agenda for
the 1990s' announced by the NTUC – in a national appeal to industry and
organized labour to return to tripartite negotiation at the workplace as well
as at the national level. Such a policy communiqué epitomizes an endeavour of a reluctant labour movement, when trapped in the contradiction
between an enshrined tradition of 'tripartite centralism' and the latest drift
towards a workplace hiatus (which is somewhat lacking a structured
central policy directive and theme, from which the workplace has been
purportedly detached under the 'search for flexibility' zeal), to restore and
reinstate the previously state sanctified 'visibility [it has] lost with the
return of bilateral collective bargaining' (ibid., p. 225).

In summary, the Singaporean syndrome now emerging in the wake of
the state's attempts to restructure its institution of tripartite centralized
partnership between the ruling party, the national labour movement and
capital may have inadvertently subverted the highly prided stability and
collaborative harmony in industry which have been attributed to Singapore
as a model of non-adversarial 'Asian' unionism and industrial relations.
Paradoxically, 'bipartitism' without direct government involvement now
featuring workplace industrial negotiation – in spite of its creeping popularity to private enterprises seeking marketplace flexibilities – may work to
the detriment of the nation's industrial relations stability by instigating
again the adversarial practice of Western-style conflictual bargaining that
'it has taken decades to change' (ibid.). At the time of writing, Singapore
is still struggling to work out a balanced and prudent combination
of 'national-level tripartitism and workplace-level bipartitism'. While a
consensual type of industrial harmony may be critically buttressed in a

nationwide ideology of 'altruism' and 'commonwealth' shared among its nationals, the economic basis for its sustenance has become noticeably more fragile with a growing propensity to industrial disputes and workplace grievances. The prospects for a continuously integrated, solidaristic and resilient industrial partnership beyond the turn of the millennium will have to depend, amongst other things, upon how successfully the NTUC is able to conserve itself as a unitary union centre of the nation's labour movement, relatively immune, as it has always been in the past, from the challenge of an otherwise alternative union movement which can be stimulated, unwittingly, by workplace bargaining which the state is seemingly inclined to nurture by fostering 'Japanese-inspired' house unions and other practices (see Wilkinson, 1994, pp. 69–70).

7.7   TRADE UNIONISM IN TAIWAN

The drama of organized labour in Taiwan is perhaps a conspicuous illustration of the aftermath of rapid advances in industrial affluence which touched off, as a political sequel, the state deregulation of its once hegemonic control over the economy (see Galenson, 1979; Farh, 1995, pp. 268–9). Not atypical among most of the Asian newly industrialized economies (NIEs), like South Korea, the democratization initiatives sponsored by a once authoritarian and pro-capital governing elite in the late 1980s (when the coercive Martial Law was abrogated in Taiwan) have drastically reconstituted the industrial relations terrain by first stimulating the rise of an alternative labour movement by drifting away and challenging the orthodox national labour movement: in other words, a shift towards union pluralism from a formerly state-sponsored unitary system; second, bringing about the decay of the Singaporean equivalent of labour–capital–state trilateral partnership, because of a recalcitrant new unionism purporting itself as the standard-bearer of the working class 'independent' consciousness. Ironically, the almost 'revolutionary' increase in political tolerance of the official administration in Taiwan, just as in the case of South Korea (see Koch *et al.*, 1995) has inadvertently instigated a volatile proliferation of opposition groupings in not only the political arena but also the allied domain of organized labour. The mushrooming of a nationwide upsurge of social and industrial unrest (see San, 1993, p. 374) was, in partiality, reminiscent of the Chinese labour history 70 years ago, when the May Fourth Movement sparked off in sequence a spiral of nationwide upheavals disrupting society and industry in the Mainland up to the 1949 Liberation, which led to the Nationalist evacuation to Taiwan (see Perry, 1993).

It is hardly surprising, therefore, that the portrayal of the labour movement in Taiwan prior to the 1987 'democratic' divide is virtually tantamount to charting an extended epilogue to the political and labour disarray and contested ground pervaded by the Communist versus Nationalist conflict, first appearing in the late 1920s (following the collapse of the Canton–Hong Kong General Strike and Boycott) and reappearing shortly after the conclusion of the Second World War in the mid-1940s. The national labour movement, which under the central leadership of the Chinese Federation of Labour (CFL), has performed as the 'mainstream' labour organ of the ruling Nationalist Party – the KMT – since its withdrawal to Taiwan, up to the 1987 reforms. This officially sanctioned union centre has featured essentially as an archaic organ of the 'labour aristocracy', subsidiary to and enmeshed in the power-hierarchy of the ruling Nationalist regime. Although anxious to revitalize its activity and mass appeal as the economy modernizes, such an ambition has always been merely visionary rather than pursued with determination – probably because of the veteran leadership's inertia and its aversion to any risk of antagonizing the senior partners of the state and big business. Docile and acquiescent, it has been politically feeble in articulating the workforce's interests within the government. When compared to its Mainland counterpart – that is, the ACFTU umbrella of Chinese socialist trade unions before the 'Four Modernizations' – the CFL paled as an even less active and efficacious public organ for organizing and mobilizing workers, in spite of the historical mutuality between the two collectivities when tracing both back to the prewar trauma of organized labour agitation and its movement inside the Mainland.

In the eyes of most of its critics, the CFL is trapped today in a lukewarm image as 'an ageing organization dominated by party veterans who cannot offer inspirational (or ideological) appeal to the labouring mass and lack the technocratic capabilities to assume an effective industrial leadership, as has the NTUC in Singapore' (Maeda and Ng, 1996, pp. 184–5). A cursory revisit to the history of this single-centre labour movement during Taiwan's curfewed days of emergency 'martial' reign, between the late 1940s and the eve of its 'demilitarization' in 1987, demonstrates certain striking parallels between the CFL system and the ACFTU structure in the Mainland, the latter of which has been documented earlier in Chapters 2 and 3.

The Chinese Federation of Labour (CFL) had been launched in April 1948 at Nanking, out of the national congress of the representatives of provincial, special municipal and national trade union federations under the jurisdiction of the retreating Nationalist Government. Directed by a general council of 51 members, the CFL was made up of 19 provincial federations of labour, 10 special municipal federations and six special industrial national federations altogether, with a total membership of

5 495 703. The CFL activities were halted temporarily at the height of the Civil War but it resumed its operation in April 1950, moving its head-quarters to Taipei (Maeda and Ng, 1987, pp. 7).

The basic unit of union organization within the CFL umbrella is either the industrial union or the craft union. In general, the industrial union corres-ponds to the plant union while the craft union organizes workers in the same trade or occupation, often without a fixed workplace. At the succes-sive tiers of the city, provincial and national levels, union federations may be formed for a specific industry or craft or on a general basis (for further details, see Wilkinson, 1994, pp. 144–9). The Trade Unions Law has prescribed, anyway, the general rule that a single union be allowed for organizing the enterprise, the industry, the occupation and so on. The rate of unionization has risen to around 30 per cent, mostly organized at enter-prise level (see Table 7.3 for background statistical data). In short, the law epitomizes an organizational principle against 'multi-unionism' which, by implication, justifies ideologically the logic of a single trade union centre under the leadership of the CFL. Directly affiliated to the CFL are such industrial bodies as the Taiwan Provincial Federation of Labour, the Taipei Municipal Federation of Labour, the Kaohsiung Municipal Federation of Labour, the Taiwan Federation of Industrial Workers' Unions of Processing Zone, three special trade national federations, one national seamen's union and 31 national industrial unions (such as highway, railway, postal, telecommunication, electric power and petroleum). A labour union, if affiliated to a union organization at a higher level, is also obliged to subscribe at monthly intervals 10 to 15 per cent of its monthly income (Maeda and Ng, 1987, p. 7).

Table 7.3   Selected background statistical data on Taiwan (1995, except where indicated)

Population (millions)	21.50
Labour force (millions)	8.94
% Real GDP growth	6.40[*]
GNP per capita (US$)	> 13,510[*]
% Inflation	3.60
% Unemployment	1.80
No. of union members (millions)	>2.50
% Unionized	> 30.00

[*] 1995 estimates at current market prices.
Sources: Various (Taiwan Government statistics, World Bank, World Factbook, etc.).

Before the landmark liberalization of tight political control once levied by the state in 1987, the CFL has been locked into a low-profile and conceivably, passivistic posture of a junior partnership to the authoritarian reign of the Nationalist administration (see Hwang, 1993). For one thing, it had supported in a doctrinal stance the highly circumscribed view of the state's regulation of the freedom to strike. In addition, conservatism has reigned within the CFL leadership, inasmuch as it has articulated a vested interest in conserving the *status quo* of the 'single-union' rule. It has, however, begun to concede to a reformist strategy to advance and enhance a proactive 'industrial partnership' with the state and employers as well as management in enterprises. This step was intended to consolidate a wider latitude of workers' rights and freedom, as well as to institute 'a trilateral dialogue' between the labour administration and the two sides of industry on all aspects of labour and industrial relations affairs by erecting the shopfloor work-council system and sponsoring a parallel arrangement of regular industrial relations forums at the regional level, attended by union, management and government representatives. The advents of changes brought about by political democratization for the labour sector were apparently recognized by this state-sponsored 'mainstream' labour movement when it openly acknowledged a renewed agenda 'to act as the guardian and spokesman of their (workers') interests and welfare, in the search for a more happy and stable industrial and work life' (Maeda and Ng, 1987, pp. 11–12). As the Federation's General Secretary acknowledged shortly after the uplifting of martial rule in Taiwan, the better prospect for a less regimented, more affluent, permissive and pluralistic society made possible by its economic prosperity, signaled the 'imperative' need to offer the labourforce a better deal when 'the most difficult hours of austerity have now become history' (ibid.). In the 'watershed' era of the late 1980s, the labour movement in Taiwan was almost in similar impasse, caused by the economy's advances and the imminent inflation of grass-roots' expectations of affluence, analogous to the Mainland movement under the ACFTU today: either of these two trade union centres being 'in search for an enhanced agenda to revitalize its popularity and steering role as labour's representative organizations' (ibid., p. 36).

As a sequel, the 'monistic' organization of the national labour movement led by the CFL steadily eroded in the late 1980s in spite of its internal rationalization endeavours, giving way slowly to a new realm of 'union pluralism'.[5] Ironically, the collapse of the monopoly of the CFL in labour organizations owes much of its source to the political withdrawal of the governing elite, the once hegemonic Nationalist Party, from its former total domination of the administration – as electoral opportunities were gradually opened up to the alternative or opposition parties (see Farh, 1995, p. 268). The state, by its swing to a policy of liberalizing a once highly centralized and coercive governing bureaucracy, has helped upset the *status quo* in the arena of organized labour, by first emasculating that feeble yet once unitary national labour movement and second, by stimulating the formation of recalcitrant new unions outside the established organizational ambit of the CFL. At the same time, the labour force has become less acquiescent, acquiring a more 'refractory' mood – inspired in part by the liberalized culture of political pluralism and in part provoked by the rapid industrial advances which bred a syndrome of urban poverty and deprivation. Rural migration to the cities led to an urban sub-class, whose members were increasingly unable to return to their rural homeland (the process of 'deruralization', noticeably after the Oil Crisis of the late 1970s). Their 'underprivileged' position created 'a mass of the ... "city proletariat"' (Maeda and Ng, 1987, p. 35). When the governing Nationalist elite and its labour ally, the CFL, were unable to cope effectively with these spiralling grievances at the workplace and a creeping disillusion with the social ills endemic in growing affluence, the gaps are quickly filled by a mushrooming of new unions offering an alternative home to the socially and industrially deprived.

Led by the Chinese Labour Federation of Independent Unions (CFIU) created in 1988, these rival unions are politically sympathetic to the opposition party(ies). Given a newly nurtured aptitude for industrial agitation, they coalesced to break the formerly state-prescribed mould of tripartite collaboration in industry and at the workplace. After waging in succession a chain of industrial militancy in the late 1980s and early 1990s (in particular, in staging the 1988 episode of 'labour march'), these rival unions outside the CFL 'mainstream' are poised to form 'a national coalition' of all labour organizations to compete with the official union system – thereby fragmenting the Taiwanese labour movement and threatening to split it into two rival union clusters, one remaining loyal and attached to the veteran CFL and the other constituted by the alternative movement – made up of a group of purportedly independent union federations outside the officially sanctioned ambit of trade union legislative framework. Within this alternative loose coalition of the 'opposition' movement four union federations are identifiable, namely:

(i) The T'ao-Chu-Miao Brotherhood Workers Union (TBW), allied initially to the Labour Party and later to the Workers' Party, a splinter political organization breaking away from the former after its internal schism;

(ii) the National Federation of Independent Unions (NFIU) backed by the Taiwan Association for Labour Movement (TALM); the latter was formerly the Taiwan Association for Labour Rights (TALR) the early pioneer of such rights;

(iii) the Federation of Union Cadres (FOUC); and

(iv) The Labour Rights Association (LRA).
(Ho, 1990, pp. 72–8).

This cluster of new unions is, however, internally segmented and diversified – compounded largely by the highly politicized debate inside Taiwan about whether it should first, conserve the *status quo*; second, seek independence as a sovereign state outside China; or third, work to negotiate re-unification with the Mainland across the Strait. Such a political divide is likely to persist, further sustaining the compartmentalization of the Taiwanese labour movement which has already been fragmented between the mainstream 'CFL' sector and this newly evolved yet proliferating number of 'non-conformist' union centres. Such a disintegrated state of union pluralism is naturally detrimental to and heavily impeding whatever solidarity organized labour is able to marshal in order to advance the cause and interests of waged labour against capital in Taiwan's industry (ibid., pp. 79–84). For this reason, collective bargaining has remained feeble and immature in the private business sector – with the unions posing little or no effective challenge to the employers at the workplace. The upshot has been a syndrome of workforce dependence upon the protective leverage of the government, which is almost common to that 'league of new industrial societies' characterized by what has been labelled as 'state controlled labour administration' (Thurley, 1983, pp. 106–20; also Maeda and Ng, 1996, p. 183). Equally, perhaps for the same reason, the Taiwanese government has deemed it as sufficiently non-threatening to the employers' prerogative, the State's security and society's industrial stability to initiate introduction of amendments to the Trade Union Law for a three-fold liberalization of the legislative control, namely:- to rescind first, the mandatory nature of union membership, thereby making union participation a voluntary right of the worker as his/her freedom of association; second, the single union shop arrangement; and third, the requirement that 'all companies or industrial sectors with 30 workers or more "should form" unions and substituting it with the more liberal provision that they may form unions instead' (Ho, 1990, p. 100).

7.8 CONCLUDING REMARKS

The industrial successes in these three East Asian societies of Chinese culture and demographic character appear to attest to the optimistic assumption of big business that their managerial resources and free market prescriptions are the best choice to organize and marshal the complex economic apparatus of advanced industrial societies. In fact, their 'mainstream' opinion may have helped anchor the *raison d'être* behind the national 'corporatist' strategies adopted by these three societies of creating a favourable environment for business so as to erect, amongst other things, commensurate infrastructural facilities and furnish a disciplined yet docile labour force.

In this context, the State and its governing elite, in spite of their paternalistic or reluctant (in the instance of the Hong Kong case) intervention into the economy, have characteristically restrained administrative and legalistic control in order to avoid impeding private enterprise incentives. With the exception of Hong Kong, which has been doctrinally bound by the logic of free market capitalism, the earlier iron grip of state centralism in the 1950s and 1960s in these three societies has been giving way slowly to the imperatives of market decentralization, privatization and voluntarism in the once politically feeble domain of industrial relations and labour organizations. However, the prospect of an 'organic' labour movement, as based upon the workers' 'home-grown consciousness', in Selig Perlman's (1949) terms, is still not in sight for either of those societies.[6] In Taiwan (in the aftermath of its political liberalization) and in Hong Kong (mindful of its sovereignty changeover from a British colony to a Chinese Special Administrative Region (SAR), it appears that the new unionism emerging in the wake of recent democratic reforms has been unable to free itself from the abstract grip of ideologies, nor to appeal pragmatically to the native 'job consciousness' of the labour force.

The lessons for Mainland China (and especially for the ACFTU) are therefore clear. The Overseas Chinese trade union movements in Hong Kong, Singapore and Taiwan present potential 'corporatist' models for those in the PRC in terms of their non-adversarial strategies (akin to other East Asian examples, such as the Japanese, but less so as far as the South Korean trade union is concerned). Even so, they all reveal the need for organizational adaptation and renewal *vis-à-vis* the changing demands of their members against the fast-changing backdrop of economic growth in modernization. In the next chapter we go on to present some tentative conclusions, taking into account this theme.

8 Conclusions: Summing-Up

8.1 INTRODUCTION

By the year 2000, it will be just over 50 years since the CCP took power in China and founded the People's Republic (see Fairbank, 1987). In these five decades, its economy will have changed out of all recognition, from a state of backwardness to one closer to an 'economic super-power' (see World Bank, 1990; 1993; Lardy, 1994). We must not exaggerate or extrapolate these trends unduly, but even so, China has become:

> a major participant in the world economy. It is virtually certain to become even more important because of its size, dynamic economic growth, and continuing policy reforms. Yet there is relatively little understanding of many of the fundamental elements of China's emergence, ranging from the actual magnitude of its economy to the extent of its openness to external influences. (Lardy, 1994, p. vii)

As a result of these changes, there has been a 'profound change in labour force dynamics' (Yang, 1996, p. 13). In turn there has followed an 'increasingly differentiated employment structure' (ibid., p. 14).

Over the last 40 years, the Chinese labour force has grown by leaps and bounds. As Knight and Song have noted:

> The labour force grew on average by 2.7 per cent per annum: 2.2 per cent in rural areas and 4.7 per cent in urban areas. Urban employees, known as 'staff and workers', increased by 5.7 per cent per annum, from being 8 per cent of the labour force in 1952 to 25 per cent in 1992. (Knight and Song, 1995, p. 98)

If the rural workforce more than doubled over the period, many are perhaps potentially classifiable as urban, as the TVEs in which they work are often at or just beyond the city limits of many conurbations. The degree of overlap between the industrial sectors in China should be noted, in that in some cases urban collectives and TVEs are sub-contractors for SOEs. China's labour force will thus have been transformed from a predominantly agricultural and rural one to an increasingly industrialized and urban one. If in 1950, out of the total population then one Chinese person

159

in *fifteen* lived in towns or cities, after the year 2000 this will have increased to well over one in *four*. In a nutshell, China is on track to become an industrialized urban society, possibly one day in the distant future catching up with its neighbours in Greater China and even Japan.[1]

Of the original small core of industrial workers, most were unionized by the mid-1950s. By 1990, while most state sector employees were still in the ACFTU-affiliated unions, most of those working in non-state firms were not. Very few of those in the burgeoning TVE sector belong to unions and only a modest proportion of those in larger JVs, let alone the smaller FFEs, or privately-owned firms – as we have noted earlier in Chapter 6. *In relative terms, then, Chinese industry becomes less and less proportionately unionized by the day.*

So far in this study we have said very little about unionization in urban collectives, TVEs or privately-owned firms (see Sabin, 1994), for the simple reason that not a great deal has been written in detail about union activity in these sectors.[2] Urban collectives employed over 30 million workers and accounted for around 13 per cent of industrial output in the early 1990s (see Naughton, 1995, p. 164). They fall into three groupings: first, the large light-industry cooperatives in the handicraft sector; second, the 'street industries' (mostly small workshops in cities); third, collective firms managed by large SOEs, often providing jobs for dependents of state workers. It is likely that the larger enterprises in the first and third of these categories have ACFTU representation. Urban collectives enjoy a modest degree of unionization, with about a quarter of the total number of ACFTU basic trade unions compared with SOEs (see Table 3.2) but given that they have one-third of the workforce in state-firms, this is not surprising.

TVEs now employ over 125 million workers (more than in the state-sector) (*The Economist*, 16 November 1996, p. 86). Unionization of this sector is said to be low; only a small proportion of the 25 million or so enterprises have basic trade unions. This fact is not remarkable, given that most of them are small-sized firms (see White *et al.*, 1996). If we look at Table 3.2, we can see that work-units employing between one to ten workers only accounted for just under a total of 15 000 trade union committees in all, out of nearly 600 000 in aggregate. If we turn to Table 6.2, this category only has over 111 000 employees in unionized work-units. By elimination, we can also see that if we deduct the SOEs and urban collectives categories, the number of trade union committees remaining falls to very small absolute numbers (just under 30 000 or about 5 per cent for JVs, FFEs and others). Similarly, if we look at Table 6.2, the number of employees in unionized enterprises outside SOEs and urban collectives falls to just over four million.

As China develops a nascent labour market in the wake of the economic reforms, it is crucial to have an understanding of how changes in its institutional infrastructure are affected and in turn interact with it (see Schoepfle, 1996). As China moves further along the road to a 'socialist' market-driven economy, the old institutions which characterized employment and work are undergoing considerable changes (see Gao, 1994). The existing labour movement is being by-passed by many of these, as we have seen earlier in this study. Not only the workers in SOEs (see Fan, 1994) but also those beyond the state sector are now increasingly exposed to the insecurities of the market, whether they are urban employees or rural peasant workers (see Han and Morishima, 1992). Together, such Chinese workers number almost as many as the total labour forces in the EU and US put together. A vast army of migrant workers (*mingong*) are on the move already, often seen in shanty towns around the larger cities, as we have seen in Chapter 3) with perhaps another similarly-sized number set to follow them from the countryside in the next decade (see Thompson, 1992/3; Solinger, 1995).

8.2 AN OVERVIEW

At this stage, we now present in summary the main points covered in our study. Our main goal was to examine the role of organized labour *vis-à-vis* management in the Chinese economy. The study, as a whole, was divided into three main parts. First, the *growth* of the Chinese labour movement particularly since the 'Liberation' in 1949 was reviewed. Second, the *reforms* of the Chinese trade unions and their role *vis-à-vis* management since the 'Open Door' and 'Four Modernizations' policies were introduced. Third, *comparisons* with management–labour relations in Overseas Chinese societies were outlined.

In Chapter 1 we set out to look at the main issues facing a study of Chinese trade unions and their role *vis-à-vis* management. We noted how the ACFTU was the largest trade union federation in the world and therefore of intrinsic interest as such, as well as representing key groups of a Chinese labour force in what had become the fastest-growing economy anywhere. We have used an 'institutional' approach in studying the role of the ACFTU and the organizational environment with which it has to deal. Given the fast rate of economic and social change in contemporary China, we therefore asked if the *status quo* institutional nexus was the most effective *vis-à-vis* the changing expectations of Chinese workers and representational needs. We also raised the question of whether 'corporatism' represented a route to 'civil society' and whether there were possibilities of change available within this *status quo*. The nature of Chinese trade unions was then compared with their counterparts elsewhere and the problem of 'family resemblances' was explored.

In Chapter 2, we reviewed the recent history of the Chinese labour movement since 1949 in order to understand better the current developments. We saw how Chinese trade unions evolved from the 'top-down' Leninist model imported into China in the 1950s and how the notion of the union as a 'transmission belt' was adapted to Chinese circumstances. The way in which various shop floor representational models were experimented with was also discussed and how the notion of the Workers' Congress resurfaced with the economic reforms of the late 1970s and early 1980s. The prospect of worker participation on Yugoslav lines had then been raised as a possibility, if only to inoculate Chinese workers against a Polish-style *Solidarity* movement. The rebirth of the ACFTU after the vagaries of the Cultural Revolution was also noted and how it was revived by Deng Xiaoping as a prop to the economic reforms.

In Chapter 3, we set out the key organizational rationales of the Chinese trade unions, with an examination of their strategy and structure. We then looked at the criteria for union membership and how the new Trade Union Law of 1992 tried to clarify the main functions of the unions in the context of changing economic and social circumstances, although without substantially departing from the original ideological and political terms of reference set out in the earlier 1950 version of the Law. We then went on to look at what is involved in the unionization process in the PRC and how meaningful the high nominal rates of membership are, given the non-representation of large parts of the labour force, such as those in the TVEs and FFEs, or those seeking work like, the many millions of transient migrant workers, (as noted). After this, we reviewed the emergence of challenges to the ACFTU's monopoly on workplace representation, such as those openly appearing before June 1989 and clandestinely so after those tumultuous events.

In Chapter 4, we outlined the *legal* context in which Chinese unions and management operate. We devoted most of the chapter to a detailed description and analysis of the recent 1994 Labour Law. After setting out the main headings of the Law, we turned to specific sections dealing with such major issues as labour contracts, redundancy, consultation, collective agreements, wage-determination, health and safety, conciliation and arbitration, compliance and compensation, and so on. We then examined the legal changes and innovations *vis-à-vis* the benchmarks set by the International Labour Organization (ILO) and how the Chinese Government was not only trying to conform formally to many international standards for reasons of diplomacy, but also to modernize its labour legislation *vis-à-vis* an increasingly globalized world economy. We concluded that the new Labour Law was a step forward in that it represented a limited degree of 'convergence' attempting as it did to balance 'social stability' with 'enterprise efficiency'.

In Chapter 5, we turned to the development of Chinese trade unions in the state-sector. Here we outlined the major role the ACFTU plays in organizing most SOE employees, who in turn constitute the lion's share of its aggregate membership. We then discussed the role of the Workers' Congresses in the late 1980s and early 1990s and the development of collective contracts in both their pre- and post-1994 Labour Law guises. The trade unions seem to have lost some of their overall influence if we compare the earlier with the later phases of the economic reforms (see Laaksonen, 1988; Child, 1994; Warner, 1995, for example), although their presence in SOEs is still comprehensive and highly institutionalized as more recent empirical investigation has indicated (see Warner, 1996b). New challenges to the existing roles played by the ACFTU have appeared both helping to shape and being shaped by the new 1994 Labour Law, as discussed above.

In Chapter 6, we set out to look at the role of the unions and management in the non-state sector, which is now on course to upstage the long-established SOEs (see Tsang, 1994). In this analysis, we looked at the role of the unions in the JV and foreign-funded firms which by 1995 constituted nearly 15 per cent of the nation's total industrial output value and nearly 40 per cent of total imports and export volume, employing over 17 million people according to official State Statistical Bureau figures (see *Beijing Review*, 28 November 1996, p. 18).[3] Of the numbers working in such firms, only a modest percentage are in fact unionized, ranging from around 88 per cent in Shanghai in larger JVs and FFEs, to none at all in many smaller foreign-funded examples. Many have neither trade union nor Workers' Congress. In recent years, the lack of union representation has in fact led to a growing number of 'wild-cat' industrial disputes in such ventures.

In Chapter 7, we turned to comparisons of unions and management in the three major *Overseas Chinese* societies, namely Hong Kong, Singapore and Taiwan. In this analysis we look in turn at each system of industrial relations and their respective varieties of 'corporatism'. A major theme in this chapter is the essentially *non-adversarial* nature of their industrial relations (IR) and how this may point to a 'family resemblance' with those of Mainland China but at the same time suggesting a way of perhaps combining both 'Asian' (as opposed to 'Western') labour practices and possibly a greater degree of pluralism (see Thurley, 1983; 1988). The three systems have long been associated with a favourable climate for business and a disciplined, even docile labour force, but in many cases have not yet developed unions based on what, in Perlman's (1949) terms, might be called a 'home-grown consciousness'. Convergence between the Mainland and Overseas Chinese models may be a possibility, given time (see Warner, 1997). The ACFTU, for example, has already shown interest in the Singaporean system, as we have noted earlier.

8.3   CONCLUDING REMARKS

To sum up, Chinese trade unions still remain very prominent at the apex-level, given the close state–Party–ACFTU nexus. On the other hand, at the grass-roots level, their role is increasingly problematic, not only in the SOE sector as redundancies grow by the day, but also in the fast-growing non-state sector where their representation is at best patchy. Once the 'iron rice bowl' is phased-out (see Wedley, 1992; Wood, 1994), the unions will find their position further weakened in the former but with an uncertain future in the latter.

What exactly trade unions do in a socialist market economy 'with Chinese characteristics' has hardly been clearly conceptualized. To be sure, moves towards a form of 'shadow' collective bargaining have been made with the introduction of collective contracts, but this is, at the time of writing, still an organizational experiment with a limited degree of effective implementation (see Table 5.2). The introduction of the 1994 Labour Law has perhaps clarified the role of the ACFTU compared with its earlier position *vis-à-vis* the most recent economic reforms across both the state and non-state sectors. As Josephs (1996) notes:

> The apparent reluctance of the Chinese government and the Chinese Communist Party to give statutory legitimacy to labor relations in a society where workers and peasants were supposedly the masters is a very intriguing phenomenon. This reluctance continued long after the resurrection of the Chinese legal system in the 1970s. One might conclude form the history of the Labor Law that the Chinese government takes the law-making process very seriously, and especially in the area of labor relations, did not want to undertake any commitments it could not reasonably expect to fulfill. (p. 24)

The above view represents a reasonable interpretation of fact but some may remain skeptical of the Chinese official intentions in the legal field in general here, given the differences with respect to interpretations of the term 'rule of law' as understood in Western usage, and with the implementation of 'human rights' in particular. Perhaps the author's use of the phrase 'apparent reluctance' is ironic. It is true, however, that IR legislation is now taken seriously and that the 1994 Labour Law reflects even more of the built-in 'corporatist' characteristics of the Chinese system, aspiring to ILO recognition, plus or minus.

Whether Chinese unions have in fact achieved a 'mature' degree of corporatism is another matter. Indeed, the very initial term implies a degree of parity between the 'social partners; which the ACFTU hardly possesses, subordinate as it is to the state–Party nexus, which also dominates the 'official' employers representative body (cf. White, 1996). To go even further, to significantly contribute to a 'civil society' is, at the moment, a step beyond the present ACFTU 'top-down' structure. Further decentralization of its organization is needed, if it is to fully perform a role as 'intermediary' (see Zhang, 1997) particularly with regard to the growing plant-level collective negotiating and dispute-resolution machinery introduced in the 1994 Labour Law, as noted in Chapter 4 earlier.

It is clear that the 'peak' labour organization – the ACFTU – has perhaps remained a 'mirror-image' of the old economic industrial *status quo*. Its capacity for organizational learning still remains constrained by its links with the state–Party structures. The present leadership appears to be too connected with the existing 'power-elite' to move beyond its shared mind-set and conceive of new goals and rationales. In terms of Western-based studies of union democracy (see Child *et al.*, 1973; Edelstein and Warner, 1979; for example) there is perhaps a need for a new balance between the administrative and representative rationales of the present organized labour infrastructure in the PRC. New ideas and new blood are surely needed for organizational renewal. To date, there has been insufficient evidence of either appearing as a positive response to Deng's economic reforms.

Any start in this direction must involve the ACFTU reformulating both its strategy, as well as its structure, given the changes which have taken place in its organizational environment in recent years. Not only do greater decentralization and pluralism seem appropriate directions to pursue, but also greater diversity in recognized representational bodies, even within its own federal domain. Even more bodies seeking greater autonomy may emerge in the coming years and a further loosening of political control in the industrial sphere may be needed *vis-à-vis* workers' representatives (as it has in reality occurred, both *de jure* as well as *de facto*, for managers). Given that convergence with 'Asian' non-adversarial industrial relations models may be a likely option, a greater degree of workplace pluralism may not weaken social control there – on the contrary, it may even enhance it. The institutionalization of industrial conflict, as seen in the examples cited in Chapter 7, may be best achieved by looking at what can be learned from neighbouring Asian models, rather than continuing past practices.

Faced with a potentially more prosperous future, China has nonetheless planted the seeds of greater inequality in its soil. A survey carried out in 1994 by the People's University in Beijing found that a 0.434 Gini coefficient for the nation as a whole, compared to 0.2 in 1978 and 0.385 in 1984 (cited in the *China Finance Association Newsletter*, 11 October 1996). Such a movement from a base-line of relative equality upwards does not augur well for calmer industrial relations.[4]

The erosion of the ACFTU's hegemony, resulting from the continuing economic and social differentiation now sharpening in the Chinese economy, can only increase. Given the pressures to dramatically cut-back the SOEs, with the potential massive down-sizing this implies, the future is uncertain for the 'vanguard' of the working-class. If we add to this the vast expansion of the JVs, FFEs, and TVEs we can readily conclude that the momentum of change is not on the side of the official organized labour institutions. Greater decentralization, diversify and pluralism must be now placed at the top of the reform-agenda in this domain.

Appendix: Constitution of the Trade Unions of the People's Republic of China[*]

GENERAL PRINCIPLE

The trade unions of China are mass organizations of the Chinese working class led by the Communist Party of China and formed by the workers and staff members voluntarily, are the bridges and bonds linking the Party and the masses of the workers and staff members, are the important social pillar of the State power, and are the representatives of the interests of the trade union members and workers and staff.

The Chinese trade unions take the Constitution of the People's Republic of China as the fundamental criterion for their activities, conduct their work in an independent and autonomous way in accordance with the 'Trade Union Law of the People's Republic of China' and 'the Constitution of the Trade Unions of the People's Republic of China', and exercise their rights and fulfill their obligations according to law.

The working class are the leading class of China, the representatives of the advanced productive forces and the relations of production, the main force in the reform and opening-up and socialist modernization drive, and the powerful and concentrated social forces in maintaining the social stability. Guided by the theory of building socialism with Chinese characteristics, the Chinese trade unions implement the Party's basic line of centering on the economic construction, upholding the Four Cardinal Principles and adhering to the reform and opening-up, fulfill the social functions of the trade unions comprehensively, better represent and protect the vital interests of the workers and staff members while protecting the overall interests of the entire Chinese people, and unite and mobilize the workers and staff members all over the country to strive for building China into a prosperous, powerful, democratic and civilized modern socialist country with their spirit of self-reliance and pioneering and painstaking efforts.

The major social functions of the Chinese trade unions are as follows: to protect the legitimate interests and democratic rights of the workers and staff members; to mobilize and organize workers and staff members to take an active part in the construction and reform and accomplish the tasks of economic and social development; to represent and organize workers and staff members to take part in the administration of the State and social affairs and to involve them in the democratic management of the enterprises, undertakings and offices; to educate workers and staff members to constantly improve their ideological and ethical qualities and enhance their scientific and cultural levels in a bid to build up a well-educated and self-disciplined contingent of workers and staff members with lofty ideals and moral integrity.

---

*Adopted by the Twelfth National Congress of the Chinese Trade Unions on 30 October 1993.

In the process of developing the socialist market economy, the Chinese trade unions, while protecting the political rights of the workers and staff, shall safeguard their rights to labour and work and their material and cultural interests, and take it as their major task to participate in coordinating the labour relations and regulate the social contradictions so as to propel the economic development and maintain a long-term social stability.

The Chinese trade unions shall safeguard the socialist State power of the people's democratic dictatorship led by the working class and based on the worker-peasant alliance, assist the People's Governments at all levels in their work and play the role of democratic participation and social supervision when the Governments exercise the State's administrative powers.

In enterprises and undertakings, the Chinese trade unions shall support the management to exercise the administrative powers in accordance with the laws, organize the workers and staff members to participate in the democratic management and democratic supervision, establish the system of consultations with the management so as to guarantee the legitimate rights and interest of the workers and staff members, mobilize their initiatives and promote the development of the enterprises and undertakings.

The Chinese trade unions shall persist in building themselves on mass and democratic basis, maintain close ties with the masses of their members, rely on them to carry on the trade union work. The leading trade union organs at various levels shall persistently place their focal point of work on the primary trade union organizations and whole-heartedly serve the grass-roots trade union organizations and workers and staff members in a bid to add vitality to the primary trade union organizations and make them 'homes of the workers and staff members'.

The enterprises and undertakings run by the trade unions shall persistently observe the principle of serving the reform and opening-up and the development of the social productive forces, serving the masses of workers and staff members, and serving the promotion of the trade union movement.

The Chinese trade unions shall strive to consolidate and develop the worker-peasant alliance, adhere to the patriotic united front and strengthen the great unity of the people of all nationalities in China including the compatriots in Taiwan, Hongkong and Macao as well as overseas Chinese with a view to promoting the unification of the motherland and enhancing its strength and prosperity.

The Chinese trade unions, in their international activities, follow the principle of independence and broad contacts and shall extensively develop friendly relations with trade union organizations of various countries on the basis of the principle of independence, equality, mutual respect and non-interference in each other's internal affairs with a view to striving, together with the workers and trade unions all over the world for world peace, development and workers' rights and interests as well as social progress.

Chapter 1: Membership

Article 1. Membership of trade unions is open to all manual and mental workers in enterprises, undertakings, and offices within the territory of China who live on wages or salaries as their main source of income and who accept the Constitution of the Trade Unions of the People's Republic of China, irrespective of their nationality, race, sex, occupation, religious belief and educational level.

Article 2. For admission to the Chinese trade unions, the worker or staff member shall voluntarily submit an application, which will be discussed and approved by a trade union group and subsequently approbated by a primary trade union committee, whereupon a membership certificate will be issued to the applicant.

Article 3. Trade union members shall enjoy the following rights:

(1) To elect, to be elected and to vote.
(2) To criticize any trade union organization and personnel, and to demand the removal or replacement of any union personnel, and to supervise the trade union work.
(3) To criticize and make suggestions on problems in the State and social life and to demand that the trade union organizations accurately convey their criticisms and suggestions to the departments concerned.
(4) To demand that the trade unions give them protection when their legitimate rights and interests are infringed upon.
(5) To enjoy preferential treatments provided by trade union-run undertakings and services in the field of culture, education, sports, tourism and sanatorium; To enjoy various awards given by the trade unions.
(6) To participate in the discussions at union meetings and through trade union-run newspapers and journals, on trade union work and issues of concern to the workers and staff members.

Article 4. Trade union members shall fulfill the following duties:

(1) To acquire political, economic, cultural, scientific, technological knowledge, to acquire the basic knowledge about trade unions.
(2) To take an active part in democratic management and fulfill production and work assignments.
(3) To abide by the Constitution and laws of the State, uphold social morality and professional ethics, and observe labour discipline.
(4) To handle properly the relations among the interests of the State, collective and individual, and combat all conducts harmful to the interest of the State and society.
(5) To safeguard the solidarity and unity within the working class, foster class brotherhood and strengthen mutual assistance.
(6) To abide by the Constitution of the Chinese trade unions, carry out the union's decisions, participate in trade union activities and pay membership dues every month.

Article 5. Trade union members are free to withdraw from the union. To do so, the union member shall submit a personal request to the trade union group to which he or she belongs. The primary trade union committee concerned shall then make the member or members' withdrawal publicly known, and call in his or her membership certificate.

A union member who fails to pay membership dues and to participate in union activities for six months in succession without justification, and refuses to mend his or her ways after education, shall be regarded as automatically having given up membership.

Article 6.   A union member who does not carry out union decisions or abide by the trade union Constitution shall be educated by criticism. A union member who seriously violates laws, commits a crime and thus receives due criminal sanction shall be expelled from the union. Expulsion shall be decided by the primary trade union committee after the trade union group to which the member belongs has discussed the case and given its views. The expulsion decision shall be reported to the next higher trade union organization for record.

Article 7.   Membership can be retained when the trade union member retires or waits for a job. He or she will be exempted from membership dues during the period of retaining his or her membership. Trade union organizations shall show concern for the life of their members who have retired or wait for jobs, and enthusiastically report their wishes and demands to the departments concerned.

Chapter II: Organizational structure

Article 8.   Chinese trade unions practice the principle of democratic centralism, the main contents of which are as follows:

(1)   Individual union members are subordinate to the trade union organization, the minority is subordinate to the majority, and the lower trade union organization are subordinate to the higher trade union organizations.

(2)   The leading bodies of trade unions at all levels are elected through democratic means, except for the agencies appointed by them.

(3)   The highest leading bodies of the trade unions are the National Congress of trade unions and the Executive Committee of the All-China Federation of Trade unions elected by the National Congress. The leading bodies of local trade union organization at different levels are the trade union congresses at their respective levels and the committees of trade union federations elected by the trade union congresses.

(4)   Trade union committees at all levels are responsible, and report their work, to the general membership meetings or the congresses at their respective levels. They accept supervision by the membership. The general membership meetings and the congresses have the power to dismiss or replace any delegate to congresses and members of trade union committees elected by them.

(5)   Trade union committees at all levels function on the principle of combining collective leadership with individual responsibility based on division of labour. All major issues shall be decided upon by trade union committees after democratic discussions. Members on committees discharge their duties in line with collective decision and division of labour.

(6)   Trade union leading bodies at all levels shall give briefings to the lower trade union organizations from time to time, and must pay constant heed to the opinions of them and the rank-and-file union members and discuss and solve the problems they raise. Lower-level trade union organizations shall request instructions from, and report on their work, to higher-level trade union organizations.

Article 9.   The election of congress delegates and trade union committee members at all levels must fully reflect the will of the voters. The lists of candidates shall be submitted to the voters for repeated deliberation and full discussion. The election shall be conducted by secret ballot. It may be carried out by using the system of electing the delegates or members directly from a list of candidates exceeding the number required or a preliminary election may be held to select candidates from a list of candidates exceeding the number required, so that candidates themselves will subsequently be formally elected. No organization or individual shall in any way compel voters to elect or not to elect a candidate.

Article 10. The trade unions of China apply, as their organizational and leadership structure, the principle of federating union organizations formed along industrial lines with those on locality basis. Trade union members in the same enterprise, undertaking, unit or office are organized in a single primary trade union organization. National and local industrial trade unions shall be formed, as circumstances require, for a single branch of the national economy or for two or more similar branches of the national economy. Except for a small number of industries where the administration is executed directly from top to bottom, trade unions of those industries accept dual leadership of both industrial trade unions and local trade union federations with the former as the major form, other industrial trade unions are mainly under the leadership of local trade union federations, while accepting leadership of higher-level industrial trade unions at the same time. The leadership structure of all industrial trade unions is defined by the All-China Federation of Trade Unions.

Trade union federations are set up in provinces, autonomous regions, municipalities directly under the central government, autonomous prefectures, cities and counties (banners). Trade union federation is the leading body of the local trade union organizations and local industrial trade unions in its locality. The All-China Federation of Trade Unions is the leading body of all local trade union federations and all national organizations of industrial trade unions. The system of substitution is implemented in election of members of the Executive Committee of the All-China Federation of Trade Unions and members of National Committees of industrial trade unions. This system may also be applied in election of members of the committees of the local trade union federations at all levels and members of the committees of the local industrial trade unions.

Article 11. The committees of local trade union federations at and above the county level may, as their work requires, set up agencies in their respective localities.

When necessary, the committees of local trade union federations at and above the county level may convene delegates' conferences in between the two congresses to discuss and decide upon major issues which require prompt solution. The number of delegates to such conferences and the procedure governing their election are determined by the trade union federations which convene the said conferences. Committees of national industrial trade unions, local industrial trade unions at different levels, township trade union federations and neighbourhood trade unions in urban areas may, in accordance with the principle of federalism and representation, consist of leading members of lower trade union organizations who are elected through democratic means and representatives from the parties concerned according to an appropriate proportion.

Article 12. Trade union congresses at all levels elect auditing commissions at their respective levels. The auditing commission of the All-China Federation of Trade Unions sets up its standing committee, and the auditing commissions of trade union federations of provinces, autonomous regions and municipalities directly under the central government and those of national industrial trade unions who manage their funds independently may also set up their standing committees. These commissions are responsible for auditing the income and expenditure accounts and checking on the management of assets of trade union organizations at the corresponding levels and of enterprises and undertakings under the direct management of these unions, and supervise the implementation of the economic and financial legislations and discipline, and the rational use of trade union funds. These commissions accept the guidance of auditing commissions of higher-level trade unions. The commissions are responsible, and report their work, to the general membership meetings or membership congresses or, when these are not in session, to trade union committees at the corresponding levels.

When auditing commissions at higher levels deem it necessary or when they are requested by auditing commissions at lower levels, they may audit the income and expenditure accounts and check on the management of assets of the lower-level trade unions and of enterprises and undertakings under the direct management of these unions.

The auditing commission of the All-China Federation of Trade Unions applies the substitution system in the election of its members. This system may be also used in election of auditing commission members of both local trade union federations at all levels and industrial trade unions who manage their funds independently.

Article 13.   Trade union organizations at all levels set up committees for women workers to reflect and safeguard the legitimate rights and interests of women workers. Nominated by trade union committees at the corresponding levels.

Article 14.   Trade union organizations at and above the county level may set up legal advisory agencies to provide services for the protection of the legitimate rights and interests of workers and staff members and trade union organizations.

Article 15.   The establishment or dissolution of a trade union organization must be endorsed by its general membership meeting or membership congress, and reported to the next higher trade union organization for approval. In case the enterprises stop their productions or in case the undertakings and offices are dissolved, the grass-roots trade union organizations which used to exist there are thereby dissolved, and these cases have to be reported to higher-level trade unions for file. No other organizations or individuals are allowed in any way to dissolve trade union organizations with other bodies or put them under the administration of other working departments.

Chapter III: The national trade union organizations

Article 16.   The National Congress of Chinese Trade Unions is convened once every five years by the Executive Committee of the All-China Federation of Trade Unions. Under extraordinary circumstances, it may be convened before or after its due date once it is proposed by the Presidium of the Executive Committee of the All-China Federation of Trade Unions and approved by the plenary session of the Executive Committee. The number of delegates to the National Congress and the procedure governing their election are determined by the All-China Federation of trade Unions.

Article 17.   The functions and powers of the National Congress of Chinese Trade Unions are as follows:

(1)   To examine and approve the work report of the Executive Committee of the All-China Federation of Trade Unions.

(2) To examine and approve the report of the Executive Committee of the All-China Federation of Trade Unions on incomes and expenditures and the work report of the Auditing Commission of the All-China Federation of Trade Unions.

(3) To revise the Chinese Trade Union Constitution.

(4) To elect the Executive Committee and Auditing Commission of the All-China Federation of Trade Unions.

Article 18. When the National Congress is not in session, the Executive Committee of the All-China Federation of Trade Unions is responsible for the implementation of the decisions of the National Congress and exercises leadership over national trade union work.

The plenary session of the Executive Committee elects the Chairman and Vice-Chairmen of the Executive Committee and members of the Presidium, thus forming the Presidium. The Executive Committee meets in plenary session at lease once a year; such sessions are convened by the Presidium.

Article 19. When the Executive Committee is not in session, the Presidium exercises the functions and powers of the Executive Committee. The Presidium meets in plenary session generally once every three months and such sessions are convened by the Chairman.

The Secretariat is set up under the Presidium. The Secretariat consists of a first secretary and a number of secretaries, who are elected by the Presidium from among the members of the Presidium. Under the leadership of the Presidium, the Secretariat attends to the day-to-day work of the All-China Federation of Trade Unions.

Article 20. The setting up of the national industrial trade unions are determined by the All-China Federation of Trade Unions in light of the actual needs.

The national committees of industrial trade unions are set up with the approval of the All-China Federation of Trade Unions in accordance with the principle of federalism and representation. They may also be elected by the national congress of individual industrial trade unions. When their five-year term expires, the national congresses shall be convened at their due dates to have re-elections. Under extraordinary circumstances, they may be held before or after their due dates upon approval by the All-China Federation of Trade Unions. The functions and powers of the national congresses of industrial trade unions or the plenary sessions of the committees formed in light of the principle of federalism and representation are as follows:

To examine and approve the work reports of the industrial trade unions; To elect the national committees or the standing committees of the national committees of industrial trade unions; To elect the Auditing Commissions of the industrial trade unions which run funds independently. In these circumstances, the Auditing Commissions should report their work to the national congresses or to the plenary sessions of the national committee of industrial trade unions. The standing committees of the national committees of the industrial trade unions consist of one chairperson and a number of vice chairpersons and standing members.

Chapter IV: Local trade union organizations

Article 21. Trade union congresses of provinces, autonomous regions, municipalities directly under the Central Government, autonomous, prefectures, cities and countries (banners) are held once every five years convened by the committees of trade union federations at the corresponding levels. Under extraordinary circumstances, they may be held before or after their due dates upon suggestions from the corresponding trade union federations and approval by the committees of the next higher trade union federations. The functions and powers of the congresses of the local trade union organizations at all levels are as follows:

(1) To examine and approve the work reports of the committees of trade union federations at the corresponding levels.
(2) To examine and approve the work reports of incomes and expenditures and the work reports of the auditing commissions of the corresponding trade union federations.
(3) To elect the committees and auditing commissions of trade union federations at the corresponding levels.

When the congresses of local trade union organizations of various levels are not in session, committees of trade union federations at their corresponding levels implement the decisions of the higher trade union organizations and the resolutions of the trade union congress at the corresponding levels, direct trade union work in their respective areas and report their work to the higher committees of trade union federations at regular intervals.

The trade union federations of provinces and autonomous regions may, as their work requires, set up area agencies in their respective localities, and the trade union federations of municipalities directly under the Central Government and cities with district divisions may set up district agencies or trade union organizations of district level. The trade unions federations of counties and districts in the cities may set up trade union organizations of township or neighbourhood levels.

Article 22. The committees of trade union federations at all levels each elect a standing committee which is to be composed of a chairperson and a number of vice chairpersons and standing members. The results of the election of trade union committees and their standing committees as well as their chairpersons, vice chairpersons and Auditing Commissions shall be reported to the committees of the next higher trade union federations for approval.

Plenary meetings of the committees of the local trade union federation at all levels are convened by their standing committees at lease once a year. When the plenary meetings of the committees of local trade union federations at all levels are not in session, their standing committees exercise the functions and powers of the committees.

Article 23. The local industrial trade union organizations at all levels are setupas determined by their corresponding trade union federations in light of the actual conditions in their respective localities.

Chapter V: Primary trade union organizations

Article 24. Trade union organizations may be set up and primary trade union committees formed, according to law, in basic units such as enterprises and undertakings of various forms of ownership and offices. Where there are fewer than twenty-five trade union members, an organizer or chairman and vice-chairmen may be elected to take charge of the work of the primary trade union organizations.

Article 25.   The general membership meetings or membership congresses of the primary trade union organizations are convened, in normal circumstances, once every year. The delegates to the congresses serve on a permanent basis and for a term of three to five years. The functions and powers of the general membership meetings or membership congresses are:

(1)   To examine and approve the work reports of the primary trade union committees.
(2)   To examine and approve the reports concerning the incomes and expenditures of the primary trade union committees and the work report of the corresponding auditing commissions.
(3)   To elect the primary trade union committees and the auditing commissions.

The primary trade union committees and the auditing commissions are elected for a term of three to five years.

Article 26.   The members of the primary trade union committees should be elected on the basis of repeated deliberations and full consultations among trade union members or their representatives. The chairmen and vice-chairmen of primary trade union committees may be elected directly by general membership meetings or membership congresses or by primary trade union committees. Trade union committees of large enterprises and undertakings may, as their work requires, set up their standing committees with the approval of higher trade union committees. The results of the election of the primary trade union committees, standing committees and chairmen and vice-chairmen as well as auditing commissions shall be reported to the next higher trade union organizations for approval.

Article 27.   The basic tasks for the primary trade union committees are:

(1)   To implement the resolutions adopted by their general membership meetings or membership congresses and the decisions of higher trade union bodies, and to attend to the day-to-day work of the primary trade union organizations.
(2)   To represent and organize workers and staff members to participate in the democratic management and democratic supervision in their own units through the workers' congresses and other forms in accordance with law and rules and regulations. Trade union committees in enterprises and undertakings are the working organs of the workers' congresses and responsible for the day-to-day work of the workers' congresses and for inspecting and supervising the implementation of the resolutions adopted by the workers' congresses.
(3)   To participate in the coordination of labour relations and the settlement of labour disputes, and to set up consultation systems with the administration of the enterprises and undertakings to solve, through consultations, problems concerning the vital interests of workers and staff members. To assist and give guidance to workers and staff members in concluding labour contracts with the administration of the enterprises and undertakings and to represent workers and staff members to sign collective contracts and other agreements with the administration and supervise over their implementation.
(4)   To organize among workers and staff members labour emulation and activities for rationalization proposals, technical innovation and technical cooperation, and sum up and publicize the advanced experience. To take charge of the public appraisal and selection as well as commendation, cultivation and administration of advanced workers and model workers.

(5) To do ideological and political work among workers and staff members, to encourage and support workers and staff members to learn culture, science and technology as well as management expertise and to unfold healthy cultural and sports activities among workers and staff members. To manage well cultural, educational and sports undertakings of the trade unions.

(6) To supervise over the implementation of relevant laws and rules and regulations. To assist and supervise the management to do a good job of labour insurance, labour protection and collective welfare services for workers and staff members so as to improve their livelihood.

(7) To safeguard the specific interests of women workers and staff members and combat discrimination or outrage against women workers and staff members as well as maltreatment and persecution of them.

(8) To do a good job of organizational construction of trade unions and perfect their democratic system and democratic life. To set up and develop the contingent of trade union activist. To recruit and educate new union members.

(9) To collect, administer and use trade union funds properly and to manage well trade union properties and trade union enterprises and undertaking.

Article 28.   Trade unions in foreign-funded enterprises and private enterprises shall set up a consultative and negotiating system with the administration, participate in the democratic management, represent and defend the political rights and material interests of workers and staff members according to law, and safeguard the interests of the state and the society, while respecting the legitimate rights and interests of the investors with an aim to jointly seek for development of the enterprises.

Article 29.   Trade unions in educational, scientific, cultural, health and sports undertakings as well as offices shall actively carry out trade union work in light of the fact that these are units with more intellectuals and thus make active efforts to know and show concern for the mental state, work and livelihood of the workers and staff members so as to promote the implementation of the party's policies towards the intellectuals. To organize workers and staff members to participate in the democratic management and democratic supervision in their own units so as to create fine conditions for them to give full play to their wisdom and intelligence.

Article 30.   Primary trade union committees may, as their work requires, set up branch trade union committees in branch factories and workshop (department) committees in workshops (departments). Such committees are elected at the general membership meetings or membership congresses of the said factories and workshops (departments), and their term of office is of the same duration as that of the primary trade union committees.

Primary trade union committees or committees in branch factories and workshops may, when necessary, set up various special commissions or special groups.

Trade union groups are set up in each production or administrative team or group. The trade union groups shall democratically elect their leaders and actively carry out trade union work of the groups.

Article 31.   Trade union organizations at all levels shall build up cadres' contingents in line with the principle that the cadres should be more revolutionary, younger in average age, better educated and more professional competent. These cadres' contingents must adhere to the Party's basic line, be familiar with their own profession, love trade union work and enjoy the trust of the masses of workers and staff members.

All trade union cadres must do their best to meet the following requirements:

(1)   To study diligently Marxism–Leninism and Mao Zedong thought, and the theory of building socialism with Chinese characteristics as well as economics, law and trade union professional knowledge.

(2)   To implement the Party's basic line and various principles and policies, abide by state laws and rules and regulations and be bold to open up new roads and bring forth new ideas in the reform and opening-up to the outside world and the socialist modernization construction.

(3)   To be devoted to their duties, work diligently, be honest in performing their duties, take the interests of the whole into account and uphold unity.

(4)   To seek truth from facts, conscientiously conduct investigation and study, and accurately reflect the opinions, wishes and requirements of workers and staff members.

(5)   To adhere to the principle, seek no personal gain, speak up enthusiastically on behalf of the workers and staff members, work in their interests wholeheartedly, and safeguard their legitimate rights and interests.

(6)   To be democratic in their work style, maintain close ties with the masses, and accept consciously the criticism and supervision of the masses of workers and staff members.

Article 32.   Trade union organizations at all levels undertake the management of trade union cadres in accordance with relevant regulations. They should pay great attention to training and selecting cadres from among young people, women and minority nationalities.

Chairmen and vice-chairmen of grade unions at all levels should not be transferred to other positions before the expiration of their terms. Whenever any transfer is necessary, it must be approved by the corresponding trade union committees and the next higher trade union committees.

Article 33.   Trade union organizations at all levels must set up and perfect systems for training cadres, and run well the colleges and schools for trade union cadres and various types of training classes.

Article 34.   Trade union organizations at all levels must concern themselves with the ideology, studies and livelihood of trade union cadres, supervise and urge the fulfillment of provisions concerning their corresponding treatment, support them in their work, guarantee their right to perform their functions according to laws, and resolutely combat acts of persecution and retaliation against trade union cadres.

Chapter VII: Trade union funds and property

Article 35.   The sources of trade union funds are as follows:

(1)   Membership dues paid by union members.

(2)   Appropriations made by the enterprises, undertakings and offices for the trade unions with a sum equivalent to 2 per cent of their respective total payrolls of all workers and staff members.

(3)   Proceeds from enterprises and undertakings sponsored by trade unions.

(4)   Subsidies from the people's governments at all levels and from the enterprises, undertakings, and offices.

(5)   Other incomes.

Article 36. Trade unions establish budgets, final accounts and auditing and supervisory systems based on the principle of financial independence and practise a financial system of unified leadership and management by different levels. Regulations governing the management and use of trade union funds are prescribed by the All-China Federation of Trade Unions.

Article 37. Trade union committees at all levels work out, examine and approve their budgets and final accounts in accordance with the prescribed regulations and report their incomes and expenditures to the general membership meetings or membership congresses and to the next higher trade union committees at regular intervals. The budgets, final accounts and reports on incomes and expenditures are subject to scrutiny and supervision by the auditing commissions at the corresponding level.

Article 38. Trade union funds, property and immovable property allocated by the state, enterprises and undertakings are protected by law and may not be encroached upon, diverted to other uses or arbitrarily disposed of by any organization or individual. Enterprises and undertakings sponsored by trade unions may not have their jurisdictions changed arbitrarily.

If a trade union organization is merged into another organization, its funds and property will belong to the enlarged trade union organization. If a trade union organization is revoked or dissolved, its funds and property will be disposed of by the next higher trade union organization.

Chapter VIII: Trade union emblem

Article 39. The emblem of trade unions of China is made up of two Chinese characters ZHONG and GONG superimposed in an artistic mould of a circle, symbolizing the unit and integrity of the Chinese trade unions and the Chinese working class. The standards for making the emblem are prescribed by the All-China Federation of Trade Unions.

Article 40. The emblem of trade unions of China may be hung in the offices, places of activities and meeting halls of the Chinese trade unions. It may be used as souvenirs and mark on office articles and may also be worn as a badge.

Chapter IX: Supplementary article

Article 41. The right of interpreting this Constitution rests with the All-China Federation of Trade Unions.

Notes

1 Setting Out the Issues

1. It has been estimated the Chinese economy may before long become the third (or even the second) largest in the world. A study of the International Monetary Fund found that on a purchasing power parity basis, it accounted for over 6 per cent of world output in 1990 (see Lardy, 1994, p. 3).
2. The 'iron rice-bowl' system consisted of a 'cradle-to-the-grave' welfare state for SOE employees, offering not only a job for life, but also educational benefits, housing provision, medical care and so on (see Leung, 1988, pp. 55–6).
3. The Japanese origins of the 'iron rice-bowl' stemmed from the early industrialization of Manchuria, followed by their military occupation in the 1930s (see Duus *et al.*, 1989; Warner, 1995, pp. 15 ff).
4. Since the cumulative enterprise management reforms of the mid- and late-1980s (see Lee, 1987) as well as the more recent 1992 versions, 'managers began to emerge as extremely powerful individuals. To some extent this was intentional ...' (see Naughton, 1995, p. 206).
5. The threat of bankruptcies in the SOE sector is now becoming real. In October 1996, Cao Siyuan, a well-known Chinese economist, forecast that more than 5000 State enterprises would go bust by the end of 1996, more than in the previous six years (32 in 1990, 117 in 1991, 428 in 1992, 710 in 1993, 1,625 in 1994, and 2,200 in 1995) (see *Xinhua News Agency*, 14 October 1996).
6. The best account of the Japanese 'cultural uniqueness' thesis is contained in P.N. Dale's (1986) book, *The Myth of Japanese Uniqueness* (see also Beasley, 1963; Whitehill, 1991; Ballon, 1992).

2 The Chinese Labour Movement After 1949

1. The inception of the embryonic union movement in China was associated with its maritime areas which were the first to become exposed to Western mercantile and industrial influences (Perry, 1993). In this connection, the circuit of the three city ports on the coastal fringe, Shanghai (by virtue of its international settlement), Canton (as the provincial capital of the key southern province, Kwangtung or Guangdong today) and Hong Kong (a British colony since its ceding in 1842) was always identifiable as crucial.
2. Although the 1922 seamen-led general strike in Hong Kong was echoed by a number of solidaristic strikes and workers' actions in Shanghai and China's other industrial areas (see Perry, 1993, pp. 66 ff), it appears that the Canton–Hong Kong 'nexus' had become a major nerve-centre of the emerging Chinese labour movement in these initial jubilant years – possibly because of stiffer conservative resistance in the North.

3. Alienated and no longer content 'merely to follow the sporadic and waver-
    ing political leadership of Chinese middle-class groups', China's organized
    labour 'gravitated towards leadership by Chinese Marxists ...'. Although of
    middle-class intellectual origin themselves, the latter 'saw labour as the
    vanguard force in a revolutionary process whose ultimate, though not imme-
    diate, objective was socialism' (Epstein, 1949, p. v).
4. There are reasons to suspect that the early-day militancy of the Chinese
    labour movement was more the belligerent stance of its 'elite' urban
    leadership than the labour psychology of the ordinary Chinese worker at
    the 'grass-roots' level which could be pragmatic rather than 'chiliastic' or
    'ideological'.
5. Temporary contract employment was copied from Soviet practice in the 1950s.
    There were several categories, contract workers (*hetong gong*), temporary
    workers (*linshi gong*), seasonal workers (*jije gong*) and workers contracted
    from the countryside (*mongcun xieyi gong*). See Korzec (1992, p. 30) for
    further details, as well as Howe (1971) and Takahara (1992) for background.
6. Whether there was a clear blue-print for the economic reforms is debatable
    (see Lin, 1995). The more appropriate term may be Lindblom's (1959)
    notion of 'muddling through'. A definite strategy may be discerned
    retrospectively, perhaps (see Naughton, 1995). On the overall logic of the
    reforms – see Boisot and Child (1988), Hsu (1991), Chang and Nolan
    (1994), Minami (1994), and Wood (1994) among others.

3   The ACFTU's Evolving Role

1. On structure and function of organizations generally, see most recently
    Vroom, 1996: 'The structure of an organization is a highly instructive field
    of research because it involves a deliberate and normally fairly powerful
    level of formal regulation' (p. 3381)
2. The administrative and representative rationales combine in a trade union's
    structure to include pressure upon it from the membership as well as its
    environments (see Child *et al.*, 1973, pp. 71–91).
3. By 1996, the proportion of union members in the industrial labour force
    (including TVEs) was one in four.
4. Non-state sector employment has grown dramatically, although the SOEs'
    workforce *increased* by nearly 17 per cent between 1986 and 1992 (see
    Josephs, 1996, p. 26).
5. The 'dual labour' market phenomenon characterizes the Japanese economy,
    for example, where there is a 'core' part of the labour force in large corpora-
    tions with life-time employment and a larger residual group in smaller firms
    with more flexible employment tenure (see Lardy, 1994, pp. 11–12 for a
    description of the Chinese counterpart).
6. The number of dismissals from both SOEs and JVs remains *de facto* low. In a
    recent study which one of the present writers conducted in Beijing, the average
    level of dismissals per annum was less than 1 per cent (see Warner, 1996b).
7. The threat of *ad hoc* industrial action is not new in China. In fact, in the past
    managers were 'nearly helpless if a group of disgruntled workers chose to
    disrupt production through slowdowns or absenteeism' (see Naughton,
    1995, p. 105).

8. Labour activists Li Wenming and Guo Baosheng were in trial proceedings in November 1996 for attempting to organize migrant (*mingong*) workers. As the report continues: 'The two young men focussed their attention on the tens of thousands of poor migrant labourers, known in China as *san-wu renyuan* – the "three withouts", because they have no residence permit, no identity card and no work authorisation papers. Li and Guo argued in pamphlets that Chinese activists should unite the middle class, the intelligentsia and the workers "to follow the successful path of the Eastern European experience" and the "end the totalitarian rule of the Communist party". This is described by the group Human Rights Watch/Asia as "an accurate depiction of the Communist party's worst nightmare come to life". It also provides a rare insight into the sort of challenge that the party would prefer foreign investors and governments to know nothing about. A verdict in the trial has been repeatedly delayed.' (*Sunday Times*, 24 November 1996, p. 19).

9. Accounts of worker demonstrations in China remain problematic. Accounts sometimes filter through and are reported in the Hong Kong Press or the *BBC Summary of Short-wave Broadcasts* (*SWB*).

10. Instances of Factory Directors being appointed as Party secretaries are cited in several studies (see Warner, 1995, p. 111, for example).

4 Trade Unions and Management in China and Their Legal Context

1. Most trade union legislation takes the form of *Regulations* promulgated by the State Council, often designated as *Temporary* or *Provisional*; for example, *Regulations of the PRC on Settlement of Labour Disputes in Enterprises* (1993).

2. We have given less prominence to gender discrimination, child exploitation, forced labour and the like, as they are highlighted in numerous human rights publications; for example, the *Human Rights Forum* and the international press; see also Wu (1992; 1996) on the *laogai*, or labour reform camps.

3. The iron rice-bowl policy was never previously explicitly stated in legal terms *vis-à-vis* jobs for life in any one document. There was no 'right' to permanent employment as such (see Josephs, 1995, p. 564).

4. The 1986 Regulations, amended in 1992, introduced labour contracts, but earlier regulations permitted firms to fire workers for gross misconduct and even lesser acts including slacking (see Naughton, 1995, p. 211).

5. Job security remains a politically sensitive issue. In a recent account of *Angang* Steel (which also featured in the North-East industries study – see Warner, 1995), the writer noted that the problem of redundancy had to be tackled. *Angang* 'is required to feed nearly 400 000 people' (*Beijing Review*, 28 November, p. 12). Its reform measures which will leave only 50 000 workers in the 'core' enterprise, have diverted 110 000 redundant workers from the state-owned firms there and 180 000 employees from collective enterprises, to subsidiary or branch companies.

6. Estimates of surplus labour are discussed in a number of sources. Knight and Song (1995, p. 101) list several estimates ranging from one-fifth to one-third of the labour force in the state-sector. Overmanning in SOEs is thus endemic and as many as one third of the total state-sector workforce could be dispensed with, according to recent critical accounts (see *The Economist*,

27 August 1994, p. 53, citing a report by the Hong Kong office of McKinsey, the management consultancy).

7.   Social security reform is now underway (dating from the a State Council's decision in 1991). A unified scheme was advanced in 1993 (see Warner, 1995, on the experimental schemes introduced in the *Dongbei* SOEs; *Beijing Review*, 6 January 1997, pp. 22–3, on the implementation of the most recent reforms).

8.   Factory Directors can now hire and fire, at least in theory, although China is still unlikely to achieve Western or Japanese-style HRM practices in the foreseeable future (see Warner, 1993; 1995; 1996b).

9.   Formal consultation, even negotiation between management and trade unions, appears to be the intention here, but as Josephs points out 'collective contracts are relatively meaningless without the right to take collective action' (Josephs, 1995, p. 571).

10.   Piecework and bonuses now comprise an increasing proportion of workers' remuneration. In 1984, the ceiling on bonuses was lifted. By 1995, most workers in SOEs had been covered by the 1992 experimental wage reforms introduced as part of the 'three systems reforms' (*san gaige*).

11.   Legal routes to peaceful dispute-resolution have clearly been introduced as a response to the rising incidence of industrial disputes. The new Labour Law in Article 7 refers to the union having the duty to 'protect the lawful rights and interests of workers' but the ACFTU has only recently taken to legal representation of workers' grievances and then only individual ones.

12.   The number of projected officially-sanctioned redundancies in the loss-making SOEs was stated to be set at around 14 million workers over the next five years, according to Zhu Jiazhen, China's Labour Vice-Minister (see *The Economist*, 16 November 1996, p. 7)

13.   A report on the implementation of the new Labour Law in Guangdong Province, one of China's growth areas, reveals both positive and negative findings. The official news agency noted that:

> During a two-month labour inspection campaign co-launched by Guangdong's labour, public security and industrial and commercial departments with the backing of the trade unions, a total of 7800 inspectors checked on 15 466 companies employing 4.2 million staff.
>
> The inspection found that at present 97.3 per cent of employees, or 7.3 million workers, in state-owned, collectively-owned and foreign-funded companies in Guangdong have signed employment contracts with their employers. In addition, about 40 per cent of the province's 14.7 million workers employed by township enterprises and the private sector are also protected by employment contracts.
>
> Some 1307 local enterprises have joined collective bargaining schemes. The new system of working hours and minimum wages have also been introduced in may workplaces. Furthermore, 6.475 million employees had joined the social pension scheme by the end of 1995 ...
>
> However, many forms of employer malpractice are still commonplace in the province. Workers are still forced into working overtime and their safety is often neglected. The inspection teams found that 81 320 workers in over 10 000 companies had been underpaid, mainly by employers illegally deducting wages, or their employers had failed to pay their full

social security contributions. The amount of illegal deductions and defaults under investigation currently totals RMB 17.85 million.

Among the 15 466 enterprises inspected, 1461 found of serious violations of Labour Law were punished and 787 were given official warnings about their misconduct. (*Xinhua News Agency*, 5 November 1996)

5   Trade Unions and Management in the State-Owned Enterprise Sector

1.   The phrase used here refers to the role of unions in a 'socialist' state. For further background, see Schurmann (1966) for example.
2.   One may surmise that memories of earlier Party–union rivalries influenced Deng's thinking here: see Chapter 2 earlier. In the 1950s, for example, union militancy (see Perry, 1994) had led to conflictual behaviour.
3.   The role of the Party Secretary was downgraded in the course of the enterprise reforms and 'explicitly restricted to ideological matters and supervision of overall policy ...' (see Naughton, 1995, p. 206).
4.   There were relatively few such agreements definitively implemented outside SOEs and urban collectives: at most a couple of thousand *vis-à-vis* the nearly 44 000 units in the total noted in Table 5.2.
5.   The limited space devoted to Workers' Congresses is rather odd, given the comprehensive nature of the 1994 Labour Law as a whole, applying to all kinds of business organizations, whether domestic or foreign-owned (see Josephs, 1996, p. 24).

6   Trade Unions and Management in the Joint Venture and Foreign-Funded Enterprise Sectors

1.   Re-unification poses both potential gains and losses to Deng's successors after the transfer of Sovereignty in Hong Kong in 1997. It will be interesting to see how far 'the two systems' will remain separate, especially in the areas affecting trade unions (see Yahuda, 1996, pp. 59 and 115, particularly).
2.   In solidaristic support of their counterparts in Hong Kong, the strikers' Mainland colleagues and compatriots in Canton declared a general boycott levied against the colony. These actions demonstrated not only the 'organic' solidarity of the insurgent Chinese urban workers awakening to a newly discovered consciousness against the vicissitudes of foreign capital but also the collective strength of their organized power. The general strike and boycott were effectively orchestrated by the strike committee and policed by a 'private army' of pickets which the committee controlled. The strike leaders based in Canton were able to organize, at the height of their militancy, the *en masse* withdrawal and evacuation of 100 000 strikers to Canton from Hong Kong, where as many as 200 000 to 250 000 workers stayed away from work on strike. As portrayed by Chesneaux (1968), the crisis was 'undoubtedly one of the longest strikes in the history of the

international labour movement, or at least one of the longest on a large scale' (ibid., pp. 294–5).

3. Trade unions in China have long operated a check-off system, with members paying 0.5 per cent of their wages each month to the union. The enterprise pays another 2 per cent. Of the total, 5 per cent of all union subscriptions went to the ACFTU (see Warner, 1995, p. 35).

4. Foreign and comprador-owned enterprises were set up in coastal areas in the 19th century, particularly textile factories and flour mills (Feuerwerker, 1958, p. 5).

5. In its heyday, the 'revolutionary' Chinese labour movement, it may be said, owed its inspiration to an emerging 'consciousness' newly-discovered by its working class in the urban industrial areas, when these workers started to combine at the beginning of the 1920s in response to the vicissitudes of the dual challenges of both industrial capital as well as foreign powers hegemonic influence (see Perry, 1993). The organization of the Chinese working class was in part defensive of economic interests in the workplace but, more importantly, may be described as 'chiliastic' and 'evangelistic' in nature as it articulated a 'crusading' spirit of nationalistic antagonism against the 'imperialistic' aggrandisment of the foreign powers.

6. In the terminology of labour economics, the 'dual labour market' usually has a 'primary' (or privileged) sector and a 'secondary' (or less privileged) one (see Takahara, 1992; Minami, 1994).

7. The number of strikes in China has grown cumulatively since 1988. Over 250 000 disputes had been officially recorded by 1992. Another figure, of over one million such cases had been cited (see *China Labour Bulletin*, March 1994, p. 4; June 1994, p. 5).

8. The limitations to the use of the concept and practices of HRM in China (see Björkmann and Schapp, 1994) are discussed elsewhere (see Warner, 1995; 1996b). The terms 'personnel management' (*renshi guanli*) as well as 'labour and personnel management' (*laodong renshi guanli*) rather than HRM (*renshi ziyuan guanli*) are usually used. In a set of SOEs in the North-East previously studied (Warner, 1995), the terminology of HRM was not employed at all. Many writers often use the term 'HRM' relatively flexibly as a synonym for personnel management in China (see Easterby-Smith *et al.*, 1995; Brown and Branine, 1996; Zhao, 1994; Zhu and Dowling, 1994; Verma and Yan, 1995, for example). Indeed, the Chinese notion of personnel management (see Liu *et al.*, 1988) has usually been seen as hinging on organizational control, whereas Western usage is probably more related to organizational effectiveness (Child, 1994, p. 259; Goodall and Warner, 1997).

7 Outside the Mainland: Trade Unions and Management in Three Overseas Chinese Societies

1. While it was punctuated by occasional intervals of mutual rapprochement, the theme of polarized tension between the pro-Nationalist and pro-Communist sectors had always pervaded the Chinese union movement, corresponding with the struggle between the two parties for political control of the government in the Mainland. This politico-ideological overtone of a

Nationalist–Communist divide has given the Chinese labour movement and its adjuncts (notably, the union movement in Hong Kong) their distinctive character since their birth until the present day. (By historical default, up to the present such a 'divide' has been conserved, ironically, neither in the Mainland nor in Taiwan but in British administered Hong Kong.)

2. The intense tussle between the left and right sectors in the national labour movement came to the open in 1925, when the Nationalist suppression led to the suspension of the Shanghai-based and Communist-controlled Labour Secretariat in May 1925, but it went underground and continued to retain its standard-bearing role by operating through the individual unions (see Perry, 1993). In May 1925, the Second National Labour Congress (called by the four big unions at that time, including the General Union of Railway Workers, the Chinese Seamen's Union, the Hanzhiping Labour Union and the General Labour Union of Canton) resolved to organize an all-China Labour Federation in order to join the Red International of Trade Unions (Profintern) and to work in unions with the peasant movement. The stage was set for the ensuing era of open rivalry between this left-wing Labour Congress (industry-based) and the pro-Nationalist Kwangtung (Guangdong) Provincial Federation of Labour Unions (craft-based and led by the Canton Mechanics' Union).

3. The Sino-British discussions on Hong Kong had been ongoing since at least 1979, almost continuously. Even after the Joint Declaration of 1984, the path was never smooth (see Yahuda, 1996, pp. 61–82).

4. The 'Asian' as opposed to 'Western' model is discussed in greater detail in Chapter 6 of Wilkinson (1994) although the author there highlights industrial conflict as much as harmony.

5. A greater diversity of union organization in Taiwan is discussed in further detail elsewhere (see San, 1993, pp. 371–88). Unofficial union activity grew in the late 1980s (see Wilkinson, 1994, p. 145).

6. Selig Perlman, a well-known American writer on industrial relations, in *A Theory of the Labor Movement* (1949) noted that manual groups 'had their economic attitudes basically determined by a consciousness of scarcity of spontaneity' (p. 6) which was a major determinant of their solidarity.

8 Conclusions: Summing-Up

1. In Japan, the rural population is around 6 per cent and in Taiwan, about 20 per cent (see Lin and Li, 1995, p. 89).

2. Union activity in the TVE sector has not been actively researched. Whilst there are many articles on such firms (see, for example, Nee, 1992) very little refers to ACFTU organization. More recent analyses of rural economic reforms (see Putterman, 1995; Sicular, 1995; Lin, 1997; Zweig, 1997 for instance) do not refer to unionization at all.

3. Another estimate by labour activist Han Dongfang (1996, p. 168) puts the number of workers in JVs and FFE together at over 30 million, much higher than the official figures published by the State Statistical Bureau.

4. The Gini coefficient in SOEs (and other public and collective sector firms) was 0.23; whereas it was twice as big, 0.49 in FFEs (see Zhao, 1993, pp. 75–6). As the latter sector grows, so overall wage-inequality will rise (see Knight and Song, 1995, p. 107).

References

ACFTU (1953) *The Seventh National Congress* (Beijing: ACFTU).

ACFTU (1988) *The Eleventh National Congress of Chinese Trade Unions* (Beijing: All–China Federation of Trade Unions).

ACFTU (1993) *Constitution of the Trade Unions of the People's Republic of China* (Beijing: All–China Federation of Trade Unions).

ACFTU (1994) *The Twelfth National Congress of the Chinese Trade Unions 1993* (Beijing: All–China Federation of Trade Unions).

ACFTU (1996) *Chinese Trade Union Statistics Yearbook*, Beijing: Chinese Statistics Press.

Anderson, P. (1967) 'The Limits and Possibilities of Trade Union Action', in R. Blackburn and A. Cockburn (eds), *The Incompatibles* (Harmondsworth: Penguin) pp. 263–80.

Andors, S. (1977) *China's Industrial Revolution* (London: Martin Robertson).

Associated Press News Agency, various.

Ashwin, S. (1997) 'Shopfloor Trade Unionism: The Prospects of Reform, from Below', *Work, Employment and Society*, vol. 11, no. 1, pp. 115–31.

Ballon, R.J. (1992) *Foreign Competition in Japan: Human Resource Strategies* (London: Routledge).

Banks, J. (1974) *Trade Unionism* (London and New York: Collier/Macmillan).

Barling, J., Fullager, C., Kelloway, E.K. (1992) *The Union and Its Members: A Psychological Approach* (Oxford: Oxford University Press).

Barnowe, J.T. (1990) 'Paradox Resolution in Chinese Attempts to Reform Organizational Cultures', in J. Child and M. Lockett (eds), *Reform Policy of the Chinese Enterprise*, Vol. 1 (Part A) of *Advances in Chinese Industrial Studies* (Greenwich, Conn., and London: JAI Press) pp. 329–48.

Beasley, W.G. (1963) *A Modern History of Japan* (London: Routledge).

Beijing Review, various.

Beissinger, M.R. (1988) *Scientific Management, Socialist Discipline and Soviet Power* Cambridge, Mass: Harvard University Press).

Björkman, I. and Schapp, A. (1994) 'Human Resource Management Practices in Sino-Western Joint Ventures', *Working Paper*, Swedish School of Economics, Helsinki.

Boisot, M.H. and Child, J. (1988) 'The Iron Law of Fiefs: Bureaucratic Failure and the Problems of Governance in the Chinese Economic Reforms', *Administrative Science Quarterly*, vol. 33, no. 3, pp. 507–527.

Bond, M.H. (ed.) (1986) *The Psychology of the Chinese People* (Hong Kong: Oxford University Press).

Bond, M. and Hwang, K.K. (1986) 'The Social Psychology of the Chinese People', in M Bond (ed.), *The Psychology of the Chinese People* (Hong Kong: Oxford University Press) pp. 213–66.

Borisov, V., Clarke, S. and Fairbrother, P. (1994) 'Does Trade Unionism have a Future in Russia?', *Industrial Relations Journal*, vol. 25, no. 1, pp. 15–25.

Brandt, C. (1958) *Stalin's Failure in China, 1924–1927* (New York: W.W. Norton).

Brown, D.H. and Branine, M. (1996) 'Adoptive Personnel Management: Making Sense of Managing the Human Resources in China's Foreign Trade Corporations', in D. H. Brown and R. Porter (eds) *Management Issues in China: Domestic Enterprises* (London: Routledge) pp. 191–213.

Brown, E.C. (1966) *Soviet Trade Unions and Labor Relations* (Cambridge, Mass: Harvard University Press).

Brugger, W. (1976) *Democracy and Organization in the Chinese Enterprise, 1948–1953* (Cambridge: Cambridge University Press).

Bu, N. (1994) 'Red Cadres and Specialists as Modern Managers: An Empirical Assessment of Managerial Competencies in China', *International Journal of Human Resource Management*, vol. 5, no. 2, pp. 357–85.

Byrd, W. and Tidrick, G. (1987) 'Factor Allocation and Enterprise Incentives', in G. Tidrick and J. Chen (eds), *China's Industrial Reforms* (Oxford: Oxford University Press) pp. 60–102.

Chan, A. (1993) 'Revolution or Corporatism? Workers and Unions in Post-Mao China', *Australian Journal of Chinese Affairs*, no. 29, pp. 31–61.

Chan, A. (1995) 'The Emerging Pattern of Industrial Relations in China and the Rise of the Two New Labour Movements', *China Information: A Quarterly Journal*, vol. 9, no. 1, pp. 36–59.

Chan, M.K. (1981) *Historiography of the Chinese Labour Movement* (Stanford, Calif: Stanford University Press).

Chang, H.J. and Nolan, P. (1994) 'Europe *versus* Asia: Contrasting Paths to the Reform of Centrally Planned Systems of Political Economy', Paper to Conference on Management Issues for China in the 1990s, St John's College, Cambridge, 23–25 March 1994.

Chen, M (1995) *Asian Management Systems* (London: Routledge).

Chen, P.K. (1985) *The Labour Movement in China* (Hong Kong: Swindon Books).

Cheng S.M. and Chang, A.H. (1996) 'Quality of Working Life and Employee Participation in Singapore', in I. Nish, G. Redding and S.H. Ng (eds), *Work and Society: Labour and Human Resources in East Asia* (Hong Kong: Hong Kong University Press), pp 199–218.

Chesneaux, J. (1969) *The Chinese Labor Movement, 1919–1927* (Stanford: Stanford University Press).

Chi Hsin (1978) *Teng Hsiao-Ping: A Political Biography* (Hong Kong: Cosmos Books).

Chiang, C. (1990) 'The Role of Trade Unions in Mainland China', *Issues and Studies*, vol. 26, no. 2, pp. 94–100.

Child, J. (1990) 'The Structure of Earnings in Chinese Enterprises and some Correlates of their Variation', in J. Child and M. Lockett (eds), *Reform Policy and the Chinese Enterprise*, Vol. 1 (Part A) of *Advances in Chinese Industrial Studies* (Greenwich, Conn. and London: JAI Press) pp. 227–46.

Child, J. (1994) *Chinese Management During the Age of Reform* (Cambridge: Cambridge University Press).

Child, J. and Xu, X. (1989) 'The Communist Party's Role in Enterprise Leadership at the High-Water of China's Economic Reform', *Working Paper* (Beijing: China Europe Management Institute).

Child, J., Loveridge, R. and Warner, M. (1973) 'Towards an Organizational Study of Trade Unions', *Sociology*, vol. 7, no. 2, pp. 71–91.

China Daily, various.

188   *References*

China Labour Bulletin, various.
China Finance Association Newsletter, Various
China News Analysis, various.
China News Digest, various.
Chinese Trade Unions, various.
Daily Telegraph, various.
Dale, P.N. (1986) *The Myth of Japanese Uniqueness* (Oxford: Oxford University Press).
Davis, D.S. (1993) 'Job Mobility in Post-Mao Cities: Increases on the Margin', *China Quarterly*, no. 132 (December) pp. 1062–85.
Davis, D.S. (1995) 'Urban China', in Davis, D.S. *et al.* (eds) *Urban Spaces in Contemporary China,* pp. 1–22.
Davis, D.S., Krans, R., Naughton, B. and Perry, E.J. (eds) (1995) *Urban Spaces in Contemporary China* (Cambridge: Cambridge University Press).
Deery, S.J. and Mitchall R.J. (1993) *Labour and Industrial Relations in Asia: Eight Country Studies* (Melbourne: Longman Cheshire).
Deng, X. (1985) *Building Socialism with Chinese Characteristics* (Beijing: Foreign Languages Press).
Dicks, A. (1989) 'The Chinese Legal System: Reform in the Balance', *China Quarterly*, no. 119, September, pp. 541–76.
Dobb, M. (1966) *Soviet Economic Development Since 1917* (London: Routledge).
Duus, P. (1989) 'Introduction', in P. Duus, R.H. Myers, and M. Peatie (eds), *The Japanese Informal Empire in China, 1895–1937* (Princeton, NJ, Princeton University Press) pp. ix–xi.
Duus, P., Myers, R.H. and Peattie, M.R. (eds) (1989) *The Japanese Informal Empire in China, 1985–1937* (Princeton, NJ: Princeton University Press).
Easterby-Smith, M., Malina, D. and Lu, Y. (1995) 'How Culture Sensitive is HRM? A Comparative Analysis of Practice in Chinese and UK Companies', *International Journal of Human Resource Management,* vol. 6, no. 1, pp. 31–60.
Echoes from Tiananmen (Hong Kong), various.
The Economist, various.
Edelstein, J.D. and Warner, M. (1979) *Comparative Union Democracy: Organization and Opposition in British and American Trade Unions* (New Brunswick, NJ: Transaction Books).
Epstein, I. (1949) *Notes on Labour Problems in Nationalist China* (New York: Institute of Pacific Relations).
Fairbank, J.K. (1987) *The Great Chinese Revolution: 1800–1985* (New York: Harper & Row).
Fan, Q. (1994) 'State-owned Enterprises in China: Incentives and Environment' in Q. Fan and P. Nolan (eds), *China's Economic Reforms: The Costs and Benefits of Incrementalism* (London: Macmillan) pp. 137–58.
Fang Dan and Lin Yungao (1990), *Study of the Status and Functions of Trade Unions, (Gonghui Diwei Yu Zhieng Yanjiu),* (Shenyang: Liaoning Renmin Shubansha)
Farh, L. (1995) 'HRM in Taiwan (ROC)', in L. Moore and P.D. Jennings (eds), *Human Resource Management on the Pacific Rim: Institutions, Practices and Attitudes* (Berlin: De Gruyter) pp. 265–94.
Fathers, M. and Higgins, A. (1989) *Tiananmen: The Rape of Peking* (London: *The Independent* and Doubleday).

Feinerman, J.V. (1996) 'The Past – and Future – of Labor Law in China', in G.K. Schoepfle (ed.), *Changes in China's Labor Market: Implications for the Future* (Washington, DC: US Department of Labor) pp. 119–34.

Feng, T.Q. (1996) 'Workers and Trade Unions under the Market Economy: Perspectives from the Grass-Roots', (Special Issue) *Chinese Sociology and Anthropology* vol. 28, no. 3, Spring.

Feueurwerker, A. (1958) *China's Early Industrialization* (Cambridge, Mass.: Harvard University Press).

Financial Times, various.

Friedman, B.L. (1996) 'Employment and Social Protection Policies in China: Big Reforms and Limited Outcomes', in G. Schoepfle (ed.), *Changes in China's Labor Market: Implications for the Future* (Washington, DC: US Department of Labor) pp. 151–166.

Galenson, W. (1979) 'The Labour Force, Wages and Living Standards', in W. Galenson (ed.) *Economic Growth and Structural Change in Taiwan* (Ithaca, NY: Cornell University Press), pp. 384–447.

Gao, S. (1994) 'Market Economy and the Labor Force Market', *Beijing Review*, 3 January, pp. 14–16.

Goldman, M. (1989) 'Vengeance in China', *New York Review of Books*, vol. 36, 5 November, pp. 10–13.

Goldman, M. (1994) *Sowing the Seeds of Democracy in China: Political Reform in the Deng Xiaoping Era* (Harvard: Harvard University Press).

Gong, Y. (1989) 'Chinese Trade Unions' Function of Democratic Participation and Social Supervision', *Chinese Trade Unions*, vol. 2, no. 1, pp. 2–5.

Gong, Y. (1990) 'Trade Union Organizations in Foreign-Funded Enterprises Play an Important Role', *Chinese Trade Unions*, vol. 3, no. 1, pp. 2–5.

Gongren Ribao (Workers' Daily) various.

Goodall, K. and Warner, M. (1997) 'Human Resources in Sino – Foreign Joint Ventures: Selected, Case – Studies in Shanghai and Beijing', *International Journal of Human Resource Management*, vol. 8, no. 4 (in press).

Granick, D. (1987) 'The Industrial Environment in China and the CMEA Countries' in G. Tidrick and Y. Chen (eds), *China's Industrial Reforms* (Oxford: Oxford University Press) pp. 103–31.

Granick, D. (1990) *Chinese State Enterprises: A Regional Property Rights Analysis* (Chicago and London: University of Chicago Press).

Granick, D. (1991) 'Multiple Labour Markets in the Industrial State Enterprise', *China Quarterly*, No. 126 (June), pp. 269–89.

Guillermaz, J. (1972) *A History of the Chinese Communist Party* (New York: Random House).

Han, D. (1996) 'The Prospects for a Free Labor Movement in China', in G.K. Schoeple (ed.) *Changes in the Labour Market*, pp. 167–84.

Han, J. and Morishima, M. (1992) 'Labour System Reform in China and its Unexpected Consequences', *Economic and Industrial Democracy*, vol. 13, no. 3, pp. 233–61.

Harper, P. (1969) 'The Party and the Unions in Communist China', *China Quarterly*, no. 37, January, pp. 84–119.

Hearn, J.W. (1977) 'W(h)ither the Trade Unions in China?', *The Journal of Industrial Relations*, vol. 19, no. 2, pp. 158–72.

Henley, J.S. and Chen, P.K.N. (1981) 'A Note on the Appearance of Dual Functioning Trade Unions in the PRC', *British Journal of Industrial Relations,* vol. XIX, no. 1, pp. 87–93.

Henley, J.S. and Nyaw, M.K. (1986) 'Introducing Market Forces into Managerial Decisionmaking in Chinese Enterprises', *Journal of Management Studies,* vol. 23, no. 6, pp. 635–56.

Ho, S.Y. (1990) *Taiwan – After a Long Silence: The Emerging New Unions of Taiwan* (Hong Kong: Asia Monitor Centre).

Hoffman, C. (1974) *The Chinese Worker* (Albany, NY: SUNY Press).

Howe, C. (1971) *Wage Patterns and Wage Policies in Modern China, 1919–1972* (Cambridge: Cambridge University Press).

Howe, C. (1992) 'Foreword', in M. Korzec, *Labour and the Failure of Reform in China* (London: Macmillan) pp. vii–x.

Howell, J. (1995) 'Divided Loyalties: Trade Unionism in China', *China Review,* vol. 1, no. 1, pp. 22–5.

Hsu, R.C. (1991) *Economic Theories in China, 1979–1988* (Cambridge: Cambridge University Press).

Huang, M.Y. and Bao, W.W. (1991) 'The First Federation of Trade Unions in Foreign-Owned Firms', *Chinese Trade Unions,* vol. 4, no. 1, pp. 7–8.

Hussein, A. (1993) 'Reform of the Chinese Social Security System', *Working Paper,* STICERD, London: LSE, October.

Hwang, Y-C. (1993) 'Taiwan (ROC)', in S.J. Deery and R.J. Mitchell (eds), *Labour and Industrial Relations in Asia,* pp. 270–95.

The Independent, various.

Jacka, T. (1992) 'The Public-Private Dichotomy and the Gender Division of Labour', in A. Watson (ed.), *Economic Reform and Social Change in China,* (London: Routledge) pp. 117–143.

Ji, L. (1992) 'Management by Objectives and China's Reform of the Employment System', in W.C. Wedley (ed.), *Changes in the Iron Rice Bowl: The Reformation of Chinese Management, Vol. 3 of Advances in Chinese Industrial Studies* (Greenwich, Conn., and London: JAI Press) pp. 169–81.

Josephs, H.K. (1988) 'Labour Reform in the Workers' State: The Chinese Experience', *Journal of Chinese Law,* vol. 2, no. 2, pp. 202–84.

Josephs, H.K. (1990) *Chinese Labour Law* (London: Butterworths).

Josephs, H.K. (1995) 'Labour Law in a 'Socialist Market Economy': The Case of China', *Columbia Journal of Transnational Law* vol. 23, no. 3, pp. 561–81.

Josephs, H.K. (1996) 'Labour Law Reflects the New Realities', *China Rights Forum,* Fall, pp. 24–27.

Kaple, D.A. (1994) *Dream of a Red Factory: The Legacy of Stalinism in China* (New York: Oxford University Press).

Kerr, C. Dunlop, J.T. Harbison, F.H. and Myers, C. (1973) *Industrialism and Industrial Man* (Harmondsworth: Penguin).

Knight, J. and Song, L. (1995) 'Towards a Labour Market in China', *Oxford Review of Economic Policy* vol. 11, no. 4, pp. 97–117.

Koch, M., Sang, H.N. and Steers, R.M. (1995) 'HRM in South Korea', in L.F. Moore and P.D. Jennings (eds), *Human Resource Management on the Pacific Rim: Institutions, Practices and Attitudes* (Berlin: de Gruyter) pp. 217–41.

Korzec, M. (1992) *Labour and the Failure of Reform in China* (London: Macmillan).

Laaksonen, O. (1988) *Management in China During and After Mao* (Berlin: de Gruyter).

Lansbury, R.D., Ng, S.K. and McKern, R.B. (1984) 'Management at Enterprise Level in China', *Industrial Relations Journal*, vol. 15, no. 1, pp. 56–64.

Lao, S. (1990) 'Trade Unions Help Joint Ventures Develop Production', *Chinese Trade Unions*, vol. 3, no. 1, p. 7.

Lardy, N. (1994) *China in The World Economy* (Washington DC: Institute of International Economics).

Lee, L.T. (1984) *The Structure of the Trade Union System in China, 1949–1966* (Hong Kong: Centre of Asian Studies, University of Hong Kong).

Lee, L.T. (1986) *Trade Unions in China: 1949 to the Present* (Singapore: Singapore University Press).

Lee, P.N.S. (1987) *Industrial Management and Economic Reform in China, 1949–1984* (Oxford: Oxford University Press).

Leggett, C. (1992) 'Trade Unionism, Industrialism and the State in Singapore', in E.K.Y. Chen, R. Lansbury, S.H. Ng, and S. Stewart (eds), *Labour–Management Relations in the Asia-Pacific Region* (Hong Kong: Centre of Asian Studies, University of Hong Kong) pp. 54–71.

Lethbridge D. and Ng, S.H. (1995) *The Business Environment in Hong Kong*. (Hong Kong, Oxford and New York: Oxford University Press).

Leung, W.Y. (1993) 'Stalinist Unions Under Market Socialism', *Working Paper*, Department of Political Science, University of Hong Kong.

Lin, C.Z. (1995) 'The Assessment: Chinese Economic Reform in Retrospect and Prospect', *Oxford Review of Economic Policy*, vol. 11, no. 4, pp. 1–25.

Lin, G. (1997) *Red Capitalism in South China*, (Vancouver: University of British Columbia Press).

Lin, J.Y. and Li, Z. (1995) 'Current Issues in China's Rural Areas', *Oxford Review of Economic Policy*, vol. 11, no. 4, pp. 85–96.

Lindblom, C. (1959) 'The Science of Muddling Through', *Public Administration Review*, vol. 19, no. 1, pp. 77–88.

Littler, C.R. and Lockett, M. (1983) 'The Significance of Trade Unions in China', *Industrial Relations Journal*, vol. 14, no. 4, pp. 31–42.

Littler, C.R. and Palmer, G. (1987) 'Communist and Capitalist Trade Unionism: Comparisons and Contrasts' in A. Pravda and B.A. Ruble (eds), *Trade Unions in Communist States* (London: Allen & Unwin) pp. 253–72.

Liu, J., Wang, W., He, P. and Liu, J. (eds) (1988) *Qiye Gongzi Gaige Shiyong Shouce* (*A Practical Handbook of Enterprise Wage Reform*) (Beijing: China Urban Economy and Society Press).

Liu, T. (1989) 'Chinese Workers and Employees Participate in Democratic Management of Enterprises', *Chinese Trade Unions*, vol. 2, no. 1, pp. 5–10.

Lockett, M. (1988) 'Culture and the Problem of Chinese Management', *Organization Studies*, vol. 9, no. 3, pp. 475–496.

Lu, P. (ed.) (1991) *The Moment of Truth: Workers' Participation in China's 1989 Democracy Movement and the Emergence of Independent Unions* (Hong Kong: Asia Monitor Resource Centre).

Lu, Y (1996), *Management Decisionmaking in Chinese Interprises*, (London: Macmillan).

Lubman, S. (1955) 'Introduction: The Future of Chinese Law', *China Quarterly*, no. 141, March, pp. 1–21.

Ma, C. (1955) *History of the Labour Movement in China* (Taipei: China Cultural Service).

Maeda, M. and Ng, S.H. (1987) *A Report on an Academic Visit to Taipei: On Labour Study* (Hong Kong: Centre for Asian Studies, University of Hong Kong).

Maeda, M. and Ng, S.H. (1996) (with Hong, J.C. and Liu, J.Y) 'The Role of the State and Labour's Response to Industrial Development' in I. Nish, G. Redding and S.H. Ng (eds) , *Work and Society*, pp. 167–97.

Meaney, C.S. (1988) *Stability and the Industrial Elite in China and the Soviet Union* (Berkeley, Calif.: University of California Press).

Merkle, J. (1980) *Management and Ideology: The Legacy of the Scientific Management Movement* (Berkeley, Calif.: University of California Press).

Minami, R. (1994) *The Economic Development of China: A Comparison with the Japanese Experience* (London: Macmillan).

Ministry of Lobour (1980) *Regulation of PRC for Labour – Management in Chinese Foreign Joint Ventures*, (Beijing: Chine Labour Press).

Ministry of Labour (1983) *Regulations of PRC on Joint Ventures Using Foreign Investment*, (Beijing: China Labour Press).

Ministry of Labour (1993) *Regulations of PRC on the Settlement of Labour Disputes Enterprises*, (Beijing: China Labour Press).

Ministry of Labour (1994) 'Circular on Provision of Collective Contracts, No 485, 5 December 1994, in *Seventeen Regulations Pertaining to The Labour Law* (Beijing: China Labour Press).

Moore, L.F. and Jennings, P.D. (eds) (1995) *Human Resource Management on the Pacific Rim: Institutions, Practices and Attitudes* (Berlin: de Gruyter).

Morris, R. (1986) 'Trade Unions in Contemporary China', *Australian Journal of Chinese Affairs*, no. 13, pp. 51–67.

Morris, R. (1987) 'The Revival of China's Organised Labour', *Journal of Industrial Relations*, vol. 12, no. 1, pp. 13–22.

Nakagone, K. (1989) 'Manchukuo and Economic Development', in P. Duus *et al.* (eds), *The Japanese Informal Empire in China, 1895–1937* (Princeton, NJ: Princeton University Press) pp. 133–58.

Naughton, B. (1995) *Growing out of the Plan: Chinese Economic Reform, 1978–1993* (Cambridge: Cambridge University Press).

Nee, V. (1992) 'Organizational Dynamics of Market Transition: Hybrid Forms, Property-Rights and Mixed Economy in China', *Administrative Science Quarterly*, vol. 27, no. 1, pp. 1–27.

Ng, S.H. (1984) 'One Brand of Democracy: The Workers' Congress in the Chinese Enterprise', *The Journal of Industrial Relations*, vol. 25, no. 2, pp. 56–75.

Ng, S.H. (1985) *Report on Thurley-Turner Visit* (Hong Kong: University of Hong Kong).

Ng, S.H. (1986) 'A Report on Professor Turner's Academic Visit to Guangzhou' (Hong Kong: University of Hong Kong).

Ng, S.H. (1994) 'Industrial Relations in JVs in China' in S. Stewart, (ed), *Joint Ventures in the PRC, Advances in Chinese Intdustrial Studies*, vol. 4, (Greenwich, Conn., and London: JAI Press) pp. 13–28.

Ng, S.H. (1995) 'A Current Note on the Chinese Labour Movement', *International Journal of Employment Studies*, Vol. 3, no. 2, pp. 61–75.

Ng, S.H. (1996) 'The Development of Labour Relations in Hong Kong and Some Implications for the future' in I. Nish, G. Redding and S.H. Ng (eds) *Work and*

Society: Labour and Human Resources in East Asia (Hong Kong: Hong Kong University Press). pp. 289–300.

Ng, S.H. and Cheng, C.S. (1994) 'Transition to More Cooperative and Consensual Pattern of Labour – Management Relations', *Asia-Pacific Journal of Management*, vol. 10, no. 2, pp. 213–17.

Nish, I. Redding G and Ng, S.H. (eds) (1996) *Work and Society: Labour and Human Resources in East Asia* (Hong Kong; Honh Kong University Press)

Nolan, P. (1994a) 'Introduction: The Chinese Puzzle', in Q. Fan and P. Nolan (eds), *China's Economic Reforms: The Costs and Benefits of Incrementalism* (London: Macmillan) pp. 1–20.

Nolan, P. (1994b) 'Large Firms and Industrial Reform in Former Planned Economies: The Case of China', *Cambridge Journal of Economics*, vol. 20, no. 1, pp. 1–30.

Nolan, P. (1995) *China's Rise: Russia's Fall* (London: Macmillan).

Observer The , various.

OECD (1994) *OECD Employment Outlook* (Paris: Organization for Economic Cooperation and Development).

Pearson, M.M. (1991) *Joint Ventures in the PRC: The Control of Foreign Direct Investment under Socialism* (Princeton: Princeton University Press).

People's Daily/Renmin Ribao, various.

Perlman, S. (1949) *A Theory of the Labor Movement* (New York: Kelley).

Perry, E.J. (1993) *Shanghai on Strike: The Politics of Chinese Labor* (Stanford, Calif.: Stanford University Press).

Perry, E.J. (1994) 'Shanghai's Strike Wave of 1957', *China Quarterly*, no. 137 (June), pp. 1–27.

Perry, E.J. (1995) 'Labour's Battle for Political Space: the Role of Workers Associations in Contemporary China' in D.S. Davis *et al.* (eds) , *Urban Spaces in Contemporary China,* pp. 302–25.

Poole, M. (1981) *Theories of Trade Unionism: A Sociology of Industrial Relations* (London: RKP).

Poole, M. (1986) *Industrial Relations: Origins and Patterns of National Identity* (London: Routledge).

Potter, P.B. (1994) 'Riding the Tiger: Legitimacy and Legal Culture in Post-Mao China', *China Quarterly*, No. 138, June, pp. 325–58.

Pravda, A. and Ruble, B.A. (eds) (1987) *Trade Unions in Communist States* (London: Allen & Unwin).

PRC (1992) *Trade Union Law of the People's Republic of China* (Beijing: Ministry of Labour).

PRC (1994) *Labour Law of the People's Republic of China*, (Beijing: Ministry of Labour).

Putterman, L. (1995) 'The Role of Ownership and Property-Rights in China's Economic Transition', *China Quarterly*, no. 144, November, pp. 1047–64.

Redding, G. (1990) *The Spirit of Chinese Capitalism* (Berlin and New York: de Gruyter).

Renmin Ribao (Peoples Daily), – various.

Reuters News Agency, various.

Richman, B. (1969) *Industrial Society in Communist China* (New York: Random House).

Riskin, C. (1987) *China's Political Economy: The Quest for Development since 1949* (Oxford: Oxford University Press).

Rosen, S. (ed.) (1989) Introduction to Special Issue: 'The All-China Federation of Trade Unions' Survey of China's Workers and Staff', *Chinese Economic Studies* (Summer), pp. 1–12.

Sabin, L (1994) 'New Bosses in the Workers' State: The Growth of Non-State Sector Employment in China': *China Quarterly*, no. 140, December, pp. 944–970.

Saich, T. (1993) 'The Fourteenth Party Congress: A Programme for Authoritarian Rule', *The China Quarterly*, no. 132 (December), pp. 1136–60.

San, G. (1993) 'Taiwan', in M. Rothman, D.R. Briscoe, R.D. Nacamulle (ed), *Industrial Relations Around the World: Labor Relations for MNCs* (Berlin: De Gruyter), pp. 371–38.

Schoeple G.K. (ed.) (1996) *Changes in the Labor Market: Implications for the future* (Washington, DC: US Department of Labor).

Schram, S. (1963) *The Political Thought of Mao Tse-Tung* New York: Praeger)

Schurmann, F. (1966) *Ideology and Organization in Communist China* (Berkeley, Calif.: University of California Press).

Shenkar, O. and Ronen, S. (1987) 'Culture, Ideology or Economy: A Comparative Exploration of Work Goal Importance Among Managers in Chinese Societies', *Academy of Management Journal*, vol. 30, no. 3, pp. 564–7.

Schell, O. (1994) *Mandate of Heaven* (New York: Simon & Schuster).

Sicular, T. (1995) 'Redefining State, Plan and Market: China's Reforms in Agricultural Commerce', *China Quarterly*, no. 144, December, pp. 1020–46.

Sit, V.S.F. and Wong, S.L. (1990) *Changes in the Industrial Structure and Role of Small and Medium Industries in Developing Countries: The Case of China* (Tokyo: Institute of Developing Economies).

Solinger, D. (1995) 'The Floating Population in the Cities: Changes for Assimilation', in D. Davis *et al.* (eds) *Urban Spaces in Contemporary China,* pp. 113–43.

South China Morning Post, various.

SSB (State Statistical Bureau) *Statistical Outline of China (Zhongguo Tongji Zhaiyao)* (Beijing: China Statistical Press) various years.

Sun, Z. (1990) 'Urgent Problems Facing China's Wage Reforms' in Institute of Labour Studies, Ministry of Labour, PRC (eds), *Sino–US Scholars on Hot Issues in China's Economy* (Beijing: People's Press) pp. 246–67.

Sunday Times various.

State Statistical Bureau (SSB) *Statistical Outline of China (Zhongguo Tongji Zhaiyao)* (Beijing: China Statistical Press (various).

SWB (various) *BBC Summary of Short-Wave Broadcasts: Far Eastern* (London: British Broadcasting Corporation) various.

Takahara, A. (1992) *The Politics of Wage Policy in Post-Revolutionary China* (London: Macmillan).

Tanner, M.S. (1994) 'The Erosion of Communist Party Control over Lawmaking in China', *China Quarterly*, no. 138, June, pp. 381–403.

Thirkell, J. Scase, R. and Vickerstaff, S. (1994) *Labour Relations and Political Change in Eastern Europe: A Comparative Perspective* (London: University College London Press).

Thompson, P. (1992/3) 'Afloat in a Better Sea', *China Now*, Winter, no. 143, pp. 26–8.

Thurley, K. (1983) 'Role of Labour Administration in Industrial Society', in S.H. Ng and D.A. Levin, (eds), *Contemporary Issues in Hong Kong Labour Relations* (Hong Kong: Centre of Asia Studies, University of Hong Kong) pp. 106–120.

Thurley, K. (1988) 'Trade Unionism in Asian Countries', in Y.C. Yao, D.A. Levin, S.H. Ng and E. Sinn (eds), *Labour Movement in a Changing Society: The Experience of Hong Kong* (Hong Kong: Centre of Asia Studies, University of Hong Kong), pp. 24–31.

Tidrick, G. and Chen, J. (eds) (1987) *China's Industrial Reform* (Oxford: Oxford University Press).

Tsang, E.W. (1994) 'Human Resource Management Problems in Sino-Foreign Joint Ventures', *International Journal of Manpower*, vol. 15, no. 9/10, pp. 4–21.

Tung, R.L. (1991) 'Motivation in Chinese Industrial Enterprises' in R.M. Steers and L.W. Porter (eds), *Motivation and Work Behavior* (New York: McGraw Hill) pp. 342–51.

Tung, R.L. (1996) 'Managing in Asia: Cross-Cultural Dimensions', in P. Joynt, and M. Warner (eds), *Managing Across Cultures* (London: ITBP) pp. 233–45.

Tung, R.L. and Havlovic, S.J. (1996) 'Human Resource Management in Transitional Economies: The Case of Poland and the Czech Republic', *International Journal of Human Resource Management*, vol. 7, no. 1, pp. 1–19.

Turner, H.A. *et al.* (1980) *The Last Colony, But Whose?* (Cambridge: Cambridge University Press).

Turner, H.A., Fosh, P. and Ng, S.H. (1991) *Between Two Societies: Hong Kong Labour in Transition* (Hong Kong: Centre of Asia Studies, University of Hong Kong).

Unger, J. and Chan, A. (1995) 'China, Corporatism and the East Asian Model', *Australian Journal of Chinese Affairs*, no. 33, January, pp. 25–33.

Verma, A. and Yan, Z. (1995) 'The Changing Face of HRM in China', in A. Verma, T. Kochan, and R.D. Lansbury (eds), *Employment Relations in the Growing Asian Economies* (London: Routledge) pp. 315–35.

Vogel, E. (1991) *The Four Little Dragons* (Cambridge, Mass.: Harvard University Press).

Vroom, C. (1996) 'Organization Structure', in M. Warner (ed.), *International Encyclopedia of Business and Management* (London: ITBP) vol. 4, pp. 3881–90.

Walder, A.G. (1986) *Communist Neo-Traditionalism: Work and Authority in Chinese Industry* (Berkeley, Calif.: University of California Press).

Walder, A. (1989) 'Factory and Manager in an Era of Reform', *China Quarterly*, no. 118 (June) pp. 242–64.

Walder, A.G. and Gong, X. (1993) 'Workers in the Tiananmen Protests: The Politics of the Beijing Workers' Autonomous Federation', *Australian Journal of Chinese Affairs*, no. 29 (January) pp. 1–29.

Walder, A.G. (1991) 'Workers, Managers and the State: the Political Crisis of 1989', *China Quarterly*, no. 127 (September) pp. 467–492.

Wales, N. (1945) *The Chinese Labour Movement* (New York: Day).

Wang Aiwen (1993) *Social and Labour Relations: An examination of the Processes of Change (Shefui Laodong Guanxi: Yanbian Guocheng De Kaocha Yu Fenxi)*, (Beijing: Hongai Chubanshe).

Wang, Z.M. and Heller, F.A. (1993) 'Patterns of Power Distribution in Managerial Decision Making in Chinese and British Industrial Organizations', *International Journal of Human Resource Management*, vol. 4, no. 1, pp. 113–28.

Warner, M (1979) 'Beatrice and Sidney Webb', in T. Raison (ed.) *The Founding Fathers of Social Science*, revised edition by P. Barker, (London: Scolar Press pp. 174–84)

196   *References*

Warner, M. (1986) 'Managing Human Resources in China', *Organization Studies*, vol. 7, no. 4, pp. 353–66.

Warner, M. (ed.) (1987a), *Management Reforms in China* (London: Pinter).

Warner, M. (1987b) 'Industrial Relations in the Chinese Factory', *Journal of Industrial Relations* vol. 23, no. 2, pp. 217–32.

Warner, M. (1989) 'Microelectronics and Manpower in China', *New Technology, Work and Employment*, vol. 4, no. 1, pp. 18–26.

Warner, M. (1992) *How Chinese Managers Learn: Management and Industrial Training in the PRC* (London: Macmillan).

Warner, M. (1993) 'Human Resource Management "with Chinese Characteristics"?', *International Journal of Human Resource Management*, vol. 4, no. 1, pp. 45–65.

Warner, M. (1995) *The Management of Human Resources in Chinese Industry* (London: Macmillan).

Warner, M. (1996a) 'Chinese Enterprise Reform, Human Resources and the 1994 Labour Law', *International Journal of Human Resource Management*, vol. 7, no. 4, pp. 779–96.

Warner, M. (1996b) 'Joint Ventures-v-State Owned Enterprises: Management and HRM in China', *Working Paper* (University of Cambridge: Judge Institute of Management Studies).

Warner, M. (1997) 'Introduction', in M. Warner (ed.)' Human Resource Management in Greater China', (Special Issue) *International Journal of Human Resource Management*, vol. 8, no. 4 (in press).

Webb, S. and Webb, B. (1894) *The History of British Trade Unionism* (London: Longman Green).

Webb, S. and Webb, B. (1897) *Industrial Democracy* (London: Longman Green).

Webb, S. and Webb, B. (1935) *Soviet Communism: A New Civilization?* (London: Longmans Green).

Wedley, W.C. (1992) (ed), *Changes in the Iron Rice Bowl: The Reformation of Chinese Management*, vol. 3 of *Advances in Chinese Industrial Studies*, (Greenwich, Conn, and London: JAI Press).

Wei, M. (1994) 'Labour Dispute Settlement', *Chinese Trade Unions*, vol. 7, no. 5, pp. 7–9.

Wei, M. (1995) 'ACFTU's Deadline for Unionization in Overseas-Funded Firms', *Chinese Trade Unions*, vol. 8, no. 1, pp. 6–7.

White, G. (1987) 'Labour Market Reform in Chinese Industry', in M. Warner (ed.), *Management Reforms in China* (London: Pinter) pp. 113–26.

White, G. (1996) 'Chinese Trade Unions in the Transition from Socialism', *British Journal of Industrial Relations*, vol. 34, no. 3, pp. 433–57.

White, G., Howell, J. and Shan, X. (1996) *In Search of Civil Society: Market Reform and Social Change in Contemporary China* (Oxford: Oxford University Press).

Whitehill, A.M. (1991) *Japanese Management: Tradition and Transition* (London: Routledge).

Whitley, R. (1990) 'Eastern Asian Enterprises Structures and the Comparative Analysis of Forms of Business Organization', *Organization Studies*, vol. 11, no. 1, pp. 47–74.

Wilkinson, B. (1994) *Labour and Industry in the Asia-Pacific: Lessons from the Newly-Industrialized Countries* (Berlin: De Gruyter).

Wilson, J.L. (1987) 'The People's Republic of China', in A. Pravda and B.A. Ruble (eds), *Trade Unions in Communist States* (London: Allen & Unwin) pp. 219–52.

Wilson, J.L. (1990a) 'The Polish Lesson: China and Poland 1989–1990', *Studies in Comparative Communism*, vol. XIII, no. 3/4, pp. 259–79.

Wilson, J.L. (1990b) 'Labor Policy in China: Reform and Regression, *Problems of Communism*, Sept.–Oct., vol. XXXIX, pp. 44–65.

Wilson, J.L. (1995) 'The Situation of Workers' Rights in China', Paper for Second Annual Harvard/Columbia Chinese Legal Studies Conference, Columbia School of Law, April, pp. 25.

Wood, A. (1994) 'China's Economic System: A Brief Description with some Suggestions for Further Reform', in Q. Fan and P. Nolan (eds), *China's Economic Reforms: The Costs and Benefits of Incrementalism* (London: Macmillan) pp. 21–45.

Workers' Daily (Gongren Ribao), various.

World Bank (1990) *World Development Report* (Washington DC: The World Bank).

World Bank (1993) *World Development Report* (Washington, DC: World Bank).

Wu, H. (1992) *Laogai: The Chinese Gulag*, (Boulder, CO: Westview Press.)

Wu, H. (1996) *Troublemaker: One Man's Crusade Against China's Cruelty* (New York: Times Books).

Wu, J. (1994) 'Protection of Women Workers' Rights in Overseas-Funded Firms Urged', *Chinese Trade Unions*, vol. 7, no. 5, pp. 3–4.

Xia, J.Z. (ed.) (1991), *Issues of China Labour Legislation (Zhongghuo Laodong Lifa Wenti)* (Beijing: China Labour Publisher).

Xiang, R. (1980) 'A Glimpse of Factory Life', *Beijing Review*, 11 March, pp. 17–25.

Xinhua News Agency, various.

Yahuda, M. (1996) *Hong Kong: China's Challenge* (London: Routledge).

Yang, X 'Labor Force Characteristics and Labor Force Migration in China, in (ed) G.K. Schoeple (ed.), *Changes in the Labor Market*, pp. 13–44.

Yu, K.C., Wang, D.C. and He, W. (1993) 'A Study of the Organizational Committment of Chinese Employees' in W.C. Wedley (ed.), *Changes in the Iron Rice Bowl: The Reformation of Chinese Management, Vol. 3 of Advances in Chinese Industrial Studies* , pp. 181–96.

Zhang, G.X. (1988) 'Changes in the Chinese Trade Union Management in the Light of the Current Reforms', MA Thesis, Institute of Social Studies, The Hague (Netherlands).

Zhang, Y. (1997) 'An intermediary: the Chinese perception of Trade unions since the 1980s', *Journal of Contemporary China*, vol. 6, no. 14, pp. 139–52.

Zhao, R. (1993) 'Three Features of the Distribution of Income During the Transition to Reform' in M. Grilton and R. Zhao (eds), *The Distribution of Income in China* (London: Macmillan) pp. 20–35.

Zhao, S. (1994) 'Human Resource Management in China', *Asia-Pacific Journal of Human Resources* vol. 32, no. 1, pp. 3–12.

Zheng, H.R. (1987) 'An Introduction to the Labour Law of the People's Republic if China', *Harvard International Law Journal*, vol. 28, no. 2, pp. 385–431.

Zhou, P. (1981) 'An Important Step Towards Democratic Management', *Beijing Review*, 2 September, pp. 14–16.

Zhu, C. and Dowling, P. (1994) 'The Impact on the Economic System upon HRM in China', *Human Resource Planning*, vol. 17, no. 1, pp. 1–21.

Zweig, D. (1997), 'Rural People, the Politicians and Power', *The China Journal*, no. 38, July, pp. 153–70.

Index